Introducing Change
'From the Top'
in Universities and Colleges

Introducing Change 'From the Top'

in Universities and Colleges

10 Personal Accounts

Edited By
Susan Weil

KOGAN
PAGE

First published in 1994

Apart from any fair dealing for the purposes of research or private study, or criticism or review, as permitted under the Copyright, Designs and Patents Act, 1988, this publication may only be reproduced, stored or transmitted, in any form or by any means, with the prior permission in writing of the publishers, or in the case of reprographic reproduction in accordance with the terms of licenses issued by the Copyright Licensing Agency. Enquiries concerning reproduction outside those terms should be sent to the publishers at the undermentioned address:

Kogan Page Limited
120 Pentonville Road
London N1 9JN

© Susan Weil and named contributors, 1994

British Library Cataloguing in Publication Data

A CIP record for this book is available from the British Library.

ISBN (paperback) 0 7494 1236 4
ISBN (hardback) 0 7494 1506 1

Typeset by Saxon Graphics, Ltd
Printed and bound in Great Britain by Biddles Ltd, Guildford and King's Lynn.

Contents

Notes on Contributors

Ned Binks is an Anglican priest who has worked in the college sector of higher education for the past 29 years. He has been a chaplain, lecturer in church history, director of a careers advisory and counselling service, and warden of a large student residence. Wherever he has worked, he has pressed for closer collaboration between college staff and employers of graduates, and he has led a range of major projects in experiential learning and the development of transferable skills. He became principal of Chester College in 1987. Ned believes that, from a personal point of view, he could not have gone to Chester at a more appropriate time. Most of the old rules were being scrapped, growth and diversification were being publicly funded and, above all, the College itself wanted to change. In such circumstances, a general breadth of experience and contacts were more necessary in a principal than a record of personal scholarship. An openness to innovation and a willingness to take risks were more important than formal management training.

Professor John Bull, BSc (Econ), FCCA, vice-chancellor and chief executive of the University of Plymouth was appointed to the post in 1989 to the then Polytechnic of South West where he had been deputy director (academic) since 1985. Originally trained as an accountant with the Ford Motor Company, he was a research fellow for the English Institute of Chartered Accountants and then held appointments at three former polytechnics. He was closely involved with the Business Education Council in the early years of their work, and a member and chairman of several Council for National Academic Award boards, holding an appointment to its council by the Secretary of State for Education. He was actively engaged in financial and educational consultancy and has published in the fields of accounting and educational management. He has held a variety of external appointments and is currently a non-executive director of the Plymouth Health Trust and is chairman of the Open Learning Foundation.

Dr Kenneth Edwards has been vice-chancellor of the University of Leicester since 1987, having spent the previous 21 years at the University of Cambridge where he was head of the genetics department and chairman of the Council of the School of Biological Sciences, and then Secretary General of the Faculties (one of the three principal administrative offices). He graduated from the University of Reading with first class honours in agricultural botany in 1958 and completed his PhD in 1961 at the University of Wales, Aberystwyth. He did post-doctoral work at University of California (Davis Campus). He became chairman of the Committee of Vice-Chancellors and Principals in 1993, and chairs the advisory committee of the Leicester Common Purpose Initiative. He has published widely in the field of genetics, the field in which he maintains research interests. He is married with three children.

Colin Flint is principal of Solihull College in the West Midlands, one of the largest colleges of further education in Britain, with a total of 35,000 students. He has worked previously in further and higher education in Sheffield, Liverpool, Teesside, Manchester and Birmingham. He was a founder of the Further Education Campaign Group, a consortium of principals working together to help change the image of the sector and secure it its due recognition. He is now a council member of the Association for Colleges, the body which represents nationally the interests of FE and its students. He believes strongly that Britain needs a revolution in its education systems and structures, that the country will need to move much further away from the elitist model of the past if it is to compete successfully in the 21st century. He is a former FE correspondent of *The Times Higher Education Supplement* and continues to write regularly in the education press.

Ruth Gee was the director and chief executive of Edge Hill College of Higher Education and a Professor of Lancaster University from September 1989 until August 1993. She moved there following a three-year period as assistant director of the Polytechnic of North London (now the University). She began her educational career in 1970 as a teacher of English in a comprehensive school in County Durham and taught subsequently in Hertfordshire and Haringey. She combined the early years of parenthood with political activity, which culminated in her being deputy leader of the Inner London Education Authority from 1983 to 1986. She has been the chief executive of the Association for Colleges since September 1993. She is a Fellow of the Royal Society of Arts, a Fellow of the Institute of Management and a graduate of London and Newcastle upon Tyne Universities. Between 1990 and 1993 she was a regular columnist in *The Times Higher Education Supplement*.

Professor Michael Harrison received his BA and Masters in sociology from the University of Leicester and has made his career in higher education, culminating in 1985 in his appointment as director of Wolverhampton Polytechnic (designated as a University in June 1992). The University, which is a large institution comprising 25,000 full- and part-time students housed on five campuses, has extensive international links. Mick Harrison chairs the British Council's CICHE (Africa) Committee and serves on CVCP's International Advisory Committee. Business visits during 1994 included Nigeria, Finland, USA, Siberia, Thailand and the Solomon Islands. He is a governor of Thomas Telford School (one of the new City Technology Colleges supported jointly by government and industry) and of Bilston Community College. He takes an active interest in Wolverhampton and is on the council of the Chamber of Commerce and Industry, a trustee of the Black Country Heritage Trust and a member of the board of the Wolverhampton City Challenge project.

Rhodri Phillips is head of research and strategy at the Committee of Vice-chan-cellors and Principals, where he is developing a long-term strategic framework for higher education. He is on secondment from his post as deputy vice-chancel-lor at South Bank University, London, where he has been responsible for resource management and external relations since 1990. He joined the Civil Service from university in 1970 and worked for 20 years in senior posts in the Department of Employment, mainly on education and training programmes. During this period, he also undertook several major organization reviews on behalf of the Prime Minister's Office. He was seconded in the mid-1980s for two years to the former Inner London Education Authority to advise on major organi-zational changes. He was the first secretary of the Polytechnics and Colleges Funding Council when it was set up in 1988. He writes and lectures on strategic management issues in higher education.

Chris Price has spent 40 years involved in teaching, politics, the media and higher education management. Between 1956 and 1966 he taught classics in grammar schools and was involved, on Sheffield City Council, in the early stages of Britain's comprehensive schools movement. Between 1966 and 1983, he was an MP, involved in education and civil libertarian issues. He wrote and broadcast widely, editing and writing for *New Education*, and fronting an educa-tion programme, *School Report* on Thames Television. In the early 1980s, he chaired the House of Commons Select Committee on Education, Science and the Arts.

Over the past ten years, he has been involved in the management of polytech-nics in London and Leeds. He came to Leeds Polytechnic as Director in 1985, and retired as Principal of Leeds Metropolitan University in 1994. He has been a member of the European Parliament, Academic Representative in Europe on the Erasmus Advisory Committee, and Chairman of the National Youth Bureau. He is now a Visiting Senior Fellow at the Office for Public Management and Co-Chairman of the Campaign for Freedom of Information. He lives in Settle, North Yorkshire, and Kentish Town, London.

Patricia Roberts trained as a town planner and surveyor and worked in Chicago, London and Milton Keynes before starting her teaching career at Oxford Polytechnic (now Oxford Brookes University). She moved to the South Bank Polytechnic, London (South Bank University) and stayed there for 17 years. The move to a major management position came with being elected dean of the faculty of the Built Environment. A change at the top of the institution resulted in appointed deans (on a three-year rotating basis) but, despite the odds, she was appointed. After three years of management the move back to senior lecturer was to prove personally frustrating. Currently, she is deputy principal in charge of academic affairs and quality assurance at Chester College of Higher Education.

Jenny Shackleton was born in London and educated in Guildford, Surrey. She entered University College, London as a mature student in 1968 where she spent five years in English study and research. Her career in further education spans various college and local authority posts. Currently, she is principal of Wirral Metropolitan College, a large college of further and higher education in

Merseyside. Since the mid-1970s Jenny's work has involved her in partnerships with the Employment Department (TEED) and other national bodies. She presently works most closely with the National Commission on Education and The Prince's Trust Volunteers. She is also a member of the Independent Inquiry into the Role of the Police, the Council for Industry and Higher Education, and of a local Community Health Trust.

Adrian Webb is vice-chancellor of the University of Glamorgan. After graduating at Birmingham University in 1965, he studied at the London School of Economics (LSE) and was offered a lectureship in 1986. During eight years at LSE he taught a wide variety of courses, but specialized in the personal social services. He was appointed Professor of Social Policy at Loughborough University of Technology in 1976, became head of the Department of Social Sciences in 1981, director of the Centre for Research in Social Policy in 1982, dean of the School of Human and Environmental Studies and was senior pro-vice-chancellor when he left for Glamorgan in 1993. He is the author or co-author of ten books and numerous monographs and articles in academic journals.

Susan Weil joined the Office for Public Management in 1991, as head of HE and Fellow in Organizational Learning. Previously, she was associate director of the Higher Education for Capability initiative at the RSA. She came to the UK in 1974 for three weeks on her way to Harvard to do a PhD, but remained. She has worked for many years across the public/voluntary sectors on processes of learning and change that support new organizational purposes and cross-boundary working. In the USA she worked for the New Orleans Consortium of Universities and Colleges, on new curriculum and professional development initiatives to support greater diversity and community responsiveness. She was educated at Northrop Collegiate School and Tufts University (Jackson College), where she was elected to Phi Beta Kappa upon graduation and received honours degrees in Classics and Music. She has published numerous articles, chapters and management development materials. From 1982 to 1988 she held academic posts at the University of London, finishing at the Centre for Higher Education Studies where she continues to work as a consultant and visiting lecturer. Her PhD, looking at learner experience and organizational change in the context of more diversified access, was awarded in 1989 (London). She was elected chair of the Society for Research into Higher Education from 1989 to 1991, is a Fellow of the RSA, and was granted an Honorary Fellowship from the University of Wolverhampton in 1994.

Professor Alan Wilson was born in Bradford in 1939 and educated at Queen Elizabeth Grammar School, Darlington, and Corpus Christi College, Cambridge, where he read mathematics. He took up his first post in the University of Leeds as Professor of Urban and Regional Geography in 1970. He was appointed pro-vice-chancellor for the academic years 1989–1991, and vice-chancellor from October 1991. He has served on a variety of public bodies. In July 1993 the Secretary of State for Health appointed him as chairman of the newly-formed NHS Complaints Review Committee and he has recently been appointed to membership of the Northern and Yorkshire Regional Health Authority. He has authored or co-authored 15 books and over 200 papers. He was given the Gill Memorial Award by the Royal Geographical Society in 1978; in 1987 he was given the Honours Award of the Association of American Geographers, and in 1992 he was awarded the Founder's Medal of the Royal Geographical Society.

Preface

INTRODUCTION

The role of those 'at the top' of colleges and universities has always been problematic. The complex cultures, the competing professional and disciplinary traditions, and the various histories that characterize such institutions make this inevitable. But throughout the world, unprecedented developments are forcing men and women 'at the top' of colleges and universities to revise their understanding of and approach to their role, and to initiate significant change.

In response, a range of management styles and approaches to change are being created 'on the run'. There has been no other choice. Competing demands are multiplying, but an institution cannot afford to spin in this sea of change with neither sails nor rudder. New external pressures are producing challenges that strike at the heartland of traditional assumptions, values and practices. None the less, talent and potential must continue to be released, in increasingly diverse staff, student and surrounding communities. Alternative understandings of leadership and management need to be enacted and not just 'at the top' but throughout institutions. These need to build on the best of former traditions yet equip the institution to prosper and achieve new educational purposes.

To date, there have been neither mentors nor literature to guide processes of stimulating and sustaining significant cultural change in colleges and universities. Those 'at the top' have had to work out for themselves how best to 'move forward' and whether and how to bring others 'along with them'.

Admittedly, many sagas, stories and lessons about managing change and being a chief executive in the private sector line airport and other bookshop shelves, but these are of limited value when it comes to being wise about such things up, down and around educational institutions. As Price says in Chapter 2,

> ... there are no existing role models, no books, no accounts of the way in which it may be possible simultaneously to maintain staff morale, pack the students in and preserve the traditions of the place.

THE BOOK'S APPROACH: LEARNING THROUGH STORY

This book begins to redress this gap. It complements the volume that also launches this series, *Implementing Change from within Universities* and *Colleges* (Slowey, forthcoming). Uniquely, both volumes provide access to reflective narratives written by people who have been stimulating and supporting change in colleges and universities in Britain in recent years.

This particular volume offers ten personal accounts from men and women who are doing this 'from the top' of their institutions. The contributors have been selected because they are perceived within the UK and their institutions to be successful, controversial or both, in terms of how they have defined their role and approached change. They represent a range of traditions within Britain: research universities, polytechnics (that have now become universities through legislation), colleges of higher and further education.

Contributors have told their stories, not as histories recounted at a distance, but rather as living struggles with 'grotesque turbulence' (Webb, Chapter 3). Wilson (Chapter 7) captures the spirit of the book aptly:

> *There are many ways of reporting and reflecting on the management [of change in recent years]; it is simplest to tell the individual, and certainly idiosyncratic, tale in the hope that this provides empirical data from which, combined with others, generalizations can be drawn.*

The power of story and its wider relevance to concerns that are at the heart of this book, is revealed on many levels throughout. For example, the 'I narrative' provides access to contributors' different interior landscapes and so to their values, feelings and distinctive perspectives on what is at issue and what is not, in the enactment of their role. Understandably, there are different degrees of openness, as many continue in their roles. None the less, these stories provide a rich mix of experience, styles and interpretations of priorities. They also provide considerable insight into the complexities, challenges and paradoxes of effective change management and leadership in today's colleges and universities.

The cumulative effect of so many stories also reveals the paradox that colleges and universities are simultaneously the same as, and totally different from, one another. Each contributor has managed the same external conditions as another, yet each individual and institutional unique history mediates understanding and choice. Enter any college and university and it will feel both familiar yet different. Increasingly, the influence of those 'at the top' is shaping that difference as felt by all who inhabit, or engage with, that institution.

The transparency of the first person narrative also signals an acknowledgement that change touches people's lives. Had these accounts been written by 'chief executives' in the third person narrative, by virtue of the authors being 'at the top' the perspectives would most likely have been 'panoramic, indeed Olympian, tending towards the authoritative' (Chapter 12). The use of personal story emphasizes the importance of insight, reflective self-assessment and the taking of risks that involve management and affect the 'I' in self and others. It entails remaining open to being challenged and changed oneself, acknowledging that as in any story, it is not possible to know everything, nor to predict and control responses and outcomes. In every organization there are competing and complementary narratives. How can these best be worked with, so as to release creativity and commitment and strengthen a sense of community and common purpose? These themes recur throughout, but will be developed in some detail in the final chapter.

My 'story' is also present throughout the book. My values and priorities are made transparent in how I mediate what I see as foreground and background about managing change. I set the scene at the beginning. I also introduce each chapter with personal reflections on the key issues I see at play in the story to follow and how I believe these connect (or not) with others across the book. In the closing chapter, I explore the notion of story in the context of my experience as a consultant who helps those within colleges and universities to work effectively with the different narratives that characterize a college or university. My hope is that the understandings and strategies I explore will offer insights and ideas for tackling some of the key concerns that resound so loudly across this book. Thus, the centrality of story in this book creates a very different kind of resource.

INTENDED READERSHIP

We have set out to produce a stimulating and readable resource for those who are effecting, or are being affected by, change in colleges and universities throughout the world. Those of us who are represented here hope that it will usefully support reflection, development and debate at political and institutional levels. It is also likely to challenge and deepen existing ways of thinking about effective management and change within colleges and universities. Some serious questioning of such things is absolutely essential if colleges and universities are to make their full contribution to the development of individuals, knowledge and the society of which they are a part.

We are confident that the book will provide insights of relevance to men and women throughout the world who are introducing significant change and reviewing their assumptions and approaches as leaders and managers in educational institutions. As importantly, it will support explorations about the relevance and appropriateness of different management styles and approaches. It will also be of value to those who are interested in the complexities of significant cultural change, and the impact of different approaches on professional cultures. Finally, there is much here for those interested in specific developments in Britain in recent years and their effects on the management and character of its colleges and universities. Chapter 1 more generally, and the Appendix specifically, also provide useful background information for such readers.

Acknowledgements

This book represents many people's learning, many people's efforts. At its heart are the contributors who have put themselves at the centre of their stories, thereby adopting a style that for many was unfamiliar and, predictably, not always comfortable. I thank them for taking this risk and collaborating on such an unusual venture. I am also delighted that the stories of many people whom I respect and like will have the wider hearing they deserve and can therefore influence the creation of new stories. I also want to thank the PAs who work alongside these men and women 'at the top' for matching my determination to keep to deadlines with so much effective 'upward management' and such goodwill on the telephone. Thanks also to Rhodri Phillips of the CVCP for his excellent appendix.

I would like to acknowledge those who wanted to be part of this project. They too offered much support along the way, but could not see their contribution through due to unpredictable pressures. For this reason, Scotland is unfortunately not represented. In particular, I want to mention Dick Leeson and Mike Fitzgerald, of Thames Valley University, and Anne Wright, from the University of Sunderland, whose own exploration of organizational story offered encouragement to my own.

I want to express my appreciation to Cari Loder and Professor Gareth Williams at the Centre for Higher Education Studies, University of London, for their support and confidence over many years, as well as for their assistance with the Glossary.

I am grateful to my colleagues at the Office for Public Management for their contribution to my own thinking and practice related to managing change in public services. Some key aspects of this are explored in Chapter 1. But as importantly, the Office's mission, 'managing for social result', enables me to keep my own values and commitments at the centre of my work. Thanks to Greg Parston, for his support for my work on this venture, to Laurie McMahon for how much he has taught me about exploring 'future stories', and to Helen Brown and Sue Richards for their assistance with the first chapter and their support as colleagues. Caroline Kelly, my personal assistant, began to work with me during the rush to publication at the end. She immediately demonstrated her skill, sensitivity, commitment and wonderful sense of humour, and I continue to value her immensely. I also want to acknowledge the influence of clients, and participants on programmes and longer-term learning networks.

I thank Donald Schon, for providing the right blend of challenge and support at the right time, and for the opportunity of 'side-by-side learning', after being dependent on his books these many years!

I want to honour Lesley Cook, Carlis Douglas, Ruth Gee, Cathy Hull, Sheila Marsh, Christopher Price, Phillida Salmon and Vivienne Wylie, each of whose friendship, insights and distinctive gifts provided inspiration and sustenance to the writing of my own chapters.

I also express my appreciation to Maria Slowey, editor of the second volume in this series, for being such a fun, stimulating and supportive collaborator, and to Kogan Page for their backing for this volume and the series which it launches.

Finally, I celebrate the man who is at the centre of my own story and who does so much to support its fuller expression. I thereby dedicate this book to Michel Joly.

Susan Weil
London
May 1994

Chapter 1

Management and Change in Colleges and Universities: The Need for New Understandings

Susan Weil

INTRODUCTION

Being 'at the top': a changing role

The title of this book will raise eyebrows. Perhaps less so than, say, three or five years ago, but this reaction will be triggered none the less.

The idea of the 'chief executive' of a college or university has been given new meaning and weight in recent years. In Britain, the power of those at the top of such institutions to exert influence behind the scenes, to ensure a privileged public sector position, is legendary. When Margaret Thatcher initiated her systematic challenge to UK public services, it was believed that colleges and universities would be spared. This proved anything but the case. Legislative changes and various government funding council practices have had a profound influence on both the conception and the enactment of the role in relation to the management of significant change.

Britain offers a powerful case study of such developments but the themes that figure in the story of its changes in recent years are echoing throughout the world. Those charged with leading universities and colleges are being compelled to revise their role and to introduce significant change. There is the force of external pressures (such as through government intervention in Australia, or the effects of economic recession, across the whole of Europe) or the force of challenges that demand new forms of leadership and management (such as in relation to increased diversity in the US or in pursuing new social and economic purposes for education, such as in the Pacific Basin). Themes of public accountability and consumer choice are also acquiring new meanings in many different societies.

My approach to this opening section

The purpose of this opening piece is to set the scene for the chapters that follow. In keeping within the personal narrative approach of the book (please see Preface), I offer my own particular perspective on the context within which the role of the head of a college or university and the management of change 'from the top' have been placed at issue in recent years. I speak personally and without any pretence of historical distance or objectivity, which is customarily afforded by the third person narrative. Inevitably, therefore, what is foreground for me will be background for another, and my own priorities and values will remain transparent throughout, as is the case in subsequent chapters.

RAISED EYEBROWS: A STARTING POINT FOR DEBATE?

A key purpose of this book is to offer reflective, action–oriented material that can stimulate discussion across the college and university sector about appropriate management styles and approaches to change. But even before such explorations might occur, a variety of reactions to this book will be prompted by the title alone. Drawing on my own work with staff at all levels of colleges and universities, let me envisage some of these.

First, there will be those who will reject outright the starting premise that there is indeed, or should be, a person who sees him or herself as 'at the top' of a college or university. They will say, 'Whatever do you mean, exactly?' Using the phrase runs the risk of my being dismissed as foe, not friend – someone who is colluding with the forces of 'managerialism' that are seen to be invading colleges and universities and the territorial power and autonomy traditionally enjoyed by academics.

Then there will be those who will be amused. They continue to regard the role of chief executive as something manufactured by government forces, and an imposition to be resisted at all costs. Those who hold this position can dismiss those at the 'top' as 'failed academics' who through the over-assertion of their managerial role undermine professional and collegial values.

There are others who will argue that change in colleges and universities is the result of external forces and not the responsibility of those 'at the top'. Those 'at the top' instead must react to new pressures as best as possible, in collaboration with their professional colleagues.

The title and my authorship may also raise eyebrows because my own perspective has been shaped greatly by my experience of stimulating change from outside traditional structures, both in the US and the UK. I have researched processes of learning and change, as well as worked alongside people at all levels, as an adviser or consultant: with managers, professionals and students, who are effecting, or are affected by, the style and culture of an institution (eg, Stephenson and Weil, 1992; Weil, 1989a, 1989b; Weil and McGill, 1989; Weil *et al*, 1985). As such, I bring the different experience, and I hope some of the wisdom, that can come with an 'outsider's' perspective – the value of which is identified by a number of contributors to this volume. (An elaboration of this work is offered in the final chapter.)

IN THE MIDST OF A SEA CHANGE

Challenges to public sector managers

Although the public that has been denied access to colleges and universities may have difficulty perceiving such institutions as public services, none the less those at the top have been subject to the same pressures as other public managers.

I have found the work conducted by Sue Richards, and the Public Management Foundation (PMF, 1994; Richards, 1993; Rodrigues, 1993) particularly useful in deepening my own understanding of recent developments in public sector management. This exploration of the changing role of public managers lays emphasis on the political framework within which they operate. This 'imposes particular constraints on their authority as well as conferring particular forms of legitimacy' (Rodrigues, 1993). The nature of these constraints as well as the forms of legitimacy that have been conferred to public service managers are seen to have undergone three major paradigm shifts in the post-war years.

The first of these is referred to as the 'administrative paradigm'. In this, politicians made the policy but professionals gave this their own meaning through their control of the service production process. They therefore also played a key policy role, legitimated by the perceived inviolability of professional values, the possession of expert knowledge, and the ways in which membership of professional groups was regulated. Within this paradigm, there were no managers but rather administrators with 'no authoritative independent basis for action. They reconciled and realised the objectives of others' (Rodrigues, 1993, p. 4).

By the end of the 1970s, the government took the position that the continued growth of public services and the strain on public expenditure that was sustained by the administrative paradigm, had to be stopped. This coincided with what the introduction of the PMF work refers to as the 'efficiency paradigm'. (Richards, 1993). The notion of the public service manager developed new currency, fuelled by agendas of the politicians who began to see the manager as a powerful agent for change and not merely a mediator. This shift was characterized by new emphases and priorities, including, for example, on increased accountability for individual and organizational performance, reconfigurations of public service provision (such as through the introduction of purchasers and providers in the Health Service), the development of new management structures and processes that made executive responsibility clearer, and new roles for non-executive directors from the private sector in the governance of public service institutions.

Richards argues that in the 1990s the original key actors of politician, manager and professional remain, but a fourth emerges: the 'consumer'. This represents a direct challenge to the traditional dominance of professional over client or consumer interests in public services, and indeed, the growing dominance of the politicians. In the 'consumer paradigm' further legitimacy for managerial action comes not only from politicians but also from new ways of understanding and consulting those who are intended to benefit from public services. Inevitably, the demands from the constituencies of 'consumer', the professionals and the politicians do not necessarily align – and it becomes a further task of the manager to reconcile conflicting accountabilities and, some would say, to provide the organizational steer, since not all can be satisfied. Those 'at the top' can therefore begin to create a vision and a mission which brings new influences and new players actively into the interpretation of policy. The chapters by Shackleton, Harrison and Webb are particularly useful in illustrating these issues, while at the same time revealing the kinds of contradictions and paradoxes that need to be managed to maintain the legitimacy of this space.

I believe that the template provided by the notions of administrative, efficiency and consumer paradigm shifts is a useful one through which to understand the issues raised by the majority of the contributors to this volume.

Another useful template is provided by Parston (1994), who explores the idea of conflicting accountabilities. Chief executives in colleges and universities like others across the UK public sector, along with their governing bodies, have had to assume responsibility for coping simultaneously with multiple and often competing demands. Working from his ideas, I cite some of the key ones that challenge those at the top of colleges and universities:

- meeting demands for improved comparative performance (on an uneven playing field) while complying with government policy and regulations
- achieving 'efficiency gains' and, especially, increasing volume and through-put at reduced cost in a 'mythical market' where government controls the numbers
- maintaining accountability with a wider range of stakeholders (eg, students, employers, the community, politicians, etc.) whose influence and indeed power (as supported by, for example, legislation or developments such as student charters) have grown considerably in recent years
- providing high quality services, alone and in partnership with others, that will serve the needs of that institution's constituencies within the terms of their distinctive mission
- generating alternative sources of income when the squeeze on public sector expenditure grows ever tighter, the recession continues and pressures on alternative funding sources have grown enormously
- steering a course between professionally determined criteria of effectiveness and those set by other stakeholders, including students and government; between those criteria that uphold traditional notions of quality and excellence and those that are appropriate to new kinds of educational purposes, processes and outcomes and therefore different notions of colleges and universities

These themes will be seen to figure with different degrees of emphasis in all of the accounts that follow.

The challenges to universities and colleges

These general public sector trends and their specific expression in governmental policy have touched the lives of students, college and university staff, professionals, managers, governors and all those who interact with colleges and universities, such as community organizations and employers. The policy changes have given new legitimacy to particular groups such as students, with the introduction of student charters, and employers, through the introduction of developments such as Enterprise in Higher Education. (This was a massive programme of investment by the Department of Employment in curriculum change related to the needs of industry and commerce.) These voices have traditionally been unheard in colleges and universities. They have especially not tended to influence the professionals' control of the design and delivery of education.

The developments led by government have also coincided with (and, many assert, have been prompted by) significant demographic, social and economic developments. At the same time, the nature and rhythms of knowledge creation and dissemination have changed dramatically, supported by the revolution in technology. It can be argued, and I would agree, that particular configurations of these developments, at a time when the world has become a smaller place, have made certain traditions unsustainable. Amongst these I would include the restriction of access to post-school educational opportunity for only the 'bright young few' or indeed the view that colleges and universities are places solely for servicing the minds and social development of the (largely, affluent) young.

Disturbance of the 'taken for granted'

As external changes are reacted to and their effects are experienced in the day-to-day life of institutions, even our most basic ideas about what a college or university means begin to demand a re-think. As Ronald Barnett (1990) argues in relation to higher education:

In an age when our current concept of higher education has become so enfeebled that it has almost been lost from view, it is important to realise that higher education has stood for notions of substance. Our idea of higher education remains largely buried in the past, but it need not remain there. It can and should be reconstituted, so that it gives our current practice ... a sense of being linked with historical tradition – which has largely been lost – and a view of the way forward.

The expansion of higher education, now shifted to further education colleges, combined with a decrease in what government is prepared to fund, has had considerable effect on the character and practices of colleges and universities. 'Mature students' now comprise the majority of those entering colleges and universities (see Appendix). The student profile has substantially altered, especially within the former polytechnic and college sectors. Even the more traditional universities can no longer assume 'homogeneity of intake', if indeed that mythological notion ever had any validity. Part-time and modular students increasingly rub shoulders with full-time students. Eighteen-year-olds sit beside 45-year-olds. Science students learn alongside humanities students, as more begin to make use of credit-based systems to cross traditional disciplinary and departmental boundaries, wreaking havoc with organizational structures, internal funding arrangements and academic notions of 'the coherent course'. Employers, students and tutors consult and agree learning contracts and those who have learned through living and working gain credit for this experience. Further education colleges offer 'access routes' to HE and increasingly are validated to provide higher education courses directly, in partnership with validating institutions.

Taken-for-granted ways of thinking and doing things, traditional structures and relationships (intra- and extra-institutional), and implicit assumptions about quality in relation to educational process and purpose have all been disturbed. As Dick Beckhard (1992) argues, you cannot add 2000 pounds of weight to a deer and keep the same legs. The animal must fundamentally change. We are no longer talking about 'rules of engagement [between administrators, professionals and politicians] that [illustrate] a gradual, incrementalist, negotiated order' (Richards, 1993), as under the administrative paradigm. Instead, many heads of colleges and universities are having to manage fundamental change clearly from the top (Beckhard and Pritchard, 1992). This in turn has given rise to new notions of organization, management and community.

The emergence of new notions of organization, management and community

I have been fortunate to work alongside students, staff and senior managers as they have struggled with issues of reconstitution and indeed the revitalization of professionals and institutions, in the context of what Adrian Webb in Chapter 3 describes as 'grotesque turbulence' within the public sector. Such efforts have given rise to new notions of organization and management. In the former poly-technics, certain managerial developments have been reinforced by tradition and legislation, the details of which are set out in the Appendix. Across the sector, they have been prompted by developments such as the Jarratt report (1986), the policies and practices of Funding Councils, who now seek mission statements, strategic plans and evidence of quality (in teaching and learning and in research) and of efficiency gains.

Five years ago, to refer to a university or college as 'an organization' ran contrary to the deeply embedded currents of professional autonomy and 'colle-giality' in decision making. The plurality of professional loyalties and interests – often extending well beyond the walls of an institution – seemed to defy any possibility of winning allegiance to institutional core purposes or values, much less to an overall strategic direction. The 'academic community', and participa-tion into its tribes and territories (Becher, 1989), had its own meanings and purposes, often arcane and deeply implicit. These led to the playing out of multiple agendas within institutions, but seldom those to do with a broader sense of community or institutional purpose.

An example from my own work with the sector will illustrate just how alien new public sector themes such as of multiple accountabilities and 'consumerism' have proved for colleges and universities – in ways that I suggest would echo with common cultures throughout the world. Only four years ago, I was fortu-nate to be part of the Royal Society of Arts Higher Education for Capability (1992) and More Means Different (1989) initiatives. These projects opened up major questions of HE purpose, policy and practice, initially with heads of insti-tutions, industrialists from Britain's most successful companies and leading professional figures. I visited over 30 institutions in the course of eight months, in parallel with my fellow director, John Stephenson, who was doing the same on the other side of the country. Our intention was to carry on this debate with cross-disciplinary groups of academic and services-support staff, as well as with those who were managing change within institutions.

Both of us used to comment over and over again, 'We are definitely onto something new here!', for we often provided the first occasion for staff to come together *across* traditional disciplinary boundaries to reflect on questions such as their common purpose, their shared assumptions about teaching and learning processes and outcomes, or implicit assumptions about the role and purposes of the academic community. We helped to surface – often for the first time on a *cross*-institutional basis – explorations relating to core values and practices. For example, what constitutes a 'course'? What does 'academic coherence' actually mean and are there competing meanings when viewed from the perspective of a student? What do we consider to be teaching and learning effectiveness and quality and how do we give this value within this institution? As outsiders, we were able to surface fundamental questions that are all too difficult to raise within institutions, given how deeply implicit, often arcane and uncontested are the assumptions which govern colleges and universities. During these journeys, we were often struck by the extent to which institutions saw themselves as having to 'respond'. There was little energy or vision to support conscientious 'managing up' into the wider political arena. This was understandable, given the degree of shock that reverberated around the sector, as one 'reform' after another struck at the heart of institutional and professional identities and self-esteem.

THE LEADERSHIP AND MANAGEMENT CHALLENGE: THE TWISTER COCKTAIL

Professional resistance to such questioning, much less to managers and being managed, in the context of what has been perceived as government attacks on professional interests, did and does run deep. As I continue to move across different institutions and work with senior managers and professionals from the entire sector, I still encounter fatigue, fear, confusion, anger, hostility, even outrage. I also find hope, energy and people revitalized, as they begin to engage with questions about their broader professional roles and purposes as academics, their understandings of quality teaching, learning and student experience, and the potential role that their institutions might play in creating a truly 'adult higher education' (NIACE, 1993) for a lifelong learning community. Whereas each institution has managed the same external conditions, these differences are increasingly influenced by the management style and approaches to change that have been adopted in response.

This is not to minimize the stress and lowered morale that have come from reduced resources and the relentless pace of change being imposed or induced by the government or other forces in society. Equally, there has been the negative impact of what Trow refers to as the government's fundamental suspicion and mistrust in the 'inner motivations of teachers' (Trow, 1994). Staff become further demoralized when their managers perpetuate these stances.

The reality is that public service managers are managing conflicting and multiple tensions and accountabilities, such as those outlined above. They have no choice but to play (metaphorically) the American game of 'Twister': the dial spins and you need to place your hand on the red circle, and then it spins again, and you need to get your other one on blue, and soon you have a foot on green, another on brown, and meanwhile you need to keep your balance – with decorum of course.

Add to this Twister cocktail the rich mix of professional passions, predilections and loyalties and the pluralist commitments that characterize universities and colleges. Throw in their unique histories and traditions. Then add a healthy dash of Britain's distinctive political, educational and social history: the attitudes and behaviours generated amongst those and their descendants who have been privileged by educational opportunity, in contrast to those who have been excluded, often labelled as failures, however capable. The effects of elitism, and its expression in education, remain with us today despite political claims to the contrary.

The harsh reality is that, in higher education, over 40 years of fully subsidized student tuition and accommodation have not significantly altered the social class profile of graduates. A deep suspicion remains that more and different do indeed mean less and poorer, in terms of reduced standards. Pressures to collude with the status quo (or illusory transformations thereof) remain considerable.

We cannot afford to underestimate the leadership and management challenges facing those who head our colleges and universities. Nor can we underplay the many historical, cultural and political influences that can so subtly subvert those who dare to manage against the grain of tradition. What we certainly cannot do is assume that a big dose of good private sector management practice is all that is needed to 'shape up our universities and colleges'.

There been little attention to thinking through what 'effectiveness' in managing and leading change within colleges and universities might mean, given the multiple challenges that need to be managed. John Bull (Chapter 6) in particular picks up this point, recognizing that failure to attend to such things creates a major weakness in the institution's capacity to steer its own course while simultaneously dealing with unpredictable external forces.

THE NEED FOR NEW FORMS OF LEADERSHIP

We are at a crucial stage in the development of colleges and universities. We cannot afford to sidestep the challenges of stimulating a deeper appreciation of, and more confidence in, new forms of leadership and management in colleges and universities and in the processes that help to stimulate and support significant cultural change.

More than ever, institutions now need to define and achieve their educational and social objectives for a much changed world, harness the talents and enthusiasms of staff and students, build a distinctive portfolio of services (incorporating quality processes and practices to suit lifelong learning and a mass system of post-school education) and orchestrate limited resources to produce value (Parston, 1986). To do this in the context of ever-shifting government policies and changes within society as a whole requires fresh thinking and practice and not a naive importation of often outdated and caricatured command and control managerial styles and practices from the private sector.

The stories that follow will take us forward. The bigger story that weaves its way through each of these chapters is perhaps best captured by Phillida Salmon, who provided much inspiration for my final chapter:

> *To introduce a radical new departure in [an organization's] story is to interrupt the dance, to court the protest or the disbelief of others. Changes that are convincing, that can be personally lived out, can only be made jointly with others (Salmon, 1985).*

The inextricable intertwining of one story with another is the real nature of the challenge we are facing in colleges and universities. What follows provides an opportunity to learn from the experience of those who are trying to devise new and more effective forms of leadership and management in relation to long-term cultural change. These stories are offered in the hope that together they can jointly stimulate new forms of understanding, all the while recognizing that when pattern and story become divorced from the context of real people and real environments, we risk moving into the realm of myth.

References

Ball, Sir Christopher (1989) *More Means Different*, London: Royal Society of Arts.

Barnett, R (1990) *The Idea of Higher Education*, Buckingham: SRHE/Open University Press.

Beckhard, R (1992) 'Changing the Essence'; in *Managing Fundamental Change: Shaping new purposes and roles in public services*, London: Office for Public Management.

Beckhard, R and Pritchard, W (1992) *Changing the Essence*, San Francisco, CA: Jossey-Bass.

Becher, T (1989) *Academic Tribes and Territories*, Buckingham: SRHE/Open University Press.

Jarratt, Sir Alex (1986) 'The Management of Universities', *The Royal Society of Arts Journal*, October.

NIACE (1993) *An Adult Higher Education: A vision*, Leicester: NIACE.

Parston, G (ed.) (1986) *Managers as Strategists*, London: King's Fund.

Public Management Foundation (1994) *Public Manager in the Middle*, London: Public Management Foundation.

Richards, S (1993) *The Consumer Paradigm*, London: Public Management Foundation.

Rodrigues, J (1993) *Redesigning the State Profile for Social and Economic Development and Change: A new paradigm for public management*, London: Office for Public Management.

Salmon, P. (1985) *Living in Time*, London: J M Dent and Sons.

Stephenson, J and Weil, S (1992) *Quality in Learning*, London: Kogan Page.

Trow, M (1994) *Public Affairs Report*, 35, 2, 2, March, Berkeley, CA: Institute of Government Studies.

Weil, S (1988) 'From a language of observation to a language of experience: studying the perspectives of diverse adult learners in higher education', *Journal of Access Studies*, 3, 1, 17–43.

Weil, S (1989a) 'Access towards education or miseducation: adults imagine the future', in Fulton, O (ed.) *Access and Institutional Change*, Buckingham: SRHE/OU Press.

Weil, S (1989b) 'Influences of lifelong learning on adults' expectations and experiences of returning to formal learning contexts', unpublished PhD dissertation, University of London.

Weil, S and McGill, I (1989) *Making Sense of Experiential Learning*, Buckingham: SRHE/OU.

Weil, S *et al.* (1985) *Through a Hundred Paris of Eyes*, London: CSDHE/LGMB.

Chapter 2

Piloting Higher Education Change: A View from the Helm

Christopher Price

The book's contributions begin with some substantive advice from a former principal of a polytechnic, now a university. He anticipates reactions to the title of this book, complementing the 'raised eyebrow' themes in the opening chapter: what change can someone 'at the top' of a college or university introduce? Urging chief executives to 'eschew megalomania about their own role' in such matters, he explores the problematic notion of the 'chief executive'. He questions the wisdom and validity of it being equated with 'top down' management in colleges and universities. At the same time, he acknowledges this 'rhetoric' can be useful with 'political masters'. He suggests the expansion of higher education surfaced new needs for strategic planning and direction under the leadership of one person. He underpins these introductory explorations with a clarification of different traditions in British universities (see Appendix), offering a useful introduction to issues explored by Webb, Harrison, Wilson and Edwards. Price suggests that the real challenge is to combine the roles of intellectual leader and managing director simultaneously.

The substance of the chapter is a series of reflections on lessons borne of the experience of leading a former polytechnic at the forefront of the expansion and 'reconstitution' of higher education. He gives real life to the 'Twister cocktail' metaphor outlined in Chapter 1. He discusses key issues such as managing external politics while maintaining internal morale, the risks of 'alibi-ing', ensuring realism, communication, internal and external market research, and the transformation of committees into teams. He also considers ways in which resource management can be used creatively as an 'agent of change', and the limitations of restructuring in influencing the cultural fabric of a university. He also offers advice on managing governors and 'the community'. He concludes with words of warning to anyone thinking about taking on a role 'at the top'.

INTRODUCTION: USEFUL AND LESS USEFUL STARTING POINTS

The title of this book could be misleading. Change, sometimes startling change, has been arriving upon colleges and universities worldwide over the past decade. Many chief executives of these institutions may think that change is primarily induced by them from the top. Others, within the interstices of the organization, also like to take credit for it. But much change is neither bottom up nor top down; it is driven by a range of near-invisible, and sometimes unacknowledged, external pressures – new technology, funding formulae, performance indicators, curricular fashions, student consumer whim, institutional competition and other governmental fads – the effects of which strike participants late in the day. In this state of flux, for much of the time, what the chief executive can best do is steady the ship, cheer up the crew and gently nudge the tiller now and then. An important daily reminder for chief executives is to eschew megalomania about their own role in change.

This is not to diminish the craft of a university chief executive; part of it is the yachtsman's craft of harnessing the wind, a whole package of complicated skills and decisions – in particular when to act and when to sit tight; yachts can as easily capsize if the skipper just sits there and does nothing, as they can if fool-hardy efforts are made to tack against an impossible gale. The important message is that management is not a matter of giving orders; the worst management metaphors are military ones and Britain's worst management period was immediately after the Second World War when Montgomery's (and others generals') staff officers moved into British industry and services, fondly thinking that winning the peace was just like winning the war. I believe that nautical metaphors are somehow more apt and helpful, especially when thinking about managing change in colleges and universities.

In this chapter, I shall review some characteristics of universities generally that have made them unamenable to the idea of a chief executive, and then look at this resistance in the context of the traditional European model. I shall then consider the challenges that have arisen in the context of expansion, that have required more of a clear executive steer. I shall conclude with some lessons borne of experience that have been modified by reflection since choosing to move on, and which I hope will help those who are trying to introduce change 'from the top' or elsewhere.

THE ROLE OF THE CHIEF EXECUTIVE

The nature of professional resistance

Universities have traditionally been characterized by a 'collegiate resistance to any industrial management model. The whole concept of a 'chief executive' is viewed with abhorrence by university teachers across the Western world. In many universities the role scarcely yet exists.

The modern university and college chief executive in Britain is a child of Thatcherism. Over the past few years there have been strenuous efforts first to bring universities and colleges into line with an industrial market model; and then to try to meld this private sector model with public accountability principles using government agencies as national holding companies. The establishment of subsidiary 'funding councils' with chief officers accountable to a National Audit Office, has inevitably required in its turn accountable 'chief executives' in every university and college.

The new market culture that has been introduced into British public services, and with it the concept of a chief executive, runs against the grain of a thousand years of university development. Universities established in the European tradition have always been at heart collegiate organisms; a rector or a vice-chancellor has been elected to preside over a senate which takes the strategic decisions on the direction of development. To the extent that 'administration' was required to oil the wheels, an administrator (a registrar in traditional English universities) has traditionally been appointed to do it. Exactly the same system exists in Germany, with a civil servant 'chancellor' appointed as permanent administrator by the Land with an elected academic rector serving a limited term at the behest of colleagues.

In Britain the revolution in the public services has brought the relationship between the vice-chancellor and the registrar into a new focus. While in a few traditional universities the vice-chancellor has taken effective control, in most the registrar remains the *de facto* chief executive. I would argue that in many, the commissioned officer (the vice-chancellor) continues to represent the social and intellectual life of the place while a warrant officer (the registrar) takes responsibility for the cash and the buildings and the drains. Under this old tradition the warrant officer registrar never becomes the colonel of the regiment.

However, 1992 saw the first ever English promotion of a registrar to a vice-chancellor post – albeit to an ex-polytechnic 'new' university. This must signal some sort of a change. It is far too early, however, to pronounce the death of the old tradition in the old universities.

The need for a role resolution

A resolution of this 'chief executive' issue is crucial to the introduction of change. This presupposes, for the first time, integrated, rather than split, management. For the first time universities and colleges need to be planned as a whole. The human, physical and intellectual resources need to be developed within a finite cash envelope, so that efficiency gains can finance a substantial part of expansion of the necessary post-school opportunity.

I am not now arguing whether this strategy is either possible or desirable; but rather that the key to whether or not it happens will lie in the ability of one individual, usually from an academic pedigree, to be an intellectual leader and a managing director simultaneously. Of course it is possible to do it; but there are no existing role models, no books, no accounts of the way in which it may be possible simultaneously to maintain staff morale, pack the students in *and* preserve the traditions of the place. However, if the management iron enters too deep into the vice-chancellor soul, then the university can lose a vital defining spark.

The alternative tradition

It is useful to consider these issues in the context of the alternative tradition of the now former polytechnics. These institutions were garnered together from existing colleges by Anthony Crosland, Minister of Education under the Labour government from 1965 to 1967, with the express aim of creating a different university model. He intended that these new providers of higher education would feel responsibile for a very much wider section of the general public than the narrow social and intellectual elite which had always formed the universities' clientele. Though Mr Crosland did not live to see the day, the polytechnics he created became such successful institutions that they were used, 25 years later, to break the monopoly of the old elite university tradition and widen the nation's view of its own human potential. (see Appendix)

Paradoxically, this was because the technical colleges from which the poly-technics were formed had directors and vice-chancellors who had *always* been *de facto* chief executives. As institutions, they were strangers to all the obstructive elements in university collegiality; they had not inherited the old vice-chancellor/registrar split. Mr Crosland chose them as foils to the university tradition because of their links to the working class; John Major because of their efficient managerial style. Briefly, they became the favoured sons of both sides of the political divide and in 1992 they came to represent the Government's favoured pattern for Britain's new model university.

So the concept of the 'top' of a polytechnic was a well-defined one, delineated by years of local council hierarchical structures, both at the level of director and at that of the head of department. It was quite unlike the traditional university where vice-chancellors were often distinguished academics who saw the job as both a chore and a duty which took them away from their first love, their subject; and where the heads of department often preferred to call themselves 'chairmen' and do the job for a limited term of a few years. But this hierachical 'top' could be deceptive. Though the formal powers of the director were awesome, the local authority officers and the local councillors on the governing body could always form themselves into a sort of unofficial appeal court if directors had the temerity to use their undoubted powers in ways which the academic staff disapproved of. One, or perhaps two, radical directorial acts were tolerated, especially at the beginning; beyond that, change had to be much more carefully negotiated.

When the polytechnics were removed from local authority control, this appeal court suddenly disappeared; its analogue became the techniques of management and teamwork through which directors attempted to keep both the consent of the staff and the momentum of change alive side-by-side.

LESSONS BORNE OF EXPERIENCE

I shall now consider some lessons borne of some successes and many mistakes. What follows will be helpful hints modified by reflection in retirement.

Creating buffer zones

First, *don't infect the institution with your management of externals*. Being the chief executive under a local council in a big city involved dealing with a tangled web of party political and bipartisan priorities. Managing an autonomous university continues to involve the person at the top with a host of political masters, whom it is important to understand and cope with. But you should not share this task with any more than a few senior staff who can help and need to know. Contrary to messages in popular novels and television drama, most lecturers come into higher education for a quiet, apolitical life. The boss is paid to sort these things out and not worry them with the problem.

More specifically, although the local councillors from the days before incorporation from the Local Education Authorities (LEAs) have been removed, it is now funding councils which deluge university and college management with a daily diet of forms to fill in, forecasts to make, cash to bid for, performance indicators to meet and hurdles to jump. The principle – of buffer zones – applies in just the same way. You need to set up a small but highly intelligent bureaucracy (often recruitable from your existing lecturing staff) to get funding council returns in on time, smooth-talk their bureaucrats and massage the words and figures into a shape acceptable to them. On one level it is all a bit of a game; but it is a game with rules which you and your colleagues have to understand and stay within. And you will need a bureaucracy to help you manage these forces; but it should be kept as invisible as possible. However much these influences colonize your own sleepless nights, don't blink when in dialogue with staff and students. Your first task is to maintain *their* morale.

One difficulty is that those within the faculties and departments of your institution will resent your bureaucracy, which they will see as a privileged praetorian guard. They will want to set up competing sub-bureaucracies of their own. It is important not to let them; and in all public pronouncements insist that the bureaucracy exists only to serve the staff and students in helping maximize the income and standing of the university as a whole. If your senior bureaucrats begin to develop any other agenda, you should stop them in their tracks. You will spend many hours with them, helping them get their words and figures just right; but this should be a relatively private part of your university life; your main role will be to give the university an honest and overall account of institutional progress, uncontaminated by irrelevant minutiae.

The management buck really does stop at the top

So, secondly, *don't alibi*. Remember that anything that happens is always your fault and you should always take responsibility for it. Alibi-ing can go upwards or downwards. The 'old' universities made themselves unpopular throughout the 1980s by refusing to cooperate with government policies and constantly whingeing in public. It was the sort of stance which Oxford and Cambridge could afford but the others could not. One university governing council I used to attend consisted of a catalogue by the vice-chancellor of his long, and usually lost, battles (as David) against the iniquities of a philistine, Goliath government. It was not a stance which assisted his standing or credibility. The whole point of being a vice-chancellor is to take responsibility for the institution and trust the lecturers to be sufficiently streetwise and realistic to assume you are battling daily with a range of outside Goliaths. Worse still is alibi-ing downwards. You will have to deal with subordinates who are not up to the job and are drowning in a new environment with which they cannot cope. You should first encourage and develop them and if that doesn't work shift them. As a final resort sack them. But don't make a big deal of it to anyone else; and in particular, don't blame them in public. When you are chief executive, the buck almost always stops with you.

Ensuring that realism reigns

Third, *realism*. Many university lecturers like living in slight fantasy worlds. Almost without exception, they were clever kids at school who decided to invest their cleverness in an 'academic' career. A few have worked in private industry or commerce, but not many. A lot simply don't know the wider score of life in the outside world and don't particularly want to. The sharing throughout the university of a sense of constitutional and economic realism can be one of the most difficult tasks you face.

The constitutional side – the framework set by the government, the funding council and the board of governors – is especially important. The staff need to understand that you only operate as chief executive within this context: specifically, in ex-polytechnics, articles of government lay down where the governors have precedence, particularly over the *mission* of the institution. This is by far the most important concept to get across to the staff – not as something which is negotiable but as a fixed statement which, until it is reviewed, guides all decisions.

At the same time, the mission is quite useless as a statement until it gets some sense of ownership within the place. It will contain academic, economic and social elements; it should act as some sort of reminder that, whatever they used to be, universities cannot today be ivory towers and do what they do in relation to the community. In essence a mission statement is an ethical document; it should be able to justify the university to the outside world. When things are simply not working, it is often because different staff are pursuing their own different missions. Every moment of effort spent by the chief executive in winning assent for the ideas in the mission statement is worthwhile.

The other larger element of necessary realism is economic and technological. Universities operate today within a context of tightening budgets and technological change. The whole business of teaching and learning is changing fast in front of the eyes of both lecturers and students. It is important to get over the reality that the leisured environment of the old university is not going to return; and that students' pressure to set their own agenda for the shape of their courses, and to gain the access to staff time and technology they believe they need, can only increase each year. Universities have become unalterably different places. The infusion of these constitutional, economic and technological realities into the university psyche is one of the most difficult tasks the chief executive will face.

Communication and briefing

So fourth, therefore, *communication and briefing*. Like all large and changing organizations where plenty of staff have time to gossip, universities are rumour factories. Who's up, who's down, what's in, what's out? The only antidote to rumour is open government. There are peculiar difficulties here with universities in the 1990s. Universities are awash with paper, much of it written in turgid prose, inevitably for a range of different audiences. One of the tasks of a university manager is to become expert in hermeneutics, interpreting to their particular group of staff just what it all means.

To help these managers, chief executives need to set the example at the top, through regular briefing sessions to as wide a range of managers as they can muster, whether by wandering into staff common rooms, talking informally to people or by finding ways of getting the staff to work in teams (of which more later) and talk to one another. Teamwork and communication are symbiotically linked.

Important in all this are *organs of communication*. All management magazines should be healthily distrusted by staff; the trick is to mix management news with anti-management news; gossip with cartoons; smooth pronouncements with letters criticizing them. Above all print internal newsletters on the cheapest possible paper; internal glossies are a turn off. A final communication injunction: remind everyone that briefing never stops; saying things only once is quite inadequate; to get the message home you have to say them over and over again.

Market research – inside and out

Next, *market research*, both about your staff and your students, actual and potential. Fifty years ago, in small universities, everyone knew everyone; this may be still the case in some Oxbridge colleges. But modern universities with 10,000 or 20,000 students actually know very little about themselves. They return detailed figures on cash flow, academic staff, administrative staff, usable square metres, student numbers (full- and part-time), pass rates, courses, programmes, modules and research publications; and not only for this year but for each of the five years to come. All this tells you something, but not much. It gives little hint of reality about what any of the staff and students are thinking in terms of the environment and performance of the institution.

That is why universities need continuous market research to know how people rate them. Market surveys of such attitudes are initially painful to read; all the senior managers turn out to be blissfully content, while the troops are moaning hard; but each time you do it, you understand the place better and morale perks up a bit; and for all the staff say, the management gets appreciation for doing the exercise at all.

Building the potential for teamwork: the challenge of committees

An important role of any university chief executive is to translate flaccid obstructive committees into active dynamic teams. In origin, the university committee is the epitome and fountainhead of what was always perceived to be university democracy. They are forums in which intelligent men and women can play politics, reconcile views, learn a little bit more about each other, fight their corner, concede points. In some universities there was always the unspoken assumption that if change was wanted or called for from above, it had to await committee unanimity from below; today, this culture is a recipe for structural arthritis. Change does indeed take place in universities in spite of committees, driven by external events and canny colleagues; but in too many universities, committee structures perform a purely elegant and formal role to maintain a myth of academic democracy which is thought by some essential for the academic tranquillity of a range of (usually senior) dons in myriad departments and faculties.

Committees, in this old sense, are yesterday's mechanisms. Yet they need to be replaced by something; and that something must not be an old fashioned industrial management model. In most of industry, command economy structures are being superseded by teamwork; in universities it is even more important for managerial decisions to be validated by colleagues. In the best university, the formal committee merges into the less formal team and the two cultures begin to come together. The ability of chief executives to practise the teamwork they preach will be vital to any permeation of this new form of 'management by consent' throughout the university.

Creative resource management as a 'change agent'

An environment of teamwork can immeasurably assist the management of the two issues with which all chief executives become obsessed and entangled: resources and structure. First *resources*. Resources are not just cash. They are time, buildings, space and above all, people. Staff time and talent is probably the most valuable resource, if the most difficult to harness for the objectives of the university; great savings in management time and management staffing can be made by reducing bureaucratic process to the minimum necessary; space, which needs heating, lighting and maintaining, is often almost as difficult to manage as staff time because it is owned by small disparate units.

But the staff enthusiasm is by far the most important of the university's resource assets and staff passivity the most draining resource handicap. So integrated and sensitive management of, first, people and second, 'places and spaces' can bring massive morale and efficiency dividends; both require assent to the proposition that precious resources should be shared not hoarded.

This 'sharing not hording' principle is important. A generously resourced university very often shares naturally; a tighter budget will tend to build high fences between departments, as managers concentrate on their own private people and territory. This is where the sensible use of matrix management can help if properly implemented. If one manager is in charge of course costs and another the staff available, the subsequent negotiation can often fit staff to courses more effectively. The same is true of modular course management. By dividing courses up into smaller 'modules', substantial efficiencies can be achieved, as it gradually dawns on the university that it is teaching different groups of students the same subject matter. But neither matrix management nor modularization are panaceas; both, being partly driven by efficiency criteria, can break up the solidarity between students, their teachers and their course which can be essential to their progress. It is fatal to pursue either without a wide range of consent.

In the event, however, other technological forces are already breaking up student solidarity, driving students back on their own resources and those of their personal computers, making them independent learners and their lecturers more facilitators than teachers. Libraries are driven by CD-ROM systems more than journals and books. In principle, technology ought to be driving down costs in universities as it is in industry. It is still not clear whether a generation of students who have sat in front of their computer and video will be more or less effective or humane than their elders who sat at the feet of their guru. Certainly we need gurus in universities but, even in an elite university age, there were never enough of them to go round. Now we may have to be more content than we used to be with watching them on television.

Which brings us to the final resource: cash. Most universities now have cost centres (responsible for expenditure) or budget centres (responsible for both income and expenditure) and powerful deans and others to whom freedom to spend is delegated. This creates an annual public expenditure round in the university (a paradigm of the same phenomenon in government) and produces similar tensions between the departments and the bureaucratic centre, over which it is the task of the chief executive to arbitrate.

In all this, the distribution of resources can be used by the chief executive as a 'change agent'; in this process, the achievement of change can be 'bidding'-led or 'policy'-led. The distinction is crucial. You can top slice the budget and create a tendering process for the proceeds; or achieve a corporate set of priority change targets among your deans and hold them to it through teamwork, feedback and appraisal. The former can work, but is divisive and ultimately ineffective; the latter is a better technique in principle, though slower in delivering change and only properly works when there is widespread assent to the objectives of the university as a whole.

Cultures, not just structures

As change is slow to come through, there is a tendency to blame it all on *structure*. It is probably true that the most effective way of shaking up a university is to walk in and change the structure. Throw all the cards up in the air and see how they come down. Structural reorganization is the classic 'top down' favourite for inducing change. Get rid of the old staff officers and put a new lot in. All organizations need to undergo minor earthquakes if they are not to atrophy and die; and structural change of this kind is one way of producing the requisite earthquake. There are a whole range of options: a flat structure of 15 or 20 departments; five or six large faculties, headed by deans who effectively begin to run sub-colleges of their own; a tight centralized bureaucracy, headed up by an 'old school' registrar; or a general culture of devolution in which everyone is empowered to go more or less their own way. There are many kinds of 'wiring diagrams' with which a chief executive can delineate the organization of the university.

In all these changes, it is important to remember that structures are not nearly as important as culture. You can have the most sophisticated and structured wiring diagram in the world of who reports to whom in terms of both functional and line management; it can be comparatively flat or comparatively hierarchical. Such wiring diagrams can be comforting and useful; but they guarantee nothing. The effective operation of a university depends on the willing assent of the staff to work within whatever structure is prescribed. All your major mistakes will be people mistakes; all your major successes will be people successes. Creating the right informal atmosphere of teamwork, cooperation and purpose is immensely more important than the formal structural framework within which it purports to take place.

Changes in structure should follow some clearly articulated academic, professional or economic rationale. This will not be easy. Traditional universities are addicted, at heart, to subject-based courses; the former polytechnics to professional ones. It is difficult to find a structure which accommodates both frameworks. Problems centre upon specialists and generalists. Take mathematics. Every university student needs some tutoring in mathematics. Should every mathematician be in a department called mathematics? Or should they scatter themselves across every department? Or modern languages. Every student ought to leave university bi- or tri-lingual. But how does a chief executive make this happen? Like mathematicians, linguists like to cluster together, keep up their specialisms and spend as little time as possible on what some of them dismiss as 'service teaching' for other departments.

So it is important, in restructuring, to make the subject the servant of the student. Departmental structures should be oriented, as far as possible, to the world as it is about to become for the students, rather than the world as it was for the teachers when they did their degrees. Technologies change at a pace faster than the average undergraduate course; current university departmental structures predate the arrival of student consumer demand; computing and engineering merge at the edges; every course needs a management module within it. I am not suggesting that all these pressures should be conceded; simply that, in an increasingly competitive environment, the chief executive should try to create a culture amenable to change.

MANAGING AND MEDIATING EXTERNAL BODIES

Many of the preceding injunctions have been addressed to what a 'chief executive' should do. It should not be inferred from this that it is the role of a chief executive somehow to take action on whim or without consultation. I have talked of internal teams but there are a range of external bodies to be constantly mediated also. Two that I find most important are explored below.

The board of governors

The chief executive is accountable to 'a board of governors' in new universities (of between 15 and 25 members); and to 'a council' in old ones of anything up to 60 or 70. As boards of directors at which some bucks allegedly stop, these bodies range from the utterly toothless to the domineering and interfering with all sorts of gradations in between. In old universities their powers are vague; in new ones they are supposedly strategic but in fact few and far between. In both, their only really interesting task is to hire and fire the chief executive.

Extremes of toothlessness and interference are fatal to the operation of a university. It is the task of the chief executive in facing the governors to be just that – the only executive director on the board. This requires keeping a close personal relationship mostly with the chairman (or 'chair' as we at Leeds successfully persuaded a petulantly reluctant privy council to be allowed to name ours) but also with every other member of the board. The chief executive status has to be earned and maintained through personal trust with the individuals concerned. If that trust is maintained and the purposes of strategies explained, the governors will feel sufficiently empowered not to interfere in details which are no concern of theirs. If it breaks, all hell gets let loose; and when that happens, it tends to be chief executives, not the governors, who lose out.

The 'community'

And the 'community'. In a university some of your most persistent judges and critics are outside the walls. The local bourgeoisie, often irritated by a new university in their midst; the local councils, uneasy about their new relationship; the local newspaper editor, perhaps unready to take a new university seriously; and the mass of the local folk, many of whom will have close contact as parents, employees and part-time students, who are always quietly assessing and rating the place. Their opinions are the most important of all; the one member of senior management whose office should be next to that of the chief executive is the head of communication and public relations; and all invitations to mix outside the walls at (always pompous and often tedious) social and municipal duties, should be either accepted, or enforced on deputies. No decision should lightly be taken which would not be understood by this wider community.

FOUR FINAL TIPS

Four final 'tips', for they are no more than that. First use your honeymoon period well. Universities and colleges are deeply conservative institutions, in which the majority of staff have become comfortable about doing things their way. They are prepared to concede change in the early weeks and months of a new chief executive. But the time has to be seized over those crucial days. If you leave it too long the task will be immensely more difficult.

Second, maintain your own personality, academic or otherwise. University vice-chancellors nowadays need to be a new mix of scholar and manager. As management pressures increase, the combination becomes more difficult to find. The management criterion tends to prevail. But vice-chancellors will fail as chief executives if they do not maintain a degree of either academic credibility or some other professional hobby or quirk. Lecturers like personalities, however offbeat and nonconformist, better than managerial calculating machines. So set some time aside to pursue your favourite obsession; keep up with at least an element of your subject; do some teaching, if only to maintain a connection with students.

Third, a motto for times of trouble: strategy first, detail later. Sometimes good, sensible initiatives run into the sand. The reason is very often that they have been launched at too great a level of detail, without a preceding debate of the principles behind them. So, if you get yourself into a hole, stop digging, stand back and re-present a more strategic view of the object of the exercise and gain assent for that first. You can gain the assent to changes, whether from staff or governors, even though these changes act adversely on individuals, if they see it as part of a properly thought-out plan for the greater good.

I suppose my final message is a personal one. The old university tradition of electing the rector for a limited period had good democratic principles behind it. So if you find yourself a university or college chief executive, do not hang on too long. Set yourself some tasks and when they are done consider moving on to something else. Long vice-chancellerian reigns do not have particularly good track records. The management of change from the top needs a steady recycling of individuals through posts; that applies to vice-chancellors and principals too. If they are sensible, they set an example.

Chapter 3

Two Tales from a Reluctant Manager

Adrian Webb

This chapter explores challenges entailed in introducing change 'from the top' within two different institutional cultures: the technologically-driven research university, and the one that has emerged out of a local polytechnic tradition. Adrian Webb reinforces a key theme in the opening chapter: namely, how difficult it is to go against the grain of tradition, despite government rhetoric that seems to favour difference and change in the higher education sector. To do so requires the skilful management of contradictions if the process of cultural change is not to be completely undermined. In the traditional university, Adrian Webb offers the example of the tension between demands for greater corporateness and executive management, and funding policies that encourage departments to see financial rewards for expansion and research quality as 'theirs'. At the University of Glamorgan, the traditions and rewards associated with research excellence and, as is now emerging, teaching excellence (HEFCE/CHES, 1994) challenge an institution that is determined to be a community university, actively contributing to economic and social regeneration. Such tensions are also explored in the chapters by Harrison, Price, Flint and Shackleton.

The difficulties of bringing together professional and managerial cultures is well captured here, in the author's account of his early 'on the job management training' as head of department. He explores the limits and potential of restructuring, and the difficulties of maintaining a living dialogue between such processes and those of mission definition and focusing – issues that are also picked up by Bull, Shackleton, Wilson, and Price.

By virtue of now leading an institution that dares to be different in many ways, Adrian Webb gives further weight to the 'Twister cocktail' metaphor described in the first chapter. Considerable external pressure has been exerted to introduce greater coherence and better resource utilization in colleges and universities. But the steady onslaught of pressures and the traumas these generate within institutions have made it difficult to *manage* cultural and organizational transitions at an appropriate pace.

It could be argued that the government policy of halting expansion in HE (while accelerating it in FE) will generate more participatory and iterative processes that are supported by a clear executive steer and considerable investment in staff and organizational development. As illustrated here, this helps to build the internal capability required to manage the external forces that continue to work against many of the reforms that the former polytechnics have introduced to support wider access, flexibility and choice, as well as lifelong learning that is more student – than subject – centred. Harrison describes similar dilemmas. As long as the dominant traditions of a university are rewarded, there will be a considerable management challenge to those like the author who are determined that colleges and universities are free to define and achieve new forms of social result and expression as 'community universities'.

INTRODUCTION

An unexpected career turn

I stumbled unintentionally into senior management. From the mid-1960s to the beginning of the 1980s mine was a conventional academic career; from the 1980s onwards, however, academic management roles became increasingly dominant. The managerial progression seems, in retrospect, to be a classical and inevitable one: research leadership, departmental headship, dean of faculty, pro-vice-chancellor (all at Loughborough University) to vice-chancellor and chief executive at the new University of Glamorgan. Yet, like almost all academics, I have received no systematic training in management and, initially, I viewed management as alien to the entire academic enterprise. Indeed, a round of interviews at other universities in the late 1970s was prompted by my search for a professorship – any professorship – which would not inexorably lead, as my own at Loughborough was doing, to the burdens of departmental headship.

That the first reluctant foot on the managerial ladder led to my present post is explicable in three ways. The first is simply that as head of department at Loughborough I inherited a very skilled and experienced departmental secretary. She transformed the administrative incompetence which I effortlessly generated into a standard of efficiency and dependability which impressed my superiors. They subsequently promoted the wrong person – me not her – and the rest is history. The second was my personal realization that an increasingly turbulent environment was placing demands on higher education which made the management challenge an intellectually stimulating one. University managers increasingly needed to synthesize ideas for change and development coming from many quarters, to scan their environments, seek to span internal divisions and transcend the boundaries of the university itself so as to cope with threats and maximize opportunities. The third explanation is that I had a measure of that luck which Napoleon so valued in his generals: some key things went right – and thereby reinforced the gradual shift from academic to managerial roles. But luck is an unscientific concept and, as I will emphasize, its analytic version may perhaps be better described as a capacity to seize on serendipity: to ally opportunism to more directed and intentional forms of shaping change.

The point of this potted career history is to underline my strong sense that, just as in much else, a manager – perhaps especially an untrained one – is shaped for good or ill by early experience. I remain wedded to what emerged as my initial strengths and weaknesses: an enjoyment in boundary-spanning and a mistrust of narrowness of purpose and defence of territory; the gleaning and synthesizing of ideas from many sources rather than the pursuit of a singular, purely personal, vision; and an impatience with administrative detail. No one can hope to be a manager for all seasons and responding to turbulence while surrounded by a team which complements my strengths and weaknesses may well define my outer limits – but who knows?

Policy turbulence

It is presently impossible to write about higher education, or most other areas of what used to be called the public sector, without immediately noting the *grotesque turbulence* which has beset it in recent years. This turbulence has been the defining characteristic of the management task; indeed, it is what has made management – as opposed to old-style 'public administration' – necessary and yet virtually impossible. (See Appendix).

It is not just the broad sweep of policy change which presents problems, but the myriad modifications, adjustments and, indeed, inconsistencies which flow from a government system which is increasingly seized by radical change as a totem rather than as a means to an end. Policy analysts used blithely to contrast 'disjointed incrementalism' with a synoptic and rational approach capable of achieving more radical or fundamental transformations. The more fitting epithet over recent years might have been 'disjointed radicalism'. Fundamental change has certainly flowed from government policy, but the tides set in motion have as often produced cross currents as a surge in one, known direction. Yet this disjointedness may well have occasioned more change in previously staid public bodies – by destabilizing them – than any whole-hearted push in a particular direction.

Some themes

Several key themes have emerged out of my experience as a manager at Loughborough and now at Glamorgan, although the cultures and traditions of the two institutions hvae been significantly different.

The first of these has been the need to *manage the whole*: to try to take a comprehensive and coherent approach to managing entire institutions rather than particular bits of them. Coupled inextricably to this has been the requirement to *manage change* consciously and as systematically as possible – both irresistible change visited from outside and change planned from inside. Turbulence, and external pressures and demands, may be the harbinger of enforced change but they can also be pressed into service as catalysts of planned change; put more dramatically, the art of managing change is to make *beneficial use of containable crises.*

To concede that achieving desired change is even partly in the lap of the gods rather than in the safe hands of the rational, goal-directed manager is to return to my earlier reference to serendipity. For me, management (even, perhaps especially, forward planning) is not a jigsaw in which everything has a precise place into which it must be slotted, but a water-colour painting in which a general intention is transformed as liquid colours collide and merge in unpredicted ways. The task is to spot the 'accidents' which can be worked on to create valued passages, while subjecting others to rapid damage limitation. More formally, I am intrigued by the complex *interaction of the planned and the serendipitous*.

Beyond these general themes about the nature of management are the specific topics which characterize contemporary thoughts about how to manage higher education institutions. At both Loughborough and Glamorgan, three topics predominated. The first, *mission*, throws into stark relief the changes that have engulfed universities. Until recently they hardly knew they needed a mission; the mission was so taken for granted as not to need specification. Now, universities are enjoined to embrace diverse missions; some part of this diversity – and challenge – will be illustrated by reference to Loughborough and Glamorgan. The second, *cost-effectiveness and efficiency*, is at the very heart of the changes visited from outside yet which subsequently had to be planned from inside. The third, *management structures, processes and organizational culture*, cannot be ignored.

What I shall do below is explore how some of these general themes and specific topics have translated into management choice and action in two very different environments. Loughborough was characterized by traditions of collegiality that circumscribed management. At the University of Glamorgan, there has always been a managerial tradition, but this had been heavily influenced by the style and politics of the local authority of which the institution was part until 1992. (Incorporation in Wales came several years later than that of the English polytechnics.) The two contrasting cultures reveal similar preoccupations, but very different approaches to introducing change 'from the top'.

THE UNIVERSITY OF LOUGHBOROUGH

Early lessons as head of department

When I became head of department in the early 1980s I had no idea what I was going to be able to contribute. The details of my experience of turning a department around are beyond the scope of this chapter, but some important lessons about management emerged that stood me in good stead after I became pro-vice-chancellor.

The most fundamental problem of managing change which I encountered at this time was that of having *to face two ways at once and to bridge two significantly different cultures and sets of expectations*. The 'old university' tradition was very much one of self-directed professionals operating within an institution which, at least in ideal terms, was characterized as self-governing. However, the external world was imposing a rate of institutional adaptation which was difficult to reconcile with this model. The early 1980s were characterized by a growing expectation within the corporate centre of the university that a head of department would be able to 'deliver': to sign up to change and opportunities at very short notice. Back in the department, however, the head was expected to operate on a *collegial-consultative* basis, not to say a wholly democratic one.

I was acutely conscious of these tensions but in a sense did not directly address them. I pursued change by leading from the front in research terms. I unintentionally cut myself off from important colleagues by seeming to entrench particular interests and to enshrine a model of professional activity which was alien to many. But initial success meant that my pattern of behaviour was reinforced. I never did look at the department as a whole and achieve an agreed strategy within which it and each individual member of it could develop and move forward. The department only changed dramatically and became the extremely successful one it is today because my own contribution, which was to manage the external environment and perceptions of the department, was complemented by efforts of others.

The second lesson I learned was the importance of *anticipating, if possible, shifts and trends in the external environment and to place one's own institution in a favourable position to exploit these changes.* For example, when I arrived, I concentrated on securing large research grants. My success stimulated, over the next decade, the growth of a substantial research centre that eventually won an 'outstanding' rating in the Funding Council's first research assessment exercise. As the cash registers began to ring in the vice-chancellor's office the department's previously low status within the university was transformed.

This early success turned into a virtuous spiral because research, and particularly large external research grants, had become nationally important at precisely the right time for it to benefit my department. While good fortune certainly played its part, I learned the importance of staying systematically attuned to environmental signals and shifts of direction.

Even though a greater degree of self-consciousness and systematic anticipation of opportunities and events crept into my way of working, the management of change would be an altogether too grandiose way of characterizing my early experiences. This could hardly be equated with the then classical and more 'academic' view of managing change. However, as much of my own academic writing on policy making and planning has underlined, the preoccupation with rational comprehensive planning in the 1960s and 1970s gave undue weight to a formal, linear and apparently highly structured and rational approach. My own was to marry a broad sense of direction which was perhaps characterized more by the need to avoid failure than by any specific image of success, to opportunism and an emerging capacity 'to do deals'.

A change in career direction

Although it was not apparent at the time, the consequence of appearing to be an effective manager was that my career began to change direction. My period as head of department was brought prematurely to a close by being offered the deanship of the faculty and that role was itself terminated a year early when I was appointed as pro-vice-chancellor and later as senior pro-vice-chancellor (in effect the post of deputy vice-chancellor). These moves into more senior management required greater attention to systematic strategic planning. This tempered the rather instinctual approach which I had previously adopted, without by any means eradicating it entirely. Perhaps the biggest change as I moved up the management ladder was the loss of opportunity to lead from the front. Personal professional success and achievement still mattered but it didn't have the systemic effect it had had when I was leading a department within my own broad disciplinary field. I therefore had to find new ways of effecting change. The senior management posts also involved a significant change in function compared with being a head of department. Perhaps surprisingly in one sense, these senior roles were much more inward-looking. They involved dealing with the whole of the institution but, with the exception of specific negotiations and discussions with individual outside organizations, they did not involve a significant degree of representation of the institution to the outside world. However, the tension of 'facing both ways' and of balancing entirely different managerial cultures and expectations remained.

The need for internal changes

Changes in the environment required substantial internal structural and proces- sual changes, to achieve a greater degree of coherence and better resource utilization at a time when the rate of externally imposed and induced change in the university world was truly traumatic. The most pressing case for greater corporateness and executive management arose from the need *to instil a degree of cost-awareness throughout the university*. Like many public bodies, univer- sities had operated without any real awareness of the true costs of their activities. Departments handled budgets for recurrent expenditure but were not responsible for the staffing or premises costs of their activities. Consequently, they had little awareness of the real costs of producing teaching and research, nor did they have any real opportunity to develop their own best pattern of resource utilization and of resource substitution

More effective executive management was essential, but the best way forward was far from clear. The external pressures implied a degree of increased centralization which ran counter to the university's entrenched and previously highly successful tradition of powerful departments relating to a relatively weak centre. This inheritance facilitated incremental, even radical, change at depart- mental level but made it very difficult for the university as a whole to shift its ground or to respond corporately to the outside world. The nature and pace of externally driven change also meant that academics were being forced into a reluctant and sometimes saddened acceptance of the need for cultural transfor- mation, with little time for managing that transition.

The somewhat more contentious case for a greater degree of corporateness was that an increasingly turbulent environment might yield opportunities which could best be exploited on a cross-departmental/cross-disciplinary base, and pose threats which could best be warded off by concerted action. Prime examples of such opportunities were the increasing importance of EC monies in research and in other forms of development; such threats were characterized by the possibility of a sudden loss of student demand in scarcity disciplines.

Moving forward: restructuring and devolution

The chosen way forward comprised two components: a recasting of structures and processes, especially the committee system; and financial devolution to academic departments. In retrospect, the corporate approach was not greatly different to my own as head of department. We had a perception of where we wanted *not* to be, and indeed of the rough direction in which we wanted to progress, but we did not have a closely concerted strategy for change. In particu- lar, the two strands of change were related but not closely coordinated.

My own role included involvement in both areas of change, but more so in the reshaping of structures and processes than in the detail of financial devolution.

Structural change proceeded through three main phases: a simplification of the committee structure; a series of changes in key committees designed to allow the central management team to exercise greater influence over their work; and a re- examination of the role of faculties vis-à-vis the centre of the university and the academic departments.

The first of these, for example, allowed the number of committee cycles in the year to be reduced from six to three. This progressively and inevitably created both the need and the room for greater executive decision taking. An increasingly large body of operational matters was handled by members of the senior management team and retrospectively approved by chairman's action. The fact of greater executive action was not strongly criticized or resisted by academics and was increasingly welcomed by many heads of departments who benefited from faster decision taking. Rapid decision taking was further enhanced by the university's development of a more structured and systematic approach to corporate planning. Once plans had been agreed through senate and council, they provided the base for resource allocation decisions – especially the replacement and appointment of staff. This enabled far more decisions of this kind to be taken executively and simply reported to the next available meeting of committees.

The next phase of structural change was the one which I personally saw as most crucial. Traditionally, whole areas of the university's functioning (eg, estates, information technology, student services, etc.) had been overseen by a complex system of committees – chaired by academics or lay members – characterized by diffuse terms of reference and limited coordination. In particular, no clear distinction was made between the 'management' and 'user representation' roles of committees. Inevitably, the corporate perspective on the role and functioning of the university was much less clearly articulated than the day-to-day problems and issues of service delivery (eg, staff training and development – a vital means of managing change – was initially guided by a committee which had an entirely operational and non-corporate perspective). The need to optimize the use of university resources was most specially difficult to articulate – in respect of each individual function and even more so across the whole range of support functions.

The solution was to establish a range of management committees, each of which was chaired by or included members of the central management team, alongside a separate structure of user committees which dealt with operational detail. With the exception of capital equipment, allocated in part by a committee chaired and staffed entirely by academics, the key institutional resources were now distributed and managed through a structure which fully involved the central management team. This was a significant development for an older university and one which moved us quite a long way from the tradition of collegial governance.

The third phase of structural change was in some ways far more contentious than the previous two in that it involved the *de facto* creation of executive deans and a considerable strengthening of the previously quite weak role of faculties. The momentum for change came from two sources. Firstly, the role of the deans and the faculty structure had increasingly come under question as the central team developed a stronger executive role. The faculties had effectively existed in order to handle issues of academic policy and quality but had little direct role in resource allocation and utilization. The primary argument for change was that a stronger faculty structure would enable such key resources as space, laboratories, work shops, technical staff (and to a lesser extent, administrative staff) to be used more cost-effectively across a range of cognate departments. This was inevitably contentious in that it threatened to undermine the role and importance of the collegial boards (the primary source of decision making at the faculty level) and the autonomy of departments. It highlighted tensions between corporate directiveness and decentralization, and between managerial and more traditional academic leadership, which had run through each of the changes in structures and processes. The outcome, however, lay beyond my period of involvement; the precise nature of the change was still being debated when I left the university.

Two important features of these structural changes need to be underlined. The first is that they appear to be technical and rather boring forms of organizational tinkering. This is true and to a considerable extent they were actually managed and achieved in the way which that implies. They were the product of relatively low-key working groups and, with the exception of the change at faculty level, they were surprisingly uncontentious. Yet this kind of bread-and-butter change in organizational structures and processes can be profoundly important both in reflecting on-going cultural change and also in stimulating it. In comparatively few years the university had in fact begun to transform itself, for good or for ill, from a strongly collegial institution in which decision making – especially about resource allocation and utilization – was widely diffused and generally uncoordinated, to one in which the senior members of the university could begin to exercise some kind of corporate oversight and planning control.

With the exception of the last of the three changes, there was little attempt actively to carry members of the university with the decision-making process. The fact of a generally collegial body of committees and the presence of academics as well as lay members on working parties ensured that changes went through without the need for further widespread consultation. The changes at the faculty level did require considerable effort on the part of the central management to convince heads of departments and academics that this kind of development was necessary and appropriate. There was an understandable – perhaps entirely justifiable – fear that change would increase bureaucracy and add a further layer of governance within the university.

Taken overall, these changes resulted in a curiously hybrid approach to decision making. The move from a collegial tradition was real and yet it had not resulted in the creation of a clear system of executive management. Members of the vice-chancellor's senior 'management team' still did not directly *manage* any of the functions in the university. The impact of senior post-holders remained – at the time I left – one of personal influence or the representation of the vice-chancellor's will through a committee structure. The university had increased the chance of central coordination and direction of resource utilization, but it had not moved to the more traditional executive management structure prevalent in most of the ex-polytechnic universities and many other public organizations.

The curious nature of university governance is well illustrated by the parallel development of financial devolution to departments. This policy was conceived and implemented through committee structures of which I was only tangentially a part (despite being deputy vice-chancellor) and it certainly had a strong life of its own. It took the form of an almost complete devolution of resources including the staff budget.

The beneficial aspects of financial devolution had to be balanced against the need to retain a degree of central control and coordination. At the very least, it is essential to prevent departments with large budgets (and accumulated surpluses) destabilizing the institution by distorting its cash flow. It is also essential to ensure that long-term staffing commitments do not reflect short-term optimism about future budgets. These are minimal requirements; more generally the need is to strike a workable balance between departmental autonomy and corporate steer. In Loughborough, the weight was very much in favour of full devolution combined with residual financial *control*. In my view, this was at the expense of corporate steer.

A highly formulaic, and public, form of university funding had been imposed nationally on institutions which had traditionally denied – in theory – the very legitimacy of executive management. It was almost inevitable, therefore, especially in strongly decentralized universities, that departments should see money flowing into the university via students and research as 'theirs'. In effect, financial devolution countered, in part, the degree of corporate direction and steer being developed through the other changes outlined.

National policies for change which had begun by emphasizing the need for corporateness in universities had, by the late 1980s, reinforced a form of financial decentralization which could greatly constrain corporateness. But this was only one of the contradictions to emerge from a period of extreme policy turbulence and it was by no means peculiar to Loughborough. The opportunity to tackle these issues in my own way came with the appointment to Glamorgan as its first vice-chancellor.

THE UNIVERSITY OF GLAMORGAN

The inheritance

The university's immediate lineage was that of having been the Polytechnic of Wales – the only polytechnic in the Principality and the latest in a succession of institutions of education to occupy the same campus, beginning with a School of Mines in 1913. Both originally and proximately, therefore, its roots lie in vocationally-oriented education and in the valleys communities of South Wales. As the Polytechnic of Wales, however, it had developed an undisputedly wider role with a franchised network of 20 partner colleges throughout Wales and half as many again overseas – mainly in Europe and SE Asia.

The Polytechnic of Wales became an autonomous, incorporated institution as late as April 1992, several years after polytechnics in England had moved out of local authority control. It became a university in September 1992 and I took up post as the first vice-chancellor in April 1993. Incorporation made it one of only two universities in the Principality – the other being the federal University of Wales. Within a very brief period the institution had undergone three changes of status and funding body, three changes of governing body and three chief executives (there being an acting chief executive between the retirement of the director of the polytechnic and my taking up post).

This degree of upheaval was almost insignificant in face of the somewhat late (in national terms) but subsequently spectacularly concentrated growth. The 13,000 students enrolled in 1993/4 compared with only 6,000 five years earlier; and this entire growth took place without the addition of a single square metre of accommodation. Of the total student body, 4,000 were part-time; over two-thirds of all students were recruited from within Wales and – even more locally – almost half were from the three counties of Glamorgan. It was the largest provider of part-time post-graduate education in Wales.

Because it became independent late, the polytechnic did not receive the financial boost to research, or the assistance with capital and infrastructure, which attended the earlier pattern of growth in England. Like all other polytechnics, it began life without reserves and with a very substantial backlog of maintenance work; but also with 'negative cash' (it was carrying a deficit). One inevitable consequence was that the early financial benefits of growth had to be ploughed into reserves and maintenance; indeed, creating such reserves was a major reason for the sudden spurt in growth decreed by the university's board of governors once they came into office. The initial result, inevitably, was growth at a price – high staff:student ratios, difficult working conditions and barely adequate equipment. These were the issues to be faced.

That the university was surviving, let alone thriving, was certainly a testament to the dedication and calibre of its staff and governors. Yet, again in common with other ex-polytechnics, the university had to make a very rapid transition from being an institution administered by a local authority, with a full range of technical and managerial support provided through that authority, to one which was self-managing in an increasingly tough and competitive world. The learning curve for staff in managerial positions had of necessity to be both very sharp and steep – and only part of the needed managerial team was in place. Moreover, the new university was immediately plunged into a problem which sapped the morale of academic and managerial staff alike: that of new academic staff contracts.

Until the late 1980s, the polytechnics had operated under a contract which guaranteed long holidays and limited flexibility. In England, this was replaced by negotiation with an alternative contract. It was several years later that Wales attempted to do the same. Initially, a financial 'inducement' was offered to staff without the requirement to adopt the new contract. When I took up post just under half of the academic staff had recently moved to the new contract amidst some controversy, while the rest remained on the old contract. The institution was only operating effectively because most staff effectively waived, in the wider interest, some of the rights they had under the old contract. But to be operating on two substantially different contractual bases was a most unwelcome situation for a newly formed university.

Managing the whole

There could be no doubt that the task was to manage the whole. But where to start? The pressing and most obviously threatening issue was the contractual one, but new vice-chancellors need to come bearing broad messages rather than be immediately submerged by detail and controversy. Contracts had to wait. However, all the pressing issues were equally intractable in the short term and simply to look beyond them to sunnier, future uplands may have seemed perverse. But serendipity can take peculiar forms; in this instance it took the form of a Funding Council requirement to submit a strategic plan by June – a mere six weeks after I took up office.

Signalling a change in culture

Previous strategic plans had been developed through an essentially 'top-down' managerial process, which gave me the chance to introduce an immediate change in organizational processes and to signal a wider change in culture. Despite, or perhaps because of, the short time-scale, my first six weeks in office did result in the production of a broad strategic framework through a participative (but definitely managerially-led) process, involving two complete iterations between the central management team (including governors) and all departments in the university.

By great good fortune, a team from the Office for Public Management had begun, but had been unable to complete, a project within the university prior to my arrival. This had involved them in working with heads of departments, as well as with 'slice groups' throughout the institution which comprised over 100 or more staff drawn from all levels in the university as well as students. The focus had been on an assessment of areas of strength and weakness and hopes for the future – including for myself as the new vice-chancellor. The Office was immediately brought back in during my first week in post. The slice groups were reconvened so as to provide a 'diagonal' as well as a 'vertical' flow of ideas and suggestions about the way forward. In turn, I was able to introduce my approach to strategic planning. The result was a large measure of agreement throughout the institution about what it did and did not aspire to be. Given the very recent change to university status and the first-ever access to research funding (£500k for each of three years to assist in developing research), this focusing on the mission and strategic planning through broad-based participation was crucial.

The institutional mission

At Loughborough the only real debate about mission revolved around the university's ability in the face of changing circumstances to be what it had always assumed it should be: a research-led university. For some, this might have seemed an option at Glamorgan, but it was not a realistic one. What then was realistic – and how, if at all, was research to figure in the new university?

Glamorgan is, and will be, a 'practical' university with a powerful bias towards 'vocational' programmes. Not only is this its inherited role, it is the space left partially vacant by the more traditional role of the University of Wales; and government policy is precisely to foster a diversity of missions rather than a convergence. I went to Glamorgan with a strong belief in such diversity, but what it means in practice was the issue for the strategic planning statement. To emphasize the vocational is certainly not enough; indeed, it can be misleading. All universities – even the oldest and ostensibly most traditional – are now vocational in that they offer what is essentially professional training as well as courses which allow for the pure pursuit of knowledge for its own sake. Moreover, all universities claim that academic study is in itself a valuable preparation for a wide variety of economic (and, presumably, social) roles. Indeed, they are almost forced to make this claim by the many employers who consistently look for 'good graduates' rather than specific bodies of knowledge and by the countless ex-students who choose to follow careers which are wholly unrelated to their degree – even where that degree implies an obvious career route.

For the University of Glamorgan, like many of the new universities, the distinctive mission is, therefore, a set of interlocking commitments. These focus on access and equity; value-added rather than intake qualifications; flexible education with high choice; active student learning; personal development and transferable skills and knowledge; employer involvement, along with knowledge and skills upgrading opportunities for those in work; knowledge, or technology transfer; and the goal of being a community university for the entire locality.

Managing the pressures to conform to traditional models

Such a package of goals involves a number of careful balancing acts and a determination to uphold a distinctive mission in the face of profound pressures to conform to the dominant image of a university. Custom and practice, the detail of policies towards higher education and the dominant model of 'what a university is' – upheld widely among academics in all universities, old and new – tend to push towards convergence.

A policy of diversity is matched by great variety at present, but there are few rewards in practice for departing from traditional models. For example high ratings for research competence are presently best obtained by relatively large groupings of people who work (approximately) within conventional disciplinary boundaries, publish in the 'best' (eg most academic and esoteric) sources, and lean towards 'basic' rather than applied work. Britain's genius for basing judgements on ascribed status rather than on economic or social results pervades academe. It has tended to value research above teaching, 'real research' above applied research or knowledge transfer, high student intake levels ('A' levels) over and above the task of 'adding value' to students who suffer from woefully poor standards of pre-university education, and – perhaps primarily for reasons of administrative convenience – the single honours degree to the detriment of modular and other structures. In the latter context, it is beginning to look as if even a rating of excellence in teaching quality is easier to obtain for traditional, single honours courses than for modular programmes which pose assessment difficulties. (HEFCE/CHES, 1994).

The community university

All the elements of our distinctive mission, therefore, raise tensions. I shall develop that of the 'community university' role which I was very keen that the university should explore. Many of Britain's 'old' universities were national rather than local creations and even those civic universities with historically strong roots in a community have had every incentive to play a national and international role rather than a local one. However, polytechnics were based in local government and were expected to play, at least in part, the community university role. None the less, they too were subject to pressures to play a larger national and international role, both before and after their change of status to universities. Not least, the national system of recruitment and the British tradition of 'going away' to university enforced a national perspective, while income generation required a policy towards international markets.

One active approach to serving a community, and also promoting access, is to work with a network of schools and colleges and to give priority to their students, including those who underachieve in entry qualification terms. Given the educational need which has attended economic disadvantage in areas such as the valleys of SE Wales, such policies have a powerful appeal. During the period of rapid expansion this approach could be reconciled readily enough with the recruitment of the most able students applying from across the UK, but my arrival coincided with the slow down in growth. In popular subjects, in particular, the problem was acute: who does one turn away – the local student or perhaps a 'better qualified' student from further afield? This dilemma was in turn mirrored by the size and in-built growth of the franchise programme with colleges of further education. Once growth stops, is priority to be given to on-

campus recruitment or to students studying the university's programmes in partner colleges, often in geographically remote areas which would otherwise lack
any local access to higher education?

In addition to solving these operational issues – which in practice define the
reality of a 'community university' role – the need was also to broaden the focus.
My continuing message to my new colleagues was, and is, that the successful
university of the 21st century will deliver education where people can best
receive it; it will move out from its home base rather than merely seek to attract
students onto its own premises. One obvious example is to deliver whole
programmes – and not merely short courses – within companies and other
employing organizations. The university does and will increasingly seek to
create frameworks for employers within which the in-service training which they
require – and often provide – can be credit-rated and supplemented so that externally recognized awards can also be gained.

More difficult, however, is the delivery of 'non-vocational continuing education' – the kind of 'extra-mural' provision which used unkindly to be dismissed
as 'flower-arranging', but which is crucial to people wanting to build their confidence, get into the labour market, upgrade their qualifications under their own
steam, and enjoy retirement – or early retirement – or just enjoy learning for its
own sake. With 4,000 part-time students, the university is making a real contribution, but by no means enough in total, and especially not in this area of 'non-
vocational' (we would argue, in many cases, pre-vocational) continuing
education.

As in so many of the policy issues confronting the university, the task was
clear, but the resources sorely lacking. Funding for such work has in the past
concentrated on selected traditional universities with extramural departments.
Funding arrangements will change in the near future, but the need is to move
ahead immediately. Local schemes, in conjunction with further education college
partners, which combine delivery with the development of social and cultural
facilities are the present way forward – especially in a geographical area able to
look to the European Union for some support.

To serve an area in which the old economic base – coal and steel – has virtually disappeared, is to think in terms of social and economic regeneration. The
social role is especially about continuing education and 'reaching out' through
joint cultural and social events and activities. It is also about research which
focuses on the history and culture of the sub-region. To talk of making a contribution to economic regeneration is immediately to enter the world of *realizing
our potential* – the world of generic research and 'technology transfer'. In doing
so, it is useful to examine the notion of 'technology transfer' – or knowledge
transfer – in conjunction with the idea of the 'community university' and thereby
to consider the relationship between local, national and international levels of
operation.

The usual image which 'technology transfer' has conveyed in recent years is
that of the 'MIT model': the powerful research university in which new
knowledge is carried to market by academics either establishing their own
companies or by working directly with existing production companies. This
model does not map easily onto the British, and especially the Welsh, situation.

The sheer mass of path-breaking research in the MIT Boston region cannot be
replicated in Wales, but neither can the particular style of American entrepreneurial drive or the willingness to give publicly-funded academics free 'risk

capital' (ie, considerable time free of other duties) in order to take their ideas to market. Moreover, in Wales, the economy comprises relatively few large companies – especially few indigenous ones with their headquarters in Wales – and many small to medium companies. To be of real help, therefore, the university has to create a different model.

The aim is to help source all and any knowledge relevant to economic growth rather than focus narrowly on 'technology transfer'. Many small and medium companies do need innovative technology, but they need to be involved in its creation if they are not to be 'risk aversive' and leave it to someone else to take to market. Many may also need knowledge which is old and passé by the 'frontiers of knowledge' criterion, but which is new to them. In addition, the barriers to their growth are far more than technological. There are knowledge or skill deficits in management, marketing, finance and even in the law. Immediately, the role of a university with only a limited body of 'frontiers of knowledge' research, but embedded in its local community, becomes much clearer. It will, and we do, carry innovations to market, but sourcing *relevant* knowledge (which may not be 'new') on all and any issue which blocks growth, from *wherever* good practice may be found, to *local organizations and workforces* will be the focal task. This is an agreed strand in the university's mission and an important one which underlines the need to combine local links with a much broader access to the national and international worlds of useable knowledge.

Making progress

Defining our mission is a continuing process, but some aspects did become clearer in my first six weeks in post and have become more so since. Making progress on the ground is inevitably a slower and more frustrating task. It would be ideal to focus on one or two key issues at a time and pursue them to solution, but managerial life is not like that, especially in times of turbulence and tight resources. Consequently, during my first year, I have had to give priority to issues that did not seem the most strategically important or timely when I arrived. These have included tackling the dilemmas of having 3000 full-time students and only 600 student accommodation beds, the restructuring of senior management, the resolution of the lecturers' contract problem, and the – ever to be underestimated – task of simply meeting and establishing working relationships with the many influential people who operate in the highly political village which is Wales. The restructuring process could not be rushed, and the new managerial team is likely to be in place some 15 months after my arrival. The lecturers' contract issue is almost resolved, but not without a lot of hard work by all concerned. A new vice-chancellor may have a honeymoon period with many people, but not with trade unions and staff who feel bruised. But the contract has provided the basis for a staff appraisal system, better promotion and rewards policies and an altogether more active approach to the management of more than 1,300 staff – the institution's most important resource.

The other preoccupation of my first year – networking – brings the story back to where it began. Managing the relationship between the internal and external worlds of the organization is central to managing the whole and it is one which involves tensions. When new in an organization which is itself undergoing rapid change, the greatest tension is simply that of how to divide one's time: how to expand the working day to permit a full day of work on each front, each day.

This is especially so in Wales (or Scotland, or Northern Ireland) because the regional tier of government is so close at hand, influential and yet complex to comprehend at first as an outsider (and being born locally makes one no less an outsider when the time away has been 30 years or more). This time, however, my personal role, as chief executive, is the proactive one. Rather than simply explaining and interpreting the ever-changing outside world to the university, I also have to try to gain the understanding and support in the outside world which the university needs if its ambitions – and problems – are to be managed successfully. It is the opportunity to engage in this most strategic form of boundary-spanning activity which propels even the reluctant manager along the road to the top post; it is the ultimate piece in the jigsaw of managing the whole.

References

HEFCE/CHES (1994) Assessment of the Quality of Higher Education, London: Institute of Education.

Chapter 4

A Modest Revolution

Colin Flint

Colin Flint reveals a deep commitment to releasing the potential of FE in support of new visions and purposes for education and training in the 21st century. He demonstrates how necessary it is to combine managing change within a college with activity in the political arena. Like Webb and Harrison, he identifies the contradictions that need to be handled 'from the top': between government policy intentions and implementation; between declared commitments to widening access and specific interventions and behaviours. All this makes the leadership of educational institutions 'more demanding, more fraught than ever before'.

The author describes his approach to significant cultural change in two different FE institutions: one where the dominant motivation was survival, and another where there was obvious success and therefore considerable complacency. He would argue alongside Webb, Shackleton, Price, Harrison, Binks and Roberts, that change in colleges and universities needs to be vision driven rather than merely government induced. Building on points made in the opening chapter, many changes in society justify the need for a review of the purposes, systems and behaviours of institutions. As part of the context for this discussion, he introduces the 'congruence triangle'. This sets out the values that many contributors in this book are struggling to establish through their change efforts. He illustrates how an intervention into one part of the system requires attention to the simultaneous effects in others. New ways of working and relationships need to connect with the whole, and the mission needs to be more than a bland statement of the obvious and uncontentious. But a dynamic learning organization needs continuous revitalization – a process that keeps its mission and vision meaningful and clear for staff and students.

He offers a special example of the kinds of multiple accountabilities that confront public service managers set out in Chapter 1. The story of a failed merger illustrates the particular challenges of introducing change 'from the top' to issues of purpose and vision for the sector as a whole, and the kinds of forces that continue to constrain the most determined of efforts.

This chapter, like the previous one, raises key questions about 'managing up': against the weight of tradition (ironically, to become a genuine public service organization, rooted in the community); from 'not the top' (in this case, within the historically defined 'second class tradition' of British education); and into the wider political arena (against the forces that restrain policy intentions and rhetoric). Overall, he illustrates how these aspects of introducing change 'from the top' are inextricably intertwined in the still elitist and highly politicized world of colleges and universities.

INTRODUCTION

Further education has been, and to a surprisingly large extent still is, the best kept secret in our education system. Many of us in it are there by a mixture of accident and good fortune: few of us, having discovered its richness and seen its potential, have wanted to leave. We have seen it meeting needs, raising and realizing hopes, changing people's lives: remedying at least some of the deficiencies of the rest of the system. But we also knew that its contribution has been neither sufficiently recognized nor effectively utilized, because FE has not been seen as in the mainstream of the nation's educational purposes.

I have worked in colleges now for 30 years. My first two jobs were in institutions which are now universities, but it was when I went into FE proper that I found a sense of vocation. There, subsequently in another college, and then in two principalships I have groped towards some philosophy and style of management that has enabled the institution in question to do its job properly. In order to do that, one has to have a definition of what that job is, of course, and that's where managing colleges and seeking to change national systems become heavily intertwined – which in part is what this chapter is about. My own task has been to make the college effective so that it can make its full and crucial contribution to the delivery of an education system which is more appropriate to the present needs of the nation: which is, in short, fit for its purpose in a way that our present structures are not and have not been for most of the 20th century.

THE CHANGING CONTEXT FOR MANAGING

Dawning awareness of the importance of FE as the key engine for a significant improvement in the numbers and levels of vocational skills and qualifications in the workforce began about five years ago. The process led, perhaps inexorably, to the incorporation of the colleges in 1993.

The Further and Higher Education Act of 1992 was at least partly about biffing the LEAs, partly about freeing up the colleges from historical constraints, and very much about letting market forces rip. It has unquestionably changed the context in which we work dramatically and changed the nature of managing colleges.

It is undoubtedly true that we have been living with change for 20 years and more. Patterns of society have themselves changed dramatically in that time: unemployment at high levels is structural and apparently permanent; the nature of work itself is transformed, as is that of the workforce. In response, colleges have made major changes in most areas of the curriculum and in our patterns of recruitment, and therefore in the heart of what it is we seek to deliver to our customers.

Managing colleges during this time has been about leading the process of change to reflect these changing demands. Managing in FE has brought us closer to all of this flux than other managers in education, because the purposes of this sector change more, and more rapidly, than do those of schools and universities. We are closer to industry and to workers. Recession has had direct and immediate effects on much of what we do.

RESHAPING PURPOSES

The starting point for cultural change

Colleges which do not re-examine the nature of their key purposes are likely to get into trouble. For example, my previous college was in serious decline in the early 1980s because it was pursuing a vision of its purposes which was a good ten years out of date. It was built, equipped, planned, staffed and managed to meet the needs of employed young men in engineering, and by 1981 there were not anything like enough of them. Neither in the college itself nor in the LEA did there seem to be any strategic ambition to change anything (methods and approaches to accountability in the public sector have, of course, seen some major change since then). The old principal took early retirement, a new one was appointed and—more or less accidentally—he, who was I, was not an engineer. What we then did was change the culture, by way of a new mission.

Changing the culture of an organization is probably always difficult. Deeply embedded practices are arrived at by expediency or pragmatism and take on the pattern of authority, however mythical: for example, the organizational chart becomes perceived as being 'true' and it structures how people should behave. One of the cultural myths widely held at Garretts Green in 1981 was that staff were discouraged from talking about their work to anyone other than their immediate supervisor. This obviously had a stultifying effect on creativity and innovation. Only amongst a very small number of staff whose functions were largely peripheral to the declared mission of the college was there any debate about alternative futures; but these of course became the change agents, helping to lead the process of cultural renewal.

These processes were made much easier to achieve because of two factors. The first of these was a generous early retirement policy financed by the LEA. The second was the fear factor – fear for the future of the college – and this definitely reduced resistance. Key changes were introduced quickly and benefits were relatively soon apparent, though there was a good deal of pain to be undergone, over which memory tends to cast a veil. Achieving major cultural change is a very long process and success is rarely apparent to all, but it takes place where there is coherence of purpose and consistency of action. In this particular case, the process most certainly continued and took fresh impetus after I left the college.

This College's experience was repeated many times over during this period. Colleges were failing because the purposes for which they had been designed and managed were no longer valid. They have had to reinvent themselves. College management during this process must necessarily be transformed because it becomes a case of 'adapt or die'. Incorporation, granting us independence from the LEA, has made our critical choices more critical.

Cultural change challenge 2

Another example, leading into some analysis of how I believe processes of change in colleges are best led, comes from my present post.

Solihull College of Technology in 1987 represented a different set of circumstances from Garretts Green but many were the same: how to promote and stimulate change, how to evaluate present practices and future purposes, how to – again – lead with cultural change. In many respects the task was the more difficult because of the levels of success that the college enjoyed. It was much larger; it had a rich curriculum mix; it was full of students and achieved generally good outcomes. It saw itself, at least in parts, as responding to the needs of its customers, because if there was demand, it put on a course. In its better departments it worked well with industry and promoted new opportunities for students.

The model was none the less well out of date. It felt like the mid-1970s and it had not involved itself in many of the developmental areas and opportunities which were opening up. Any involvement with these new areas was peripheral, scrabbling for existence in the gaps between the monolithic departments, in the tenuous ownership of 'cross-college coordinators' who were largely unloved and erratically nurtured. The college's vision of itself – one which had served it well and had promoted its growth – was one in which it met the needs of school-leavers who could not or did not wish to go to the local sixth form college. It provided resit examinations – A levels and O levels – and a range of evening classes for adults. It had done fairly well out of government Training Opportunity Schemes which, for example, gave training allowances to adult returners, mainly women. Otherwise, it had not developed opportunities for adults, had not taken Access sufficiently seriously, and was generally content to be in reactive mode at a time when growth came easily. Except in isolated pockets, very small in number, it was not outward looking, a problem compounded by the fact that it was the only college of FE in a small and conservative local authority. (One of my first ambitions, to open a crèche, was initially stalled by the LEA on the grounds that since they themselves did not have one, why should the college? This provided a wonderful example of the failure to perceive what colleges were now about.)

In fact, there was little perception of the need for change, certainly not anything radical, at senior levels and not much among most of the rest of the staff. I remember a meeting early in my time in the college with the staff of one of the departments. I talked at some length about new directions for education, new client groups, new approaches to learning, and new methods of organizing the curriculum. I ended up with the usual invitation – were there any questions or comments? 'Yes', came the first response, 'we don't approve of the way you call your secretary by her first name in public'. I hasten to add that this was not a problem for most of the rest of the college, though another head of department, now retired, was known as Mr ... for the whole of his 20-years career and *not one*, not even those who knew it, addressed him by his first name.

These in themselves were not major problems, but they were symptomatic. Solihull College of Technology was a 'tight' organization with clear lines of control and demarcation, a fairly high degree of autonomy within clearly understood limits for the nine departments; no cross-fertilization, only very weak cross-college activity; development only within those departments that clearly identified an achievable target and set out to hit it. The central services of the college were seen only as supporting departmental activity: there was a seriously enfeebled administrative service and a library that was barely used because it had too little money spent on it, in turn because it had no one to champion it.

We've succeeded in some things, failed at some others. We abandoned the departmental system very early and have had radical reorganizations of the management structure (we're now on the third and most ambitious). We can with all due modesty claim to have moved the college into significant involvement with educational development across a range of work, and we have attempted to involve the whole college in a re-examination and redefinition of its mission and its objectives. We have gone from seeking to stimulate change and debate through a handful of very talented and extraordinarily committed staff operating initially as an alternative culture, to one in which (probably) a clear majority of staff are at least most of the time 'signed on' to our values and purposes.

I write of this hesitantly, aware of ever-present hubris. These are dangerous times, and both colleges and principals are perhaps more vulnerable than they have ever been before. Certainly there is no room for complacency, either about the performance of individual colleges or about the future of the sector as a whole, but there is more to be optimistic about than the reverse.

Developing a 'vision-led' learning organization

What we have been trying to do at Solihull College is to turn it into a 'learning organization'. We were doing so long before the term became fashionable, coming to it from the drive to be student-centred, learner-focused, corporate in the sense of shared mission. The British are not very easy with some of this 'vision' stuff, but we need to get over our collective discomfort. Genuinely shared vision can transform organizations, as Abraham Maslow observed long before Tom Peters. More recently Peter Senge writes in *The Fifth Discipline* (1990):

> *You cannot have a learning organization without shared vision. Without a pull towards some goal which people truly want to achieve, the forces in support of the status quo can be overwhelming. Vision establishes an over-arching goal.*

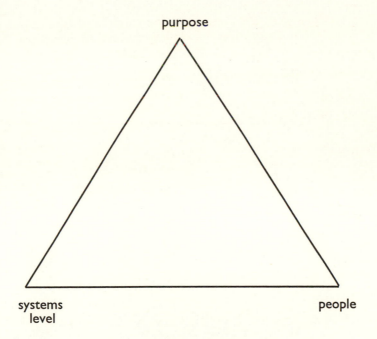

Figure 4.1 *The congruence triangle. A framework for looking at organizations*

Our means to this kind of shared vision have been around the attempt to secure a high level of congruence in our central purposes – purposes systems and people which are in some sort of harmonious relationship. My colleague Angela Myers devised 'the congruence triangle' concept, which we have used inside the college. I reproduce the three explanatory diagrams here: the reader can easily enough see where dissonances often occur in organizations.

Purposes that include:
Providing jobs for staff
Keeping students off the streets
Getting students through exams
Obeying the paymasters, D of E /Training Agency/LEA

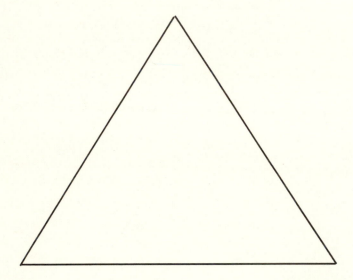

Systems that are:

Product orientated
Compartmentalized
Disabling
Rigid
Status-ridden
Closed
Rules-led
Reactive

Resistant to change
(high degree of control)

People who are:

Disempowered
Disempowering
Suspicious
Apathetic
Fearful
Passive
Aggressive
Subservient
Defensive
Didactic
Worshipful of
experts
Working in
isolation
Entrenched
Punitive

Figure 4.2

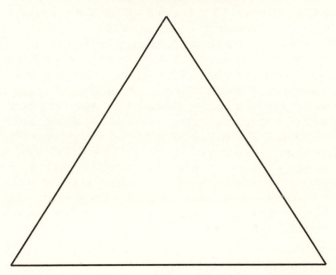

Purposes that include:
Providing access to education for *all*
Delivering a curriculum
appropriate in style and content to client needs
Accommodating to needs of industry and commerce
Anticipating future needs
Facilitating learning

Systems that are:

Process orientated
Integrated
Enabling
Flexible
Non-hierarchical
Open
Needs led
Evaluative

Open to change
(responsive)

People who are:

Empowered
Empowering
Facilitators
Confident
Autonomous
Committed
Problem solvers
Decision makers
Working
together

Figure 4.3

I am not claiming that we have yet fully managed to achieve congruence on all of the various points in the third triangle of Figure 4.3. What is important to me as a manager is the recognition that educational organizations are in any case different from the kind of Fortune 500 companies that management gurus tend to analyse. What we have achieved, I think, has been the promotion of debate amongst those interested enough to take part, about what our college vision should be, and the arrival at the 'critical mass' which accepted the concept of challenge and change.

We have invested heavily in staff development, using members of that 'critical mass' who had both the skill and the enthusiasm for the task. It seems now, looking back at that process, that there was almost endless debate, with dedicated groups committed to the redefinition of the college's mission talking late at night, long after a full day's work. I remember recalling Tracy Kidder's book, 'The Soul of a New Machine' (1993). There was a real sense of excitement about what we were doing, because we felt that it lay at the heart of what colleges were for. We were trying to change the focus of our institution from one in which *teaching* took place, some good, some not, and in which exams were sat and sometimes passed, to one in which learning and the best and most fertile circumstances in which it can be prompted, were pursued.

Over time, more and more people have accepted the new definitions and the new role, enjoying some of the consequent freedoms. There had been those in the college who fretted at the restrictions that the old regime imposed, and who wanted something other than a system driven by administrative procedures. They have become the agents of change, because they were empowered by a more open style and support for new approaches to teaching and learning. Some of these staff were already the most committed in the institution, but were operating at the lower organizational levels. There was considerable tension during the period – necessarily lengthy – in which bureaucratic control began to give way to new methods and structures. In those circumstances leadership is vital, and it has to be as consistent, congruent and aware as is possible. The message is more important than the medium, but men and women in that leadership role are inevitably identified with the message itself.

MANAGING A BIGGER AGENDA

The institution and the system

It is worth looking back at the context in which all of this was taking place, because it helps to place the efforts of a single college to find ways better to meet the needs of its students within a national picture. There have been, in fact, parallel struggles taking place: to make the individual institution more flexible, responsive, customer-friendly; analytical, effective; and to make the system one in which such virtues could be properly valued and encouraged.

In 1989, prompted by growing irritation at the failure of others to see the importance of the colleges and our own failure to put that message forward, some colleagues and I helped create an initiative called the Further Education Campaign Group. Kenneth Baker, then Secretary of State, had made what became known as his Cinderella speech. This signalled the government's change in policy towards expansion and at least marked a significant advance in the awareness of the Department of Education and Science. Some principals had also been to America to see the community colleges, and we grew even more impatient with the apparent inability or unwillingness of official FE organizations to put our case. The campaign group no longer exists, having voluntarily and enthusiastically become a part of the newly formed Association for Colleges which, it is to be hoped, will not stand in need of ginger groups to be reminded of its central purposes. But some of the content of its 1990 manifesto still is the essential agenda for change.

The mainspring of our first manifesto was a claim for recognition of FE and its key role in the education system. We claimed:

FE can be seen as the constant and stable force that has underpinned the development of fresh ideas and new approaches to post-16 education and training.

FE at its best is responsive, dynamic, pragmatic and innovative in providing learning opportunities for the diverse needs of individuals, communities and industry.

FE should be seen for what it really is – the hub of a complex vocational education and training wheel, unequalled in the richness and diversity of its range of learning opportunities.

The harnessing of these characteristics to a properly resource coherent national strategy for post-16 education and training would transform the economic and social wellbeing of the UK.

I and my colleagues still make these claims. We would recognize that four years is not long in relation to the 150 years for which Britain has been worrying about the inappropriateness and lack of relevance of its education system. None the less, the messages of the original campaign group have been only partially understood and enacted. A lot has happened since 1989, but not enough.

Incorporation of the colleges deregulates the system, and it should – and perhaps will, as the new system shakes down – lead to much greater coherence. There will, for example, be mergers between neighbouring colleges, to achieve economies of scale and greater curricular convergence. In the next section, I shall use the case study of a merger to illustrate the tensions between, on the one hand, striving to achieve changes relevant to achieving strategic objectives that we associate with college effectiveness, and those attitudes towards education that still reside in the dominant culture and the education system as a whole.

A failed merger: a case in point

In the period between the Act and the setting up of FEFC, there was much speculation about the minimum size that colleges would need to have in order to sustain the costs of infrastructure. The received wisdom was that an institution below 2,000 FTE would struggle: 2,500 was going to be just about comfortable. When I gave evidence (on behalf of the Further Education Campaign Group) to the House of Commons Select Committee on Education for 16–19-year-olds, I quoted these figures as part of an argument for better articulated planning of the sector. This got me into trouble with some principals of small colleges serving largely rural catchment areas. So far, smaller colleges do not appear to have struggled, but these are early days.

To date, most merger activity has been between HE and FE colleges, and often involves colleges of art and design. There have been two or three failed bids, as where the proposal has been abandoned before it has reached the Secretary of State. The first of the mergers between two institutions within the new sector is likely to be that between an FE college and a sixth form college in Redcar in North East England.

Another early merger proposal came up in Solihull, where we too had ambitions to be first. Had we succeeded, the wider implications of this merger would have been highly influential as far as other parts of the sector were concerned. We failed. The failure has been instructive and the story is worth recounting, I think, because it illustrates some of the underlying issues about the nature of the British education system and about the difficulties that lie ahead.

I have been arguing the case for tertiary reorganization – for a greater rational-ity in post-compulsory education – for as long as I have worked in Solihull, which is now seven years. There has been no corresponding interest either in the LEA or in our local sixth form college until very recently. A new principal of our sister college was appointed some two years ago, just before a new chief execu-tive for the education authority. Had the appointments been in the different order, the merger might have been successfully brokered by the LEA, but naturally enough the new principal was anxious to make her own mark. Incorporation then made the LEA role redundant. The incoming principal knew, however, that her college – selective, traditional, insular and dedicated to A levels – would have to change, and sought some help from us, the much larger FE college, to facilitate this process. We were prepared to offer assistance, but wanted to know where it was leading. We pointed out that there had to be a limit to our good nature, as we were helping them to compete with us (in such things as vocational curriculum, development of HE provision and community education).

Our joint meetings moved inexorably to the point where we began to talk of the logic of merger, for reasons both of curriculum and of the consequences of incorporation. All of the senior staff of the sixth form college, and then, initially reluctantly but increasingly enthusiastically, the chair and vice chair of their governors, became strongly in favour. But it was held too close for too long. There was not enough lobbying of other of their governors, nor of other influential staff, and so when the story broke, there was a lack of understanding of the reasoning behind the move. We had consulted local politicians, secondary heads, the town's MP, leading industrialists and the Training and Enterprise Council: all in favour, though the local Liberal Democrats, scenting votes, came out against. My own governors were strongly supportive as were our staff and students.

However, the sixth form college staff voted decisively against it for a variety of reasons; so did their students with a depressing absence of any idealism; there was some limited but noisy parental opposition. In the face of this, their gover-nors voted the plan out on an 11–6 vote. The six in favour comprised the chair, vice-chair, past chair, chair of the personnel committee, principal and chief exec-utive and the representative of higher education – all the best informed.

And that's that, but several issues arise, in the areas of governance, management in the newly-changed public sector, and the planning of post-compulsory education.

Governance

Two simple points about governance first of all. It is not without irony that in the business world, the strong recommendation of the chair and chief executive would almost invariably prevail. Here we had a business-dominated governing body, largely inexperienced in this field, refusing to support such recommenda-tion. Second, some of the most powerful arguments in favour of the merger were and are those which business and industry *at national levels* most strongly support. There was almost no interest in these arguments at local level. Academic/vocational divide, National Targets for Education and Training, widening participation, improving progression: these were other people's concerns; leave us and our A levels alone.

What price leadership?

In these circumstances, what price leadership in the public sector? How does one bring about change? Given that tactical mistakes were made in the Solihull case, there is still a major issue about affecting strategic change within an educational culture which is characterized most strongly by tradition, elitism, parochialism, inertia and in this case, ignorance. One understands the legitimate concerns of parents about yet more change, and there are undoubtedly real issues about the proper pastoral care of students in a very large institution, but few were listening to the equally real answers. What we had in Solihull was the defeat of rationality by prejudice.

INSTITUTIONS AND THE SYSTEM: A QUESTION OF PURPOSE

The persistence of elitism

All of which prompts, again, some big questions. What sort of post-compulsory education system do we want? What should be its purpose? Even, ultimately, what sort of country do we want?

I remember hearing Sir Christopher Ball (a prominent educationalist who leads initiatives on behalf of the Royal Society of Arts) reporting on a visit to Malaysia some years ago. Education in that country was seen as important for three things: first and paramount, to create and cement nationhood; second, to support economic development and success; third – some way behind – for individual fulfilment. Our allegedly more sophisticated systems should at least promote all three of these but have not been conspicuously successful in achieving them and arguably have been becoming less so. The Solihull merger proposal fell in the end because of issues more about class and race than about education, though that statement would be vigorously protested. Vocational education was seen (at least by the vociferous) as second class, second rate, second best, fit for those who have been adjudged unfit for A level study, and consequently more appropriate for students from the working class estates in the north of Solihull, and for the Asian or black students who come to us from Birmingham. And the longer we leave in place an education system which was designed to be elitist and avowedly remains so, any attempts to create a mass system will do no more than tinker, and the more serious the social (and economic) consequences will be.

Needs for root and branch reform

As we approach the millennium, with its overtones of apotheosis or apocalypse, we in Britain – and indeed any national system of education – need to be much clearer and more consistent about what the purposes for education are or should be. Currently there is no coherence in approaches to problems which are seen as being urgent but are addressed at best in piecemeal fashion, at worst by policies which are antithetic. We have a Prime Minister who plaintively bewails the situation in which (he says) the education of 15 per cent of our school-leavers is the envy of the world whilst that of the other 85 per cent is unacceptable, but does not appear able to make the obvious causal connection. The preparation of our so-called most able students for the narrowest high school curriculum in the advanced world, and the gearing of much of our schools and our higher education systems to that curriculum as by far the most significant arbiter of success, fatally distorts our entire structure. It needs root and branch reform.

Managing contradictions

A tertiary colleges system would at least ameliorate the effects of that distortion, but while the logic of incorporation will move colleges in that direction, elsewhere in the forest other activities prevent it from happening. Grant-maintained schools and new sixth forms with inadequate numbers and inappropriate curriculum but much parental approval condemn us to another round of marching up to the top of the hill and marching down again. Recent changes in the funding of higher education appear at the time of writing to have cut off the development of new models of HE qualification in FE colleges, in direct opposition to the apparent intention to secure democratization of participation, and to the avowed wish for more vocational higher qualifications. Professor David Robertson (1994) of Liverpool John Moores University puts it cogently:

The reform process is long overdue. The pattern of aspiration, achievement and progression throughout British post-secondary and higher education has largely been taken for granted. A minority of socially privileged, educationally-selected students have been carefully nurtured through secondary school and the 'A' level tradition to take their place in higher education: the majority have been discharged ill-prepared into the labour market, neither properly trained for survival nor seeking a return to educational opportunities.

The further education sector has been unable to find the resources or the policy commitment to fulfil an adequate role. The crisis of the sector has been a symptom of the crisis of national education priorities. Since colleges have generally defined their purpose as vocationally-focused, 'second chance' institutions, they have not enjoyed the status bestowed upon academically-focused sixth forms or universities. They have come to symbolise the rift between academic and vocational learning, between education and training, that has defined British post-secondary education. This rift has in turn retarded our national ability to reform our provision for the benefit of the majority of citizens.

The task remains an enormous one. The challenges are very clear: the means of achieving national educational targets well understood: the will never more apparent. But in every respect, circumstances are unpropitious. The capricious inconsistencies of governmental policy, which go on creating new obstacles in the path of our theoretically shared goals, the problems we are plunged into as a result of government interference, despite incorporation (currently, it is an issue of contracts of teachers, our best resource) make forward-looking leadership and the achievement of national goals more fraught than perhaps they have ever been. The stresses of the job have already produced a high rate of casualties amongst college principals. However, the vision still sustains most of us.

FINAL REFLECTIONS

In Solihull College, seven years on, there is still a great deal to do and of course there always will be. We have, I think, kept faith with the essential focus and with our main methodology, a strong commitment to staff development as the means of involving all, or the large majority of colleagues in the debate, and continued attention to the learning experience. We have devolved management and I think middle management is effective and strong. We are now reshaping senior management so that it is more supportive of those working at the point of delivery, and more responsive to the need for high-level strategic decision making. We are trying in the words of other management gurus, to 're-engineer the corporation' (Hammer and Fleming, 1993). We have to recreate the vision – even harder than seeing and selling the first one. There are now many more people who want to share in it, because we have changed the dominant ethos and culture, at least very substantially, and that is a very great gain. But the challenges now seem to be even greater, as do the risks of failure.

Clark Brundin (until very recently vice-chancellor of Warwick University and now of Templeton College Oxford) once remarked to me that he thought that ten years was perhaps the maximum for one to continue to be fully effective in a leadership role within one organization. With seven years in this job behind me, that's something to think about.

References

Hammer, M and Fleming, J (1993) *Re-engineering the Corporation: Manifesto for Business Revolution,* London: Brealey.

Kidder, T (1993) *The Soul of a New Machine* (new ed), Harmondsworth: Penguin.

Robertson, D (1994) Chapter in Burke, J (ed.) *Outcomes, Learning and the Curriculum,* London: Falmer.

Senge, P M (1990) *The Fifth Discipline,* London: Doubleday.

Chapter 5

A Productive Partnership

Ned Binks and Patricia Roberts

The approach and content of the piece that follows demonstrates effective teamwork 'at the top' in action, and how fruitfully differences can be worked with, given the starting point of common purposes and values. Written by the principal and his deputy, they trace their approach to enabling a small church college not only to survive but also to grow and thrive in the new HE environment of the 1990s. This chapter, like those of Shackleton and Harrison, places considerable importance on the development of new approaches-resourcing for teaching and learning – but at a 'measured pace'. (The importance of timing and phasing are key themes also in the chapters by Wilson, Gee, Shackleton and Webb). In this case, the student is clearly placed at the centre of the changes that are being facilitated from the top – in ways that build upon, but also break with, past traditions. Examples of an integrated approach to such change are provided to staff and organisation development.

There is considerable value placed on new forms of partnership, such as between students and employers; and in the approach taken to expansion and attaining accreditation from a validating university, ensuring that resources preceded growth. This required new forms of collaboration with the local community, but partnership, not donorship, generated capital required for new ventures. Equally, the introduction of a school structure has required attention to ensuring that heads of departments do not think power and autonomy are being taken away – a major concern in the restructuring initiative undertaken by Shackleton. Cross-boundary partnerships have also become essential to the ongoing development of institutional capacity to manage change. Finally, the two authors illustrate how risk taking and learning from each other, as well as from their experience of managing significant change, have enhanced the quality and impact of their partnership – with clear benefits for the institution. Different styles, vocabularies and personal preoccupations are used to good effect given the emphasis in the culture – on people feeling able to make 'distinctive personal contributions'.

What is refreshing is the emphasis placed on small but symbolic successes and humour (as with Gee), the planting of the trees being an apt example. This chapter, like a number of others in this volume, illustrates how a major change effort can be approached in ways that link 'caring with empowerment', for staff and students alike, while simultaneously building institutional capability for managing financial and political realities and maintaining a clear self-chosen direction.

INTRODUCTION

This chapter is a collaborative exercise between myself, as principal of Chester College, and my deputy. We have very different backgrounds, personalities and approaches to the management of institutional change. These differences could have easily led to open conflict and private stress but, so far, we feel it has proved a most productive partnership. For, despite our differences, we do share some personal Christian values and a strong commitment to the extension of educational opportunity. We also recognize that we must temper any personal passions in order to maintain the remarkable goodwill and staff enthusiasm that continues to exist throughout our particular college community.

I became principal in 1987, after 22 years in church colleges, and therefore a background in teacher training. I had also been heavily involved in helping two of the old colleges of education to diversify their degree programmes, and particularly in ways that gave greater recognition to the value of experiential learning. In the first section of this chapter I describe how I encouraged Chester College to respond to the new freedoms introduced with the Education Reform Act (ERA) of 1988 and the creation of the PCFC (see Appendix). I summarize the type and scale of changes that have come over the five years from 1989 to 1994. I discuss the key management decisions I encouraged and some of the lessons I learned from them.

In the second section of the chapter, I invited my deputy principal, Patricia Roberts, to reflect on her impressions on joining the college in 1992 from a large institution in the then polytechnic sector. She had experience of course development and of validation and professional accreditation, gained both within her own academic field of the built environment and from contributing more widely to validation across a large, diverse institution while dean of faculty. Widening access had also played a major part in her academic life. Patricia discusses leaping in to help push changes forward and some of the achievements to date.

In a jointly-written postscript we reflect on the writing of the chapter and its parallels in our daily collaboration.

THE MANAGEMENT OF GROWTH: NED BINKS

What has changed in five years?

Table 5.1 highlights the major changes that have occurred at Chester College over the years 1989–94. The general profile of change follows a pattern common to many institutions that attempted to thrive under the funding methodologies of the PCFC. On closer inspection, the figures also reveal the common tactics of the times. They show investment in academic support staff rather than in more high-cost teaching staff. They show growth in learning resources and in the use made of them, but also reflect the rising cost of books and periodicals. They record the underlying erosion of the unit of resource.

For the period, Chester's pursuit of growth, its profile of change and most of the tactics employed, may all appear quite commonplace. However, as a case study, it may still be worth closer inspection. For, unlike many other institutions, the college has consistently attempted to put resources in place before permitting growth. It has taken seriously the complete challenge of the times – to achieve rapid and substantial growth at lower unit cost *but without loss of quality*. This concern has dominated the thinking of the management team and the college's strategic plans. I have ensured that great effort has gone into the control of all

Table 5.1 Major changes at Chester College

Chester College	*Change 1989 to 1994*
Total student numbers	+ 224%
Part-time student numbers	+ 419%
Total student FTE	+ 172%
Teaching staff FTE	+ 38%
Staff development budget	+ 110%
Academic support staff FTE	+ 65%
Library expenditure	+ 145%
Book and journal library stock	+ 40%
Library issues	+ 272%
Library space	+ 50%
Library study carrels	+ 66%
Total teaching space	+ 39%
Total public account expenditure	+ 95%

expenditure, the management of all admissions, and into achieving high operational cost-efficiency in the use of all staff and all space. But I have never seen these as ends in themselves. They were the means by which crises could be avoided – to protect some continuity of academic freedom, maintain a personal care for students, and to allow new styles of teaching and learning to evolve at a measured pace.

The key management decisions

The college certainly welcomed the opportunity to take responsibility for its own development and growth that came with the ERA of 1988 – the first such opportunity in its 150-year history. Founded by the Church of England as a small teacher training college, the college had been permitted a little growth in the 1960s and made excellent use of the chance to diversify its work in the 1970s. But all change had been directed or constrained by central government and in 1988 it still had only 1,000 students, and teacher education was still the mainstay of its work.

However, when opportunity did come, the college lacked both the funds to develop and the space to grow. It had no investments and it inherited no land from a founding local education authority. So what approaches did I encourage to address these fundamental problems? Well, looking back over five years, 450 hours of senior management team meetings, and several tons of spreadsheets and *aides-mémoire*, three key decisions stand out. These changed the pace of the college's work, its student population and its community relationships.

The first decision was to increase the student:staff ratio from 14.5:1 to 20:1 in two years, to release development funds. In a small institution it was possible for me to put such a bold proposal to the whole staff in a single meeting. But, however reasonable the case, making the proposal acceptable was another matter. After much management debate, two points were recognized. First, if there was going to be pain, then the senior management team must be seen to share it. Second, if any developments were going to be 'bought' through increased staff effort, they must be ones that could be clearly seen or experienced. Consequently, the strategic plan proposed that a highly-paid senior management vacancy should be frozen, that expenditure on learning resources and staff development should be increased by 20 per cent per annum, and finally that the college's library building should be extended by 50 per cent. The package was accepted. But it carried substantial promises that had to be honoured – and were. Of course, the risks had been carefully calculated. Nevertheless, along the way, I frequently caught myself composing a plausible letter of resignation!

The second decision was to promote part-time recruitment – the only form of growth that did not require additional teaching premises. The starting point in 1988 was only 70 FTE students – all derived from in-service programmes for local teachers, but the quality of the work was very good. To get things moving, I proposed a scheme of profit-sharing from additional fee income. But this brought only a brief flurry of growth and deserved little more. My message was entirely wrong. At best, it suggested that involvement in part-time programmes was a voluntary and peripheral activity. At worst, it could be seen as greasing palms to achieve some abstract management performance targets. Part-time work needed to be highly rewarded, but within annual departmental funding allocations and because the activity was intrinsically important. I also had to learn from a lively young PhD that, when planned in association with local employers, part-time programmes could also open the door to substantial new opportunities in higher degree work. By 1994, I was wiser and 40 per cent of the college's 4,900 students were on part-time Diploma and Masters' programmes, and across a wide range of subject areas.

The third decision was to seek external investment in the institution. First I tried sharing the college's problems with the wealthy, but to no effect. They had probably heard sadder tales better told. Again lessons had to be learned, and here Ray Downes, the college bursar, proved to be my best tutor. Problems, he said, were commonplace and usually depressing. Attention must focus on the sharing of goals and visions that excited, yet without stretching credibility. Of course, this required me to know clearly what I wanted my institution to become and why. It also meant that I had to be attentive and responsive to the aspirations of those outside the institution as well as those of my colleagues. And this was much harder than defining problems. Yet even where there has been clarity only *collaborators*, not *benefactors* have emerged – the Church, the City Council, nearly 300 employer partners, two property developers, two Health Authorities, the Employment Department. £2 million in contributions to capital building projects can mean a great deal to a small college. The sharing of insight and expertise has meant even more, enabling the institution to discover its own potentiality, to grow in self-confidence and to refine its mission within the local community.

In 1992, the opportunity came to appoint a new deputy principal. The management team rightly pressed for someone with substantial experience in academic leadership and quality assurance, to help us secure the university's accreditation.

I hoped that we could also bring in experience from a very different kind of institution to our own. The college was flourishing, but it would do no harm to have its aspirations and assumptions challenged. Patricia Roberts seemed to fit the bill.

THE ROLE OF A DEPUTY PRINCIPAL: PATRICIA ROBERTS

Arrival

I was attracted to Chester College as it seemed to be an institution with an idea of itself and what it wanted to stand for. The staff were positive about the institution and a sense of caring prevailed. There was also the advantage of a campus with a quality environment – playing fields, trees and flowers – which could provide a release or thinking time when meetings or events became temporarily overwhelming. The senior management team under Ned's leadership was well established but still offered opportunities for influencing the management style. Overall in the college there seemed to be possibilities to link caring with empowerment as the nature of the student body diversified.

Part of my job was to identify and develop the role of deputy principal. I was different from my predecessor. While we had being female in common, I was coming in from a very different background both in terms of the institutions I had been involved in and the personal background of coming from inner London where my partner and I had brought up our two children. I was also appointed on a revised job description. This included formally deputizing for the principal in his absence and having a more major role in the management and planning of the college. A major part of my remit was to help the college gain accreditation for taught courses from the University of Liverpool. I had a long experience of course development and validation in the CNAA sector and professional accreditation; I had led a faculty almost the size of the college through a period of rapid change, and had participated in the first year of an MA in HE at the Institute of Education, University of London. The move away from London and the pressures of the new job have prevented me completing the programme. However, the first year was in itself valuable for the experience of high quality peer-group learning, the placing of my practice in teaching and learning in a theoretical context and for the experience, after a gap of a large number of years, of a three-hour examination – one which allowed me to use my theoretical and practical knowledge.

Over the first term at Chester College I visited each of the academic departments to meet and talk to the staff. The original intention was to follow up the visits to the academic departments with visits to the support departments which, while not part of my formal management remit, are an important part of the college. Eighteen months into the job these support department visits have not yet been made and some of the offices have still not been penetrated, though most people have been met at least in the staff common room.

To brief myself for the meetings I asked for an annotated list of staff (full-time/part-time, qualifications held or being taken), a copy of the latest department plan or annual report and a SWOT analysis (an analysis of strengths, weaknesses, opportunities and threats) on the present state of the department. This latter request was to provide unintentionally an interesting insight into the

ment work in research, academic credit and European and international links. The post-holders are seen as a source of information of what is going on across college and outside and as empowerers of others to expand the activity. The time for the post does not allow for the job-holder to undertake all the work themselves – a cost saving and a deliberate policy. Other members of staff, by being encouraged to bring forward proposals for postgraduate programmes of study or new modules in the undergraduate programmes, have also been helped to grow.

There is always the possibility of a negative feeling about such a policy – of people with responsibility such as heads of departments feeling some of their power and autonomy is being taken away. An institution the size of Chester College has the benefit of all these heads being on the academic board and thus themselves participating in the decisions on setting up these posts, any policy decisions again coming to the board after discussion within the college. A number of the policies developed are now part of the Quality Assurance Handbook and the discussion helped to embed in the body of the college the ownership for the quality assurance policies; a fact strongly recognized by the university in its final report on the granting of accreditation.

Encouraging signs of progress

Looking back there are three events which mark progress in acknowledging to myself what I was about at the college and the way I was helping to manage change. The first was the staff development week at the end of my first academic year which in the event coincided with the funeral of my mother. I gave a joint session on values with a visiting professor from Alverno College. About half the academic staff and some support staff participated in the discussion sessions and reported back with an openness perhaps not always expected before.

The second event was at Founders Day, January 1994 – a celebration of the Christian Foundation of the college – where the Foundation Committee invited me to give the address. As they did not take back the invitation when I suggested I wanted to talk about equal opportunities, I prepared an address which I recognized would be at the limits if not beyond the convictions of some of my colleagues. I discussed my understanding of equal opportunities in a Christian context. I feel the reception I received and the discussion afterwards were a statement of my acceptance into the college and an enhanced openness about the issues we could discuss and move forward with in a more open environment.

In February 1994 we achieved accredited status for taught courses from the university after a successful visit which we felt demonstrated the learning, on both sides, of the meaning and function of accreditation. My remarks in the common room one day on the amount of paper and trees we had destroyed in getting accreditation was taken up by Ned. He arranged for me to plant two trees at the next governors' meeting in some small recompense to the environment.

POSTSCRIPT

In preparing our contributions to this chapter, we were determined not to meddle in what the other chose to write. Inevitably this has revealed many of our differences – certainly in educational vocabulary, leadership style and personal preoccupation. But it also reflects the way in which we are generally trying to collaborate in our personal work and across the college – by giving one another the freedom to make a distinctive personal contribution to the institution.

To a substantial degree, this freedom already exists within the college. The institution is well-practised in agreeing and respecting clearly defined areas of responsibility, within the senior management team and wherever it is devolved to departments or individuals. And, at present, most of the work of the college is undertaken very effectively on this basis, and with considerable trust and good-will. However, for several years the institution has been tightly directed, and also enjoyed a fair wind. Currently it has very few misplaced staff. It has sustained a strong general commitment to its stated mission. What it has proposed it has managed to deliver, and this has engendered confidence. Its present cost-efficiency is permitting continuing growth and favourable funding. But are the trust and goodwill within the institution the cause or a by-product of its general effectiveness?

Fortunately the college is neither complacent nor content. Staff have seen fortunes change in other apparently effective institutions. They also know that to sustain momentum the college must continue to grow and diversify, and be willing to be changed in the process. There is therefore an acceptance of hard self-appraisal and the need to test out conflicting approaches to the next stages of development. In such a context, it would be folly for a senior manager to attempt to constrain the contribution of a colleague.

Chapter 6

Managing Change or Changing Managers?

John Bull

At the heart of this chapter is an emphasis on the importance of process in any long-term change effort being introduced from the top. John Bull explores critically how central this must be to building the leadership and management capability now required to deal with external forces and the shaping of new purposes and practices. His own particular management challenge has been to create a new unified institution out of four previous ones that were at a distance, one from the other, not only geographically but also in terms of cultures, values and views of quality. (Readers may also wish to refer to Flint's account of a merger that failed).

He cites the difficulties as well the benefits (based on hindsight) of establishing a commonly understood vocabulary and shared values and purposes at an early stage of a planned change. Like Wilson, Webb, Shackleton and Gee, he acknowledges the critical importance of iterative processes which involve all staff in exploring and creating shared values and a commonly understood mission. Sustained effort to overcome resistance to spending time on such things pays off since, otherwise, for example, new structures are seen to impose managerial values rather than to grow out of core ones, and the same cultural change dilemmas can re-emerge to impede effective performance. As with a number of others, working with organic processes is seen as preferable in a change effort that is intended to be long term and more than merely cosmetic, without ignoring that at times there will be needs for top down management rather than transformational leadership.

He explores issues of language and culture, mission and values, structures and people. His reflections on Plymouth's restructuring experience is refreshing, given the excessive emphasis that has been placed on structuring and restructuring as a solution to cultural change in universities.

The aftermath of the restructuring has led to a review of change processes used, and new priorities have been established. There has been a major investment in staff and organization development.

He concludes with a wish: that he had begun earlier to establish a genuine 'learning organization' – something that is also central in Flint's chapter. In this way, processes of action-oriented reflection and development can strengthen the 'basic philosophy, spirit and drive of an organization', but can, he asks, new approaches to introducing change from the top create the opportunity in higher education for leaders to be managers? He is still searching for the appropriate process that will help him meet this challenge.

INTRODUCTION

Twenty-first century chroniclers of higher education looking at the late 20th century will, I have no doubt, view the period as one of unprecedented change. Living in the midst of those changes, it is perhaps already possible to discern the analytical framework which they might employ. A dominant theme might be the rise of educational consumerism, an analysis of the extent to which the previously grateful and largely passive, direct and indirect recipients of higher education – the student, the employer, industry, society – had shaped, influenced or even dictated the purposes of the once autonomous universities. A second might be the substitution by Government of explicit regulation by a doctrine of accountability – for funds, for quality, for consumer satisfaction – and the influence this too exerted upon institutional strategies and purposes. In juxtaposition, our future chroniclers might explore how the universities responded to these forces which challenged their long established autonomy, their academic freedom to 'discover, transmit, conserve and disseminate' that knowledge and ideas which their members themselves, as a self-regulating community, collectively defined as their institutional mission.

If these twin challenges to academic freedom of consumerism and accountability provide the philosophical, conceptual and operational framework within which institutional managers have had to effect change – and I believe that largely they do – then I must begin with a confession; I wish I had identified, understood and articulated them more sharply much earlier. I have no doubt that the University of Plymouth has responded for the most part effectively and coherently to these forces, but we have done so largely instinctively, no doubt delaying some changes, creating some unnecessary ambiguities which might, with hindsight, have been avoided. Perhaps my first observation is that busy chief executives – indeed, all managers – need and should make time to reflect; there is a limit to which even the greatest wealths of past experience can be relied upon to generate intuitively and instinctively the most appropriate strategies and solutions.

Apart from the framework provided by these forces, the University of Plymouth has had to contend with the particularly significant externally determined changes which all former polytechnics have faced – the independence from LEA (1989) and the granting of university title (1992) (see the appendix). Plymouth's circumstances during this period were significantly overlaid by a series of institutional mergers which took place concurrently with the granting of independence in 1989. The then Plymouth Polytechnic merged with Seale Hayne College (agriculture and food), Exeter College of Art and Design, and Rolle College (primary teacher education and humanities) – disciplines which were largely complementary to the science, technology, business and social science base in Plymouth – thereby increasing student numbers from around 6200 to 8400.

While there was no doubt about the long-run strategic values of these mergers – and, in retrospect, the benefits have been substantial – they added significantly to the managerial challenges facing the institution. The three colleges had, not unexpectedly, very different, somewhat parochial cultures, little or no research base, a rather exaggerated view of the quality of their provision, and were respectively 25, 40 and 55 miles distant from Plymouth. Plymouth Polytechnic became Polytechnic South West – a title chosen in deference to the college sensitivities – which caused some difficulties in geographical and educational identity; the reintroduction of the Plymouth title in University of Plymouth in 1992 was not only a restoration of identity, but was in part a reflection of the extent to which we have been successful in creating a new, unified institution.

Like most polytechnics in this period, we experienced considerable growth in student numbers, in income and, to a lesser extent, in employment (some comparative statistics are set out in Figure 6.1). This growth was not wholly welcomed. In 1988, we took a view that growth in student numbers of around 4 to 5 per cent per year could be absorbed and managed. However, the funding methodology employed by our Funding Council (which involved competitive price bidding) forced us to accelerate our growth to around 10 per cent per year, which added considerably to the pressures on staff whose number grew by barely 2½ per cent per year, and inevitably the 'unit of resource' – expenditure per student – fell in real terms by some 28 per cent over the period. These 'efficiency gains' highlighted the important question of 'quality', and how the quality of teaching and of the student's educational experience could or could not be sustained in such circumstances.

This then is the context in which I will seek to examine the process by which the University of Plymouth has sought to manage change. On the whole, I believe we have been successful when measured against our mission and strategic objectives, but I have to admit that we should and could have managed some of the changes differently, and that we can still make substantial improvements in our management processes and in the ways in which managers manage.

LANGUAGE AND CHANGE

All organizations have cultures – widely shared beliefs about what goals and tasks their members should prioritize and pursue, and how they should behave and relate to one another at work. There was very little interest in or awareness of the influences which culture has on the success of the organization until the early 1960s; since then a succession of organizational behaviouralists have sought to develop classifications of organizational culture, to show the strengths and weaknesses of each, and to explore the reasons for and processes of cultural change. One of the preconditions for organizational change is the presence of strong external pressures, and the strongest pressure on all types of organization – manufacturing, service, commercial, professional, public – has been the shift from the producer/provider to the customer/user as the determinant of the product, a shift from the supply to the demand side. Until the late 1970s, higher education was arguably producer dominated – educationalists decided what was good for their 'customers'; now, universities, like any other organization have to take 'customer' preferences into account.

It is virtually impossible to engage in a debate about cultures, what they are or to what they ought to change, unless there is a shared and understood vocabulary. In 1989, the vocabulary of the then polytechnics underwent a remarkable transformation. In Plymouth, students became 'clients' or 'customers', heads of department 'managers'; the language of finance – cash flow, profit centres, full cost pricing, liquidity ratios – became commonplace. What, with hindsight, is apparent is the extent to which that language alienated and threatened some, was misunderstood by others, and was embraced by some with the enthusiasm of

		1989	1993
A.	*Student numbers*		
	(a) Pre-merger (Plymouth Polytechnic only)		
	Full time and sandwich	5575	
	Part time	650	
	(b) Post-merger		
	Full time and sandwich	7277	10019
	Part time	1108	1673
	plus partner colleges FE (funded through the university)		
	Full time and sandwich		1820
	Part time		787
B.	*Employees (Post-merger)*		
	Actual	1712	1879
	Full-time equivalent	1433	1580
C.	*Finance (Post merger)*		
	Gross income (actual £s)	£32 million	£70 million
	Gross assets (actual £s)	£71 million	£94 million

Figure 6.1 *University of Plymouth, Changing statistics 1989–93*

newly converted zealots – which reinforced the determination of some colleagues to resist all change. More recently, while conducting a thorough review in preparation for a management development programme, the lack of a commonly understood vocabulary surfaced again, underlining the need to give close attention to this problem at early stages of planned change.

CHANGING MISSION AND VALUES

The university has formally visited the question of mission twice in the past five years (although, informally, the debate is constantly engaged) – once in 1988/9 when independence was granted, and more recently with the grant of university title. While undoubtedly the second process was more effective and considered than the first, we still, in my judgement, have a long way to go before mission and values are owned by all staff.

Prior to 1989, the then polytechnic had neither believed it necessary, nor did it have the processes to engage in, systematic debate about its mission. The process in 1989 was limited, made complex by the concurrent mergers. The mission was shaped largely by top management, promulgated to middle management, and announced to the staff at large. Much more time was taken up in discussions of organization and structure – understandable as the incoming colleges sought to protect their traditions and practices. There was little understanding of the relationship between mission and the structures needed to deliver it, and no exploration of the values which underpinned and gave meaning and life to the mission. Much emphasis was placed on the fact that the newly independent institution could go bankrupt, justifying the need to establish strong financial systems and control.

Given that there was barely a year between the government White Paper and independence, and the politics of merger, the process was perhaps inevitable and necessary. Yet, in retrospect, our failure to engage staff more fully in the debate, and more particularly to explore and create shared values invited – and resulted in – ambiguities, some mistrust, and misconceptions between and in the then four cultures.

Nevertheless, from one debate at the board of governors, I conclude that, for all the imperfections of process, the first mission statement had not only pointed the institution in the right direction, but had begun to establish common purpose. One governor in particular felt strongly that a mission statement which made no explicit reference to financial realities was totally flawed. The staff members (and other independent governors) pressed and won recognition that the central purpose of the institute was related to quality education and teaching, and that finance, a means and not an end, should serve and not direct that vision. There was, even then, a glimpse of shared purpose!

When mission was revisited in 1992 as a prelude to the granting of university title, a more deliberate and systematic approach was established. An iterative process encouraged all managers to consider not only the formulation of the mission statement but the underpinning values and to engage their staff in that debate. That process involved a series of structured meetings throughout the institution, to discuss draft statements of mission and values (and to tear them up if need be), and an invitation to all staff to put their views in writing to me. Two important changes emerged from those discussions: an explicit reference to 'research' being part of the mission statement and a sixth value was added, that of 'scholarship'. This was significant in itself but also because it sought to assert the need to achieve and reflect the tension and balance between that and some of the other values which reflected the expectations of educational consumerism and accountability discussed earlier in this chapter. (The 1989 and 1992 mission statements are set out in the Annex to this chapter.)

It is interesting to reflect on whether the particular values grew out of or are a rationalization of our experiences between 1989 and 1992, or whether they made explicit the unspoken, unarticulated historic values of the institution. I think it is much more the latter, although the values reflect rather more the traditions of Plymouth Polytechnic than the merging colleges. Nevertheless, those colleges – now faculties – were fully supportive of the value statement only four years later.

We have learnt and will continue to learn what those values mean, but I would claim that we have made an excellent start in understanding and implementing them. For example, our concern for 'accessibility' is exemplified in flexible, modular programmes, in commitment to their different levels and modes, and in explicit transferability between the levels. 'Accessibility' linked with 'community' has driven the development of extensive links with partner FE colleges in Devon and the neighbouring counties of Cornwall and Somerset, providing opportunities for around 2,600 students – and there were no such links in 1989. In terms of 'effectiveness', our financial position has strengthened enormously since 1989, allowing us (some might say driving us) as a consequence of productivity gains (staff working harder!) to make substantial investment and improvement in buildings, reflecting our search for 'quality' in our physical as well as our educational environment.

Three questions remain in my mind about these processes. First, should we have engaged in the values debate in 1989? I took a conscious decision then, as newly appointed director, that given the time-scale of independence and the impact of mergers, such a debate would not only have been very time-consuming but could have been inconclusive and divisive. History, I think, has proved me right, but it must remain an open question. Second, although we involved far more people in the mission/values debate in 1992, we never penetrated significantly further than the middle managers. Although there were numerous meetings at a variety of levels, many colleagues are far from convinced that it was time well spent. In retrospect, we should have done more to help people understand that the university's present and future achievements will have more to do with shared 'values' – 'the basic philosophy, spirit and drive of an organization' – than with resources or organizational structures.

My third question relates to the processes needed to turn a bureaucracy – an organization driven functionally or in an integrated way by rules, procedures and structures – into a more organic or task culture – an organization which encourages the use of discretion and judgement, team building, creativity, achievement, openness and delegation to achieve its mission. A university traditionally has both cultures, which invites tensions and sometimes open warfare. The academic staff – individualists, innovative, highly educated, articulate, creative, questioning – are instinctively at home in a task culture (sometimes to the point where it can degenerate into anarchy!). Such a culture, however, is essential if scholarship is to flourish. The support staff (often equally well educated) who provide the necessary array of financial, personnel, estate, technical and other administrative services, necessarily have to implement systems which respond to the pressures for public accountability (from health and safety legislation to financial regulations) – the ingredients for the classical bureaucracy.

This exaggerates the divide, but both cultures do exist and both cultures have their place in a university. We have striven at Plymouth – and will continue to strive – to turn the two cultures into one, to eliminate the 'them and us' syndrome. At the same time, as students have increased in numbers and become more perceptive of their needs as consumers, the one culture needs also to become more customer conscious. The key, I believe, is to encourage and assist all staff to employ shared values as the framework which informs strategic and policy decisions and day-to-day operations, using rules as the constraining and not the driving force. That meant that our organizational structure which reinforced the two cultures in 1989 had to change.

CHANGING ORGANIZATIONAL STRUCTURES

Up till 1989 Plymouth, like many polytechnics, had institutionalized, albeit unwillingly, the two cultures. Support staff reported to a chief administrative officer and, in many instances, the numbers and grades of those staff were controlled by a distant LEA. Local authorities were often fragmented bureaucracies, and those characteristics were imported, with minor modifications, into the polytechnic. By contrast, the Devon LEA had, by the early 1980s, allowed Plymouth Polytechnic almost complete discretion, within national agreements, over the numbers and grades of academic staff. Indeed, Plymouth's research base developed at least in part because we were able to appoint readers and LEA research assistants. Within most departments and faculties, academic staff found considerable freedom in more organic cultures, although their contribution to broader strategic debates was limited both by an underdeveloped management structure – the very idea of a 'manager' was alien – and by a committee structure which up to and including the academic board encouraged debate often without decision or real responsibility.

To compound these problems, we needed urgently to establish a totally new financial system. Up to 1989, the polytechnic's financial systems (and that of two of the incoming colleges) had been maintained by the LEA. Problems of budgets, deficits (overspends), cash flow and asset management were almost beyond the institution's experience. Now, the new polytechnic, as an independent corporation, was responsible for its own financial affairs. As an accountant by training, I was only too aware of the disasters which could loom, as were several independent members of the new board of governors who hastily demanded insurance cover! Thus, in 1988/89 we faced five issues relating to organisational structure:

- how to integrate the 'academic' and 'administrative' cultures;
- how to define management structures, roles and responsibilities;
- how to integrate the three incoming colleges into the structure;
- how to establish systems of financial control and management; and
- how to develop a 'value-driven' rather than 'rule-driven' culture.

Given this multidimensional array which had to be addressed in a very limited time-scale, we unashamedly adopted a very top down process, in which I (then deputy director) wrote a series of papers, consulted with senior colleagues, obtained the advice and approval of the then 'shadow' board of governors, making only minor amendments before implementation. In so doing, only the first four issues were addressed, but we sought solutions which would allow the later development of a 'value-driven' culture. I believe there are times when what has been called 'transformational leadership' simply will not work – and this was one such!

One overarching issue was the extent to which the university should be 'centralized' or 'devolved' in its structures and styles, and if devolved what form that devolution should take. Plymouth, traditionally, had been centralist; in the smaller colleges the question was largely theoretical. As organizations grow larger, they move away from a functional organization towards a divisional structure, in which responsibility is pushed downwards, with the centre's role defined as planning and allocating resources, controlling and appraising performance, and providing some central services – the last being the least important.

At the time of our mergers, there were considerable pressures for a loose, 'federal' structure. That pressure now emerges in a different form, driven by an educational consumerism which tends to encourage individual academics, departments and faculties to become independent entrepreneurs. I firmly believe that the loose, holding company model in which the centre says to its subsidiaries, 'Make a profit however you like' is totally inappropriate to a university which, as an institution of learning and scholarship, draws its authority, its ability to speak for the larger body politic by virtue of its internal coherence, its members' sense of shared mission and values.

The organizational model which we evolved and which will continue to evolve has been the subject of a number of systematic debates. The 1988 [pre-independence] and 1993 models are set out by way of contrast in Figures 6.2 and 6.3. Some key features are:

- The colleges became faculties, and all faculties (academic units) and divisions (support units) have fully devolved revenue budgets and are responsible for both their staff and non-staff expenditure.
- The role of chief administrative officer was abolished, and the service divisions report to the appropriate deputy vice-chancellor. We have sought to encourage the concept of 'internal customers', stressing the importance of service given by one faculty/division to another, at the same emphazing the need to provide the best possible service to all our customers, particularly the students.
- To maintain internal coherence – the one university – we established a senior management executive composed of chancellery, deans (heads of faculty) and senior service managers; the executive advises – and collectively is very persuasive – the vice-chancellor on all aspects of strategy and policy and seeks to ensure coordination of the work of the faculties and divisions.

The original organizational model was largely 'driven down', but very recently it was most encouraging to find that a paper from the chancellery proposing some organizational changes for two faculties was debated fully, openly and constructively, with the emerging 'solution' different, and more radical, from that originally proposed. I do believe that it is a mark of confidence and maturity when members of an organisation can view possible change more as presenting opportunities than as a threat to the status quo to be resisted at all costs.

However, there are a number of significant unresolved issues in our structures which in part reflect a failure in process, a failure adequately to involve all colleagues in these important debates. It is perceived by some staff that:

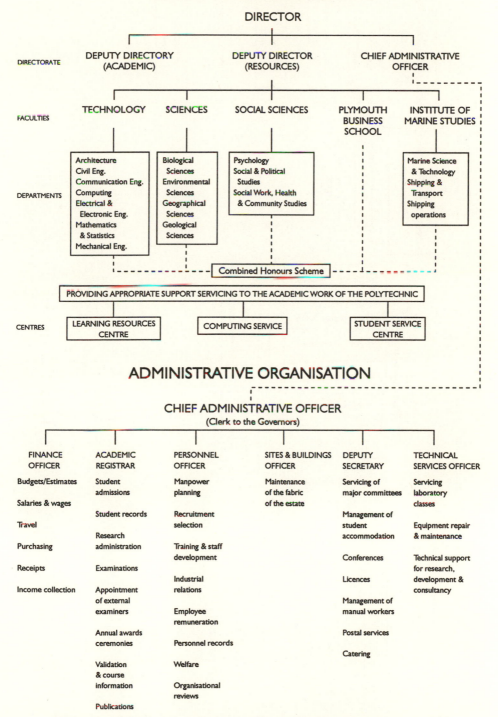

Figure 6.2 *University of Plymouth management structure, 1988 (pre-merger – Plymouth Polytechnic)*

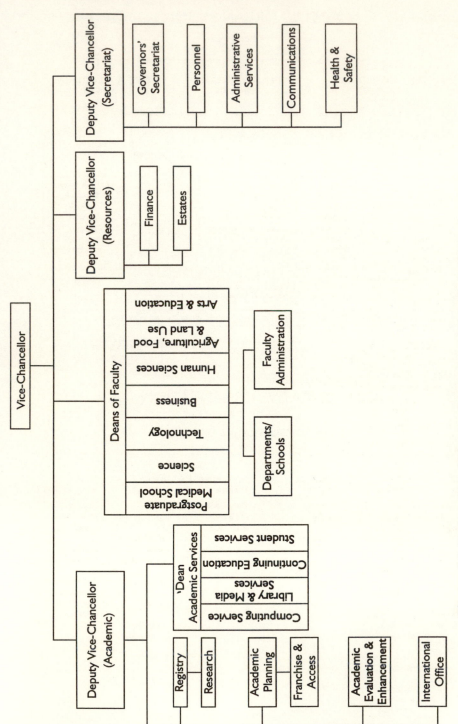

Figure 6.3 *University of Plymouth management structure, post-merger*

- In the faculties, we have not succeeded in defining with sufficient clarity the role of the heads of department, their responsibilities as academic leaders, as middle managers – indeed, some would still reject the idea of being a manager – and the ways in which they might contribute more fully to academic strategy and policy.
- Some academic staff feel disenfranchised, rendered powerless by what they consider a managerial bureaucracy – too many layers of management which, they assert, inhibits and frustrates their necessary academic freedoms.
- The academic board, formally given by the articles of government significant responsibilities in academic matters to advise the vice-chancellor, is dominated by 'managers' – particularly the academic members of the senior management executive – and has been largely reduced to a cypher.
- Too much power is still concentrated centrally, in the divisions and particularly in the chancellery. The 'devolution' has created uncertainties as to where the boundaries of authority and responsibility lie, and greater clarity is needed to be certain 'what divisional managers can and cannot do'.

The fact that these concerns, these perceptions still exist, whether right or wrong, has led us to re-examine our change processes. It would be too simplistic to identify a single cause for these problems, but I believe that there were two factors in particular to which we should have given more attention – staff training and development and internal communications.

CHANGING PEOPLE

Universities, whose mission relates to the provision of education and training, have paradoxically seldom invested much in the development of their own staff. Indeed, the culture has often been too hostile to such an activity, resenting funds 'diverted' from teaching and research. Such staff development which did exist was largely focused upon initial preparation for teaching, with other offerings very fragmented on a 'take it or leave it' basis. Management training was minimalist or non-existent.

Given the quite phenomenal rate of change which we have faced in the last five years, both from external and internal factors, our major failure has been not to provide our staff with the developmental training necessary to enable them to adapt to their new roles, and to ensure that this becomes intrinsic to the organization and everything it does. Many of the critical perceptions identified above could, I believe, have been reduced or avoided if we had taken more time to build teams, to explain, to communicate, and above all to equip our managers with the skills and understanding they need to do their job fully effectively. That we can point to considerable achievements by the university in this period is a tribute both to the enthusiasm and commitment of our staff and to some of the characteristics of the University of Plymouth which many visitors comment upon – its friendliness, openness and liveliness.

We began two years ago to address this deficiency. We are helping academic staff through a 'change agent' programme to make the necessary changes to teaching, learning and assessment which the high growth in student numbers demands and to explore how that elusive but vital concept of 'quality' might be sustained. We have strengthened and extended our induction programme to involve all new staff, to help them understand our mission and values. We have established a coherent suite of short training programmes – from word-processing skills to stress counselling – in response to staff identified needs.

One of our most exciting developments, and the process which is leading to it, is a management development programme which is being built upon a systematic evaluation of what staff themselves are saying they need to help them do their job properly, and will use both off-the-job training and work itself as opportunities to learn. In other words, we want to create a 'learning organization' for our own staff.

If, in this process, we can become more a 'value-driven' rather than a 'rule controlled' university – and I will be delighted if we can – this does not mean the hierarchies are necessarily going to wither away; removing layers in hierarchies can sometimes simply result in substantial overload for the surviving managers. But they will be less significant as the organization becomes more open and flexible, and authority is earned and negotiated rather than conferred by status.

FROM MANAGEMENT TO LEADERSHIP

I have tried to identify the need for management development in a period of rapid and radical change, but the process of cultural change is unlikely to occur in the absence of effective leadership – people of energy, vision, creativity, and imagination capable of inspiring others to share that vision and to work with them to effect change. Leadership has been an unpopular concept in the last decades; its military overtones and the ideology of the 'rational organization' have both encouraged and emphasized the virtues of 'corporate man'.

Yet I believe that in the complex, changing environment within which the university now has to work, where the managers are daily reconciling the often competing claims of consumerism, accountability and scholarship, we need not just the managers or the leaders, but rather leaders who are managers. That is a very demanding idea, and I have yet to discover any process – or if there is any process – which can train and develop such people.

CONCLUSION

Rereading this chapter, I am conscious that I have perhaps been over-critical of our processes, the ways in which we have managed change. The university, whether measured against its own goals or judged by 'outsiders', has been extremely successful, thanks essentially to the quality, commitment and enthusiasm of its members. We have transcended, in part at least, any flaws in our management of change.

Reflecting on the experiences of the last five years, I know there are processes which I would handle differently given similar circumstances. I would want to establish more quickly a common and understood vocabulary, to explore and identify our shared values at an earlier stage, to involve more people in the search for those values, to try to ensure values transcended rules, that the organizational structures grew out of those values rather than dictating them. Above all, I would begin the processes of establishing the 'learning organization' much earlier, offering our managers and all our staff more support in roles which are ever changing, ever more demanding.

BIBLIOGRAPHY

There are so many able writers on the subject of management and the management of change that any bibliography is partial. However, I am particularly grateful to the following.

Charles Handy, *Understanding Organisations*, Penguin Books, 1985.

Philip Sandler, *Managerial Leadership in Post-Industrial Society*, Gower, 1988.

Institute for Research on Higher Education, *Policy Perspectives*, June 1993, Volume 1.

Michael Goold and Andrew Campbell, *Strategy and Styles*, Blackwell, 1987.

N M Tichy and M A Devanna, *The Transformational Leader*, John Wiley, 1986.

Kevin Barham and Clive Rassam, *Shaping the Corporate Future*, Unwin Hyman, 1989.

Colin Coulson-Thomas and Trudy Coe, *The Flat Organisation: Philosophy and Practice*, BIM, 1991.

Jaroslav Pelikan, *The Idea of a University*, Yale University Press, 1992.

ANNEX

Mission Statement (1989)

To provide the highest possible quality of education relevant to society's needs.

Mission and Value Statement (1992)

The University of Plymouth aims to be a leading teaching and research University, providing education of the highest possible quality which is relevant to the needs of the individual, the region, the nation and the international community.

The core values enshrined in our Mission Statement relate to:

Scholarship – The University is committed to the pursuit of knowledge by its staff and students and will provide an environment in which intellectual enquiry and creativity are strongly supported.

Quality – The University will endeavour continually to improve its teaching, research, management administration and physical environment so that it can enhance the quality of its courses and other services.

People – The University recognises that the people within it are the source of its strength and quality. It is concerned for the well-being of its staff and students and will support and develop them within a culture which promotes equal opportunities.

Community – The University will promote the economic, social and cultural well-being of the communities that it serves; it will encourage and support the involvement of its staff and students in those communities and will, in turn, involve these communities in its own affairs.

Accessibility – The University will strive to maximise educational opportunities for students through a wide portfolio of courses which are flexible in level, entry requirements and modes of attendance.

Effectiveness – The University will promote good management, leadership and stewardship of resources.

Chapter 7

The Management of Change in a Large Civic University

Alan Wilson

Alan Wilson traces his learning as a pro-vice-chancellor (PVC) and vice-chancellor (VC) leading a large urban university through significant changes over four years. He provides insight into the external forces that compelled many traditional universities to rethink their operations and purposes. Insight into his distinctive 'from the top' style and approach is strengthened by the way he tells his story, year by year. We become party to the processes of reflection and analysis that underpin his management and leadership approach. For example, strategic planning keeps determination, design and analysis closely linked to processes of implementation, monitoring and the refocusing of effort. He thus demonstrates the developmental potential of strategic planning when it is seen as an iterative top down and bottom up process framed, but not overly constrained, by collaboratively shaped protocols and principles. Every opportunity is maximized for linking day-to-day decision making and department-driven activity to corporate objectives and values. In this way, institutional capacity for fulfilling its strategic intent can be continuously developed.

Some very specific core values have been kept transparent throughout. For example, marrying the benefits of improved management to the best of university traditions of collegiality, consultation and autonomy. The ways in which these are 'lived' rather than merely asserted come across throughout the chapter.

Readers will be interested in his account of the development of 'resource centres' in the approach to devolution, and the refocusing of committees, of which there were 150. (See also Edwards and Webb.) There are also lessons to be learned from the processes of consultation, decision making and phasing described. Combined with clear values about how management and leadership might best operate in a large university, these enabled him to introduce a 'top team' – which went firmly against the traditions and culture of the institution. We see a preoccupation with ensuring that academic, organizational and management concerns are integrated and aligned to the achievement of strategic objectives. He also illustrates how central administration/management can be kept subservient to the achievement of service and impact objectives.

This chapter offers considerable insight into the benefits of creating approaches to strategic management and leadership in universities that are 'fit for purpose'. He demonstrates how these alien notions can be introduced in ways that work *with* organic institutional processes, gradually transforming them in new directions, rather than being seen to work against tradition. External forces may have provided the catalyst for significant change but, subsequently, clearly articulated corporate values and visions can begin to yield benefits and align effort at all levels – organizational, departmental and individual. In this he echoes themes in the chapters by, especially, Gee, Webb, Bull and that of Binks and Roberts.

INTRODUCTION

In this chapter I am going to describe four years' personal experience in the senior management of a large civic university – the first two as the (sole) pro-vice-chancellor and the second two as vice-chancellor over a period of enormous change. There are many ways of reporting and reflecting on the management of that change; it is simplest to tell the individual, and certainly idiosyncratic, tale in the hope that this provides empirical data from which, combined with others, generalizations can be drawn.

I will first describe the *background* – both the university's and my own; second, I will describe the *basic model* of management which I deployed in my own job – and how that has been modified in the light of experience; third, I will describe some key features of the *experience* on a year-by-year evolutionary basis; and fourth, I will make some *concluding comments* about the chief executive's post in the light of that experience.

BACKGROUND

The University of Leeds has its origins in the late industrial revolution in the 19th century. Granted its charter in 1904, it grew steadily but modestly over the first 50 years, and then accelerated during the creation of the polytechnics during the 1960s. By the 1970s it had achieved something of the order of 10,000 (FTE – and mainly full-time) students. It remained largely static in size until 1988/9, the year before this chronicle starts. This pattern was not untypical of Leeds' peer group of higher education institutions. If there was a broad determining factor of policy, it was that further expansion was not possible without guarantees of increased funding because it would accelerate the already clearly visible decline in the unit of resource. At that time, however, the then polytechnics were expanding rapidly – clearly with a different underlying imperative.

One consequence of the failure to recognize the link between fixed numbers and the possibly *faster* decline in the unit of resource engendered by this was the fact that costs were increasing more rapidly than income was being earned. Through the 1980s, therefore, there were recurrent financial deficits and in some years, when central government cuts were particularly severe, these could be designated as crises. Many staff took early retirement to help the university to cut costs – and helped to run reserves down to a very low level. Morale declined. The creation of the UFC in the late 1980s led to some pointed questions about the development strategies of individual universities, and some of these were uncomfortable locally. There had been two rounds of research assessment; Leeds was not performing as well as it should within its peer group. By 1988/9, it was clear on a variety of counts that something had to be done – and what happened is the subject of this chapter.

During that year, I was appointed as pro-vice-chancellor for two years from 1 September 1989. I was invited to attend various key committees ahead of taking up the appointment. I began to appreciate the nature of the challenge ahead and to participate in some of the policy discussions which led to 1989/90 being designated as the first year of an expansion programme.

What of my own background was relevant to this kind of job? I was professor of urban and regional geography in Leeds and two aspects of my experience were useful: I had an academic interest in all kinds of planning; and I was involved in applied research through a university company, which involved me in corporate planning with senior managers in a range of large companies. Above all, I believed that understanding was the key to progress and problem-solving. My main approach was analytical – working on mathematical models of cities – and I believed that analysis was the key underpinning of planning.

Previous work as a scientific officer in a large government laboratory had left me with a long-standing interest in the management of research; I had been a member for one three-year term of a city council, which perhaps showed me how difficult it was to find and implement solutions to problems even when the directions of change were obvious. I undertook academic research in Oxford and in a small research institute in London. For one period I was a civil servant – probably uniquely, I was 'mathematical' adviser to the Minister of Transport.

All this experience combined to form a model of management which was certainly in my mind by the late 1960s and which has stood me in reasonably good stead since. Needless to say, recent experience has led me to modify and add to that model, which I describe next.

THE BASIC MODEL AND ITS REVISIONS

I believed that planning should underpin management. I recognized the need for different time horizons – the short-, the middle- and the long-run – and was clear that three different kinds of activity were involved: policy determination – including strategy; what in architecture is 'design' – but a concept which can be generalized to 'problem solving' or 'invention'; and third, analysis – 'understanding' again. I argued that planning activities, and therefore management, were only likely to be successful if all three components were present. Each component involved distinctively different kinds of thinking which were usually available in different people and they were often difficult to combine.

A mix of experience and management literature led me to modify this model, perhaps from an academic's conceptual view to a manager's more pragmatic one. When I am now talking to colleagues about management development, I would use three headings: strategy (and corporate planning); organization and structures; and management processes, the whole kitbag of standard 'capabilities' which are in short supply in an administrative and professional culture. Strategy still comes first: everything has to be driven by clearly formulated objectives. I had certainly underestimated the issue of organizational structures; I have now, in effect, incorporated 'design' and 'analysis' along with more specific (and valuable) technical skills in the kitbag.

The work of Henry Mintzberg has had a particular influence on my thinking. This came late into the process for me; it confirmed a number of things I had worked out for myself; it helped me to articulate these; and added considerably to my knowledge. My main source was his book *Structure in Fives: Designing effective organizations* (Mintzberg, 1983 – though reading this book led me to the rest of his work). The crucial idea is based on a triangle (see Figure 7.1): at the top are the senior managers; then the middle management; at the bottom, the front-line workers. There are two kinds of attached elements at centre-sides: the supporting services (which are familiar and obvious) and what he calls 'the technostructure'. This latter represents the staff in the organization who set the stan-

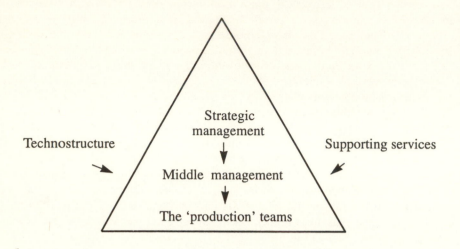

Figure 7.1 *Mintzberg's view of an organization*

dards or specify the procedures to be used. If that element dominates, you have a machine bureaucracy.

He argues that, according to the emphasis of influence in different parts of this structure, there are essentially five kinds of organization (and, of course, a particular organization can have elements of more than one). The two that particularly interested me were the *professional bureaucracy* and the *adhocracy*. The first of these is characterized by the front-line staff being high grade professionals, like hospital consultants or university teachers. A key element of his argument is that such professionals will want to keep a degree of control on the strategic development of the organization – and perhaps the management. This confirms much of what we intuitively know about the older universities: that they are controlled by committees of academics, and that there is a 'civil service' of administrators who will implement the decisions of these committees.

The vice-chancellor has to work out where to locate him or herself within this structure (there is also a tremendous administrative resource, but a tiny *developmental* one.) If something has to be decided, it will be put to the appropriate committee – perhaps to several. Needless to say, this is neither a recipe for rapid decisions nor for the generation of creative strategic thinking! Its advantages include the rapid dissemination of information and the basis for government by consent.

If the inevitability of this kind of structure is accepted, then it follows that one has to seek to change the system to overcome the disadvantages while retaining the advantages. What is clear from this analysis is that it would be a mistake to try to introduce line management in a university context, even though this might be successful in other kinds of organization. Mintzberg's analysis, therefore, to an extent underpins the strategy which was adopted and which is described in the next section.

Mintzberg offered one further valuable insight of relevance to universities. He noted that professional bureaucracies were good at delivering particular products of a high standard; such as medical care in hospitals and teaching in universities. Where they are less good, he argues, is when something more flexible is needed. *Adhocracy* needs fluid project groups with arrangements for communication between them, something less hierarchical. This is more likely to be the case for research, and so we have the intriguing question: how do we marry two kinds of organization within one, involving many of the same staff in different capacities, to achieve success in both teaching and research in a large university?

THE EXPERIENCE

Year 1 (1989/90)

In 1988/9 the idea surfaced, not for the first time, that the university should adopt some kind of cost-centering system. The then pro-vice-chancellor, and myself as PVC-elect, were delegated to investigate. We did this through a mixture of reading and consulting other universities who had already implemented such systems. I became convinced that such a delegated budget system – fully blown, including the delegation of staff costs – was necessary to help the university escape from its recurrent financial crises and to facilitate department-driven development. In the same year we decided to begin to expand. The planning and resources committee accepted an argument that we should take an additional 500 students in 1989/90.

I formally took up the post of pro-vice-chancellor on 1 September 1989. At more or less the same time, the then vice-chancellor became chairman of the CVCP and it was necessary to delegate rather more senior management responsibilities to me than might otherwise have been the case. My life was further complicated by the fact that the process for selecting a new vice-chancellor had begun. I was asked by a number of members of the committee charged with this task to give up my *ex officio* seat as they thought I ought to be a candidate.

This meant that, combining these various circumstances, four topics dominated that first year. The first was to devise a delegated budgeting system which would be both effective and acceptable; the second, to continue the planning of the increase in student numbers. The third was to begin work on the first *institutional* plan as it was then called by the UFC. Fourth, I began to think more broadly and freely (in private) about the university and its future because it became clear that I would have to make a presentation to the committee appointing the new VC.

None of this was easy. On delegated budgeting, the argument was first put that, while the idea was fine, it could not be implemented for three to four years because of software problems. It was also clear from an early stage that the redistribution of resources between departments which would be brought about by the system would be 'politically' difficult. Indeed, as these implications were revealed, it became clear that some significant restructuring of departments would have to accompany any reform, particularly in medicine and dentistry which were shown to have large 'deficits'.

I chaired a small team which met every Monday morning to try to tackle the issues. The software problems were solved by persuading a colleague from the school of geography to join us on secondment to do that work. The administration meanwhile bought an American accounting system to provide the necessary back-up. The political problems were solved in a great variety of ways: mainly through a lot of explaining and talking, and getting the principles accepted before too much of the detail was visible – this was not difficult to achieve because the calculations were still being refined until late in the year. We also had a principle of total transparency and openness: all the proposals were published in detail. As we began to do the arithmetic, that was published too – and this was a crucial feature in winning acceptance.

We had two immediate goals: to specify all the formulae determining the allocation of resources; and a set of rules governing how departments could 'earn' other income. This allowed for development incentives which were consistent with the achievement of academic objectives. There was an important continuing theme here: that we were not transforming the system of management into one which was governed by the financial accounts, but that proper underpinnings were necessary for us to achieve our academic goals most effectively and efficiently. We realized as we carried out our research, that from an accountant's point of view, what we were creating were neither cost centres nor profit centres, and indeed were more than budget centres – and so we gave them the broader name of 'resource centres'.

On student numbers, we incorporated into the institutional plan a target of 12,500 for 1994/5, which seemed very ambitious at the time. We began to gain in confidence because our first year of expansion produced an additional 700 students instead of the planned 500 – and we seemed to be coping – apart from having to accommodate 120 students temporarily in caravans.

The process of strategic planning was certainly helped by being forced by the UFC to produce a plan. It was agreed that the planning process should be simultaneously top-down and bottom-up: that is, departments should clearly play a major role, and this would enable us to tease out where the key capacity constraints (of various kinds) were.

Being forced to answer some difficult questions by the Funding Council helped us to articulate a clearer vision of our academic role. We were, in effect, being asked what our niche was and which disciplines constituted our distinctiveness and strength. Because we were very large, we wanted to say that we did everything! The view emerged that there was a national need for some large universities – and Leeds should be one – which had on campus all the basic core disciplines. This would, for example, produce physics and chemistry graduates for postgraduate work in the specialist departments of other universities (or industry). We also had our own specialist departments. But we also started to recognize more clearly we had a tremendous platform for more interdisciplinary initiatives in both teaching and research. In teaching, this led us into communications studies, international studies (development, European), women's studies and environmental studies. In research, we set up a large number of centres and institutes and this accelerated research activity levels.

My presentation on the future of the university was delivered in conditions of great secrecy in a hotel in York on a Sunday morning in July. With hindsight, it was strong on principles and targets but left an awful lot of working out to be done. None the less, I was appointed, and so was vice-chancellor-elect for my second year as pro-vice-chancellor. Needless to say, this changed the shape of my thinking for the following year.

Year 2 (1990/91)

The resource centre system had to be implemented, and this took up a lot of time. Student recruitment was again good, and we added something of the order of a further 1,000 students; indeed we had almost achieved what in the first plan we had seen as our 1994/5 target. But some things went badly wrong. When the Funding Council announced our grant for 1991/2 in February 1991, the outcome for Leeds was awful – and not even for very good reasons; for instance, our numerous combined studies students had not been properly counted. Another round of cuts was needed, and this gave ammunition to any doubters who saw the new growth and cost-centring policies as not fundamentally changing anything. It was necessary to act very quickly at that time to maintain morale and convince everyone that we could succeed. We managed to plan to continue the expansion programme in the hope that the additional finances would materialize soon.

I spent quite a lot of time thinking about the following year. Various reforms were needed and I began to sketch out a programme. A basic principle was that the centre of the university existed to support departments. If we were to improve the performance of the university in key respects, this could only be delivered in departments. This truism was not reflected in the way the institution worked and I thought that what was needed was a more focused committee system, a unified central administration (we then had a registrar and a bursar as senior officers of equal standing) and an increase in the senior management which would give us more developmental rather than administrative thinking. For me this meant having more pro-vice-chancellors (believing we were the only university to have only one). A small but important start for the following year was that senate and council agreed that we could appoint a dean for academic development, in effect providing an immediate increase in the management team ahead of any decision to have more pro-vice-chancellors. A good appointment was made. The colleague from geography who had helped to implement the resource centre system accepted an invitation to become director of planning. A core management team was being built.

According to the university calendar, there were over 150 committees in existence and this in itself was a problem. There were others: agendas tended to be unfocused, and there was inadequate coordination of academic, financial and physical planning. Many of these weaknesses stemmed from the tradition of leaving major decisions to the appropriate committee without enough staff work beforehand. For example, the planning and resources committee allocated the available funds to the main budget headings. The paper presented to the committee had no suggested allocations which meant that interested parties argued out the issues from scratch in the committee.

Along with changes in structure, some changes in working practice were needed as well. It seemed to me that it was possible to implement these without taking away the democratic control of the academic staff (through senate and its committees for academic matters) or the authority of council as the governing body of the university. These various bodies would be better informed if the 'staff work' was good – and inventive.

In keeping with my original model, I had to be clearer about policy and strategy – and this meant explicit discussion in key committees. The resource centre system started to provide a better basis for the analysis required and it was necessary to be more creative in finding solutions to problems. Committees were not always very good at this, though they were a crucial part of the system.

Stronger leadership became essential but always in a situation where consent had to be won through more traditional structures; in ways which were responsive to ideas and criticisms from that system. It has therefore been possible to marry the benefits of improved management with the tradition of collegiality; and it was necessary to proclaim that this was what we were doing. As with all major cultural changes, it can be said that much of this worked very well but that new problems and development tasks were continually added to the agenda.

The basic principle remained that the changes to be achieved in the university had to be achieved in departments. This raised all the questions about how to find ways of facilitating this by any reforms in central management structures.

Year 3 (1991/2)

I took up the vice-chancellor's post on 1 October 1991. I presented papers on the key structural reforms, via the appropriate committees, to more or less successive meetings of senate and council. There had been predictions that some of these would fall foul of what was perceived to be the culture of the university, for example, that senate would not tolerate having more than one pro-vice-chancellor, the theory being that that person was there to 'watch over' the vice-chancellor on behalf of senate. Fortunately, such predictions turned out to be unfounded and the major structural reforms were soon in place. The committee structure was reformed; it was agreed to unify the administration; there were to be three or four pro-vice-chancellors – the fourth when there was a case for some particular task or initiative.

It was possible to implement much immediately. Some of the restructuring had to await various staff changes and retirements due to take place. A new registrar and three new pro-vice-chancellors were appointed to take up office the following year. The registrar's task was to unify the administration. The new PVCs were given portfolios whose main components were teaching developments (including modularization and academic audit), research and information strategy. In effect, the portfolio of the then dean for academic development (who became PVC for research) was being divided into three. What this revealed in a different way was the previous lack of senior developmental effort which needed to applied in key areas. The system was driven forward by charting comprehensive running agendas for key staff and committees. Big questions could then be tackled, on a planned time-scale, and not perpetually deferred.

The developmental part of the system was under tremendous strain as there were few staff to do a great deal. This was particularly noticeable when we had to draft a new corporate plan at the end of our first three-year expansion cycle (student numbers were over 13,000 and we felt that we could confidently plan a second cycle). I attempted a first restructuring of the central administration into eight divisions from a much larger number of smaller offices.

Much went well, and our expansion policies finally paid off with our Funding Council grant for 1992/3. We had a substantial increase in funded student numbers and the appropriate cash. We began to experience what had happened to many organizations through the 1980s: we had cut our costs, and we were slimmer and fitter as we got into a position to expand again. We were financially in the black for the first time for many years; it was possible to plan to invest, for example, through the establishment of an academic development fund of over £2 million. We started to increase our reserves again.

Morale was better, though the unit of resource was continuing to go down and our staff were under tremendous pressure including from the sheer pace of reform. There had been the implementation of the resource centre system. We were beginning to devise a modular scheme for all our courses. Departments were under pressure to enhance their research programmes and to think about the concept of research schools when there was a new research assessment exercise to prepare for. There were many developments associated with the strengthening of our internal academic audit procedures, in anticipation of a visitation the following May.

Departments were required to develop their own plan, initially on a centrally-specified blueprint, thus taking the notion of simultaneous top-down and bottom-up planning a stage further, and providing a better link with the centre through the academic development committee and its officers. It was a formidable agenda for departments but, in most cases, the challenges were accepted.

Year 4 (1992/3)

With many of the structural changes in place, I anticipated a more straightforward year in which it would be possible to focus more on academic matters than on structural and administrative reform, but the management agenda remained a tough one. I began to learn that implementation is much harder than planning! However, the management team was enormously strengthened by the new pro-vice-chancellors and registrar and longer agendas could be tackled.

We awaited the outcomes of the main assessments of the year: the research assessment exercise (RAE) submitted the previous year; academic audit; and, as usual, the annual financial settlement, this time for 1993/4, and contingent on the outcome of the RAE. The news was mostly good. In the RAE, we had moved up half a point faster than the national average, which we needed to do because there was some catching up to do; half of our departments were now in the top two grades. This gave everyone more confidence that our policies were working. We felt able to set targets for the next RAE of having 80 per cent of our departments in the top grades. More importantly, the outcome underpinned a reasonable though not generous financial settlement. The budget was tighter than for the previous year, but we could maintain our academic development fund.

We now had almost 16,000 full-time students and, during the year, departments completed their course revisions to facilitate modularization. The most dramatic strides were being made on the research front as news accumulated month by month of increasing success rates with research grant submissions. By the end of the year it was clear that our research income had almost doubled since 1988/9 and, more importantly, the value of new contracts won had increased by 50 per cent from the previous year to £32.5 million.

CONCLUDING COMMENTS

One way to sum up what has been achieved – and what not – is to review the strengths and weaknesses of the current situation and to reflect on the chief executive's role.

Strengths

There is now a well-defined university strategy founded on dramatic success in achieving the growth targets of the last four years. We have demonstrated our ability to attract students, to increase our research activity levels and to establish a sound financial base – with opportunities for investment. Staff morale is better because of this, but there is also considerable stress because of the workloads generated by new challenges and demands.

The single most important contribution to success was probably the introduction of the resource centre system: the delegation of responsibilities to departments which, in contemporary jargon, has empowered them. Indeed, it can be argued, as we review the gurus of the management literature, that this kind of university structure is, by the standards of any organization, a very strong one: in the Leeds case, 55 or so departments, varying in size but with an average of around 60 staff (half of whom will be tenured 'academic') with effective central support within a well-defined corporate mission.

Weaknesses

Change is never fast enough! Too much of the centre is still locked into an older administrative culture. Because responsibility was not shared with committees there has been insufficient scope for central staff to exercise initiative. This culture is difficult to change. In many cases new competences are needed: software engineering, marketing and public relations skills provide three examples, and these are difficult to marry into the traditional culture. It has been very difficult to shift from a 'committee' style of working to a 'project group' base.

There is also an uneven performance across departments. Teaching is almost always very good, though pressures will force us to review our teaching methods – hopefully in a creative and productive way so that a high quality of student learning can be maintained. For research, a Pareto rule applies: in the case of funding, for example, 80 per cent is probably attracted by 20 per cent (or less) of the staff. In both cases, what is needed, and what we are putting in place, is a continuous programme of management development. In the future, we will have to increase considerably the budget for staff development.

Reflections

I can probably summarize my own role under four main headings: articulation, planning, organization and structure, management style and people.

The articulation of values and strategy is, perhaps surprisingly, not normally attempted, but forms the basis for the planning process. The corporate plan in turn anchors decision making day by day. It was important to spell out the first blueprint for departmental plans, though they will now evolve productively in a variety of ways. It is also necessary to articulate the management agenda in some detail to change the directions of individual work programmes towards institutional priorities. There is a tendency otherwise for all of us to go on doing what we most like doing!

It was necessary to do some hard thinking about the organization and its structures, particularly in the centre of the university, but also in establishing, for instance, a school of biological sciences and a school of modern languages. In each case half a dozen or so departments came under a common umbrella. We also began to establish research schools.

Management style and working with people is probably crucial. Visibility was important: being active in chairing senate and the two main committees; being involved in council; speaking at a great variety of public occasions in ways which constantly propound values and directions of change; doing the same thing on visits to departments; persuading others to undertake their internal PR programmes. It is necessary to find the solutions to difficult problems – avoiding the tendency to procrastinate. All this involves working *with* people. Perhaps the biggest single difficulty for a chief executive in a large institution is finding the time to do enough of this; in fact, it simply cannot be done. It was possible for me to establish close working relationships with the pro-vice-chancellors and a handful of administrative staff working in areas where I needed to be directly involved. I would have preferred a wider involvement to help accelerate the change in culture. It has also been the case that the main committees have become effective teams (planning and resources committee and academic development committee). They have integrated pro-vice-chancellors, deans of faculties and registry staff working creatively for the committee. This has then provided the foundation for a good relationship with senate and council. It has been particularly important that I have had a very active and supportive pro-vice-chancellor as chairman of council. It has also been useful to supplement the formal meetings involving students and academic staff (as represented by the AUT) with regular informal sandwich lunches. Issues can be aired frankly and early; ideas can be tested; and this all helps to build a consensus.

Among the successes, there were the failures: in the light of experience, I would probably now try to spend more time talking to some of the people who are still not integral parts of teams. I might have tried to find more senior managers earlier to whom major tasks could be delegated, but that is easier said than done. Some of the organizational changes I have enthused about have still not happened. So there is always a lot to learn and more to do!

Reference

Mintzberg, H (1983) *Structure in Fives: Designing effective organizations,* Englewood Cliffs, NJ: Prentice-Hall.

Chapter 8

Growing Potential: In Students, Staff, the Institution and the Community

Jenny Shackleton

This author describes a total turn around of a further education institution, based on a radical concept of the 'networked' institution – both in spirit and technologically – as well as a commitment to a clear values and achievement-driven change.

She sets out the rationale for change, which reflects a number of issues set out in Chapter 1. Change in this case was not merely a reaction to external forces; it was based on a commitment to ensuring that no longer were students to be expected to take what they were given. Like Webb, Roberts and Gee, she talks about the power of using a honeymoon period well, to review the current situation and possibilities for the future. Such processes build staff, managerial and organizational insights, and engender the capacity for collaborative effort. The author invested one year in persuading staff to accept the idea of a mission: this then led to a process of ensuring that the mission adopted was neither grafted on, nor bland. Instead the mission statement provided the values, logic and requirements against which to test *every* decision. Equally, five years have been invested in the development of the college's distinctive approach to credit accumulation and transfer. These phasings of significant change become symbolic of the institutional culture that the author set out to create, where inquiry and action-based reflection are the lifeblood of the institution. She also was determined to remove 'institutionalized unkindness'. Like Bull, Webb and Wilson, she considers in detail how a restructuring effort that fails to attend to process concerns can undermine rather than enhance the change capability of the institution. That there were no grievances out of a process that turned existing roles, responsibilities, power and priorities upside down is a considerable achievement, given the strong union-based traditions of FE institutions. It could be argued that the investment in the development of middle managers, and new roles and responsibilities for senior managers, proved beneficial – a theme also emphasized strongly by Bull. Relationships with the governing body are also considered, picking up on issues considered by Gee and Price.

The change effort has ensured that the institution was well anchored, in terms of governance, value systems, planning processes, finance, and resources, as well as friends and supporters. Resistance falls when the benefits of improved performance are experienced. The author stresses the importance of allowing for the expression of personal and group style and colour, throughout.

Working from a principle that those who share most gain most, she demonstrates how a non-confrontational culture need not be equated with a lack of robustness, and examples of resilience and strength are provided. In this, behaviours and assumptions associated with 'new management' (bringing together the best of traditional 'male' and 'female' styles) combine with those of the 'learning organization' that achieves high performance through reflective practice.

This chapter illustrates how progressive forms of organizational design and development can take us well beyond our traditional concepts of education and institution and in turn, generate leading edge challenges for the future. As the author concludes, they must continue to manage 'vulnerable circumstances in a positive fashion'.

INTRODUCTION

In this chapter I describe the process of managed radical change within a college with which I have been associated since the late 1980s, and reflect upon the reasons for that change, its nature and consequences. I conclude by considering the college's current and future positions, and the nature of my role as manager.

THE RESPONSIBILITY TO INSIST UPON CHANGE

In 1987 I moved from my post as an education officer to become the principal of the Wirral Metropolitan College in Merseyside, the sole further education college within the Borough of Wirral, which measures 8 by 11 miles and has a population of one-third of a million. The college had three main sites which between them enrolled around 20,000 students each year, and also used some 50 other centres across the borough for community education. It had an annual gross expenditure of £13.5 million, 1,300 full- or part-time staff, and was altogether more than its managers could cope with. As the (then) largest college of its type in the country there was a general view, inside and out, that it was too big to be sustained as an entity, and that its very existence in effect constituted an irresolvable problem. Its disproportionate size relative to all the other service units resourced and managed by the borough council, together with its association with vocational education and training (rather than academic study), made it particularly vulnerable in a local climate of personalized political conflict. The governing body which appointed me was convinced that something had to be done to improve matters, but there was no clear view as to what that might be.

The college, as it was then, illustrated much of the downside of the public sector. Organizational concerns and managerial inadequacy had wholly displaced issues of changing client needs for much of the college's personnel and thus diminished its role as a public service. The Local Education Authority (LEA) was doing precious little actively to fulfil its responsibilities to its local communities through the college, and was saving resources by being under no organized pressure to do so. The glorious exception to this depressing picture was the adult education department which had (through those 50 or more community centres where they could develop unseen) grown on a ridiculously small resource base to account for over a third of the college's total enrolments. Despite this, the college had been inspected in 1986 and deemed to be in the top 50 per cent of English FE colleges. In part the report constituted a necessary reminder to me at the outset that much of its well-established work was being conscientiously and adequately executed. It equally showed that the HMI's framework and resources for inspection were not designed to assess either a very large FE college, or to examine the educational needs arising from rapid and serious economic and social deterioration.

That the college required urgent and complex transformation was all too clear. This was reinforced within days of my arrival, when the director of education asked me to agree that the college budget should be reduced strictly in relation to declining numbers of 16–18-year olds in the Wirral. My startled comments about the need for measures to increase participation post-16 as part of a policy and plan for post-compulsory education and training in Wirral were politely heard and then ignored in the resulting education committee reports. Clearly no time was to be lost in analysing and communicating the need for change.

There were two (overlapping) sets of reasons for effecting radical change. One was to do with immediate survival: the college was under-working its budget and resources, which had been set at a level which deserved more provision, development and quality than was then offered. The provision built on past social and economic conditions which, with the decline of manufacturing and traditional family and community organization, no longer pertained. Yet proposals for change that did not conform to traditional characteristics tended to be derailed by arguments about values, ownership, organization and remuneration. The college also expected various client groups to take what they were given. This insensitive handling gave rise to a negative view of the college and client groups often sought alternative sources of help. Finally, the college appeared so bureaucratic and static that it presented a sitting target to a hard-pressed local authority looking for savings.

The second set of reasons for effecting radical change were more explicitly linked to the college's longer-term security and development. The college had no objective understanding of how to gain a sense of its own identity; past decisions about organization and structure had generally been made to deal with particular problems, individuals and pressure groups. The college had certain operational skills, but no discernible strategic capability. It was much more bound up with perceived internal and external threats than with its existing and future students and clients, and had no conception of the rights of other stakeholders, locally or further afield. Competition and collaboration were understood only in the sense of individually preferred working styles, and those who leant towards the former were judged to be weak. At the same time, the college had in place an unreasonable number of wholly inappropriate managerial and supervisory controls, and was disabled by fearfulness. I was astounded that an organization comprising so many talented and committed people could have got itself into such a fix. Naturally, this situation was unique neither to this college nor to the education sector.

GETTING STARTED

I joined the college knowing that the need for change was urgent and the perils of delay were great. The college had an obedience culture and was shocked by my appointment. The will for change within the governing body could not be depended upon for long. So I immediately announced a fundamental organizational review over a lengthy period (one year) to cope with the need to stimulate and develop the college's capacity to think. The review comprised the phases of position analysis, needs analysis, option formulation and option selection, in that order, so as to move from the familiar and concrete to the unfamiliar and subtle. Each phase was well supported by being broken down into straightforward tasks with guidance notes, and management time made readily available. Since the review was seen as a means of developing staff, managerial and organizational insights and quality, all staff groups were involved, as were external organizations and communities. I recognized that at each stage the prime value of the activity lay in the dawning understanding of staff, the effects of their being encouraged to work together, and their growing sense of ownership of and commitment to both the review and its results. During this activity many staff with identical roles on other sites got to know each other for the first time. It could not be expected that the review would on this occasion give rise to proposals which went beyond best current thinking for the sector. However, since it was also essential that the college be rewarded for its labours and excited by a mission which was ahead of the thinking in the UK, I took a team of five to the USA in order to crystallize understandings of human potential and achievement beyond expectations. This led to the adoption of a mission statement at the end of the review period by the overwhelming majority of staff, the core of which is as follows:

- Personal achievement is everyone's right, and the college will organize itself behind this right.
- Identifying personal capability, potential, pathways and goals is a powerful aid to learning and organizational growth. The college will assist all its clients, partners and staff to do this, within a framework of standards.
- The physical, mental and psychological involvement of learners with their own development; and that of their peers, will be adopted as an organizational principle for the college.
- To encourage the college to examine its ability and preparedness to support personal growth and achievement, positive quality assurance and control measures will be linked to learning, teaching and learner support.

The internal responses to the mission statement mirror staff reactions to change during and immediately after the review. Every member of staff received a copy of the mission statement; of these over 80 per cent acknowledged that they had received and read it. Around the same number agreed with most sections; however, 30 per cent of academic staff opposed the statements on student entitlement, and wished instead to see statements on staff entitlement. The most pointed criticism was of the term 'individual', which was seen as introducing an emphasis on individualism and consumerism and reducing the importance of group experience and development. This was a valuable concern to raise: I was intent on moving away from undifferentiated course organization, but needed to strengthen the social and contributive aspects of students' experiences.

Fancy mission statements are commonplace. Often they are worthless either because they are grafted on to an organization, or ignored when it comes to action. It took a year to move to the stage where the college would accept the notion of a mission; however, once introduced we were scrupulous in subjecting everything we did to its values, logic and requirements. From this came the recognition that the college had to de-establish itself as an institution and become, in effect, a mechanism or process within a larger delivery network and regulatory framework. There were several reasons for this, including the scale of the anticipated future need for continuing education and training and the need to popularize it; the inappropriateness of current organizational forms for mass education and training; and the need to resource continuing education and training at very much lower rates than at present. In 1988, however, the perceived importance of the mission lay in its message to college staff about the treatment of students and clients; its presence as an indicator of values and a medium through which to express them; and its availability to staff as a indicator of where the organization was going.

REORGANIZATION AND DEVELOPMENT

The reorganization consequent on the review took the whole of the following year to complete. We moved from a very tall pyramid to a fairly flat one (from seven formal tiers, not counting deputies, to three) through a procedure so carefully evolved and consulted upon that no grievance cases resulted. This was despite the removal of the formal and informal powers of many individuals and groups, and some striking inversions of previous positions and practices.

Other characteristics of the new structure included fewer senior management posts, broad faculties replacing narrow departments, standardized job descriptions, increased responsibility for middle managers, a greater emphasis on college-wide development, a growth in posts providing support for students, a specialist administration and an increased support for teaching and learning. As noted above, college roles had for some time been assigned on an *ad hoc* basis to avoid facing some difficult personnel matters, and without adequate rationale. The new structure was staffed by seeking claimants to the new positions on the basis of what they had been doing immediately beforehand. By this process women were immediately appointed to 30 per cent of the middle management roles, having previously carried that proportion of the work without recognition (they had formerly occupied only 5 per cent of middle management posts). Unsuccessful claimants maintained their salaries but were redeployed. The unfilled posts were advertised on the open market; one colleague who had been refused basic support in his middle management role three years previously thus found himself managing the equivalent of four ex-departments and supervising the performance of several of his erstwhile 'superiors'.

The expansion of student opportunity and choice was immediately apparent in increased enrolments and new provision. Prior to reorganization, access to the college and associated educational services had been at the discretion of the academic departments and had operated in an arbitrary fashion. The new faculty of college services was partly designed to provide an understandable, helpful entry point to the college for students, and progressively to expand the range of services available to the student from the start to the finish of his or her programme. The main overall purpose underlying the establishment of college services was to embed strategic thinking and development within the college. Our sketches of student services and student pathways from the USA gave us something tangible through which to carry forward achievement-led organizational development.

The new structure removed the problem of surplus senior management and brought to the fore the 100 or so middle managers whose working arrangements and management development most urgently needed addressing. Although they had had very diverse formative experiences, for all of them the reorganization was enlivening and challenging, and benefits were immediately seen from their exploring the limits of their capacities and opportunities. There were very few risks attached to this; these colleagues erred on the side of safety while they built up their confidence. They were helped to become familiar with all the senior management team at the outset through a management development programme; a simple process was agreed for weekly feedback to and from senior manage-ment; all were encouraged to use a facility for making quick checks (often taking literally seconds) with any of the senior management, including me. The senior managers had been given such broad responsibilities of their own that they recognized their dependency upon the middle management tier and were only too happy to give them their heads in a supportive spirit. The immediate result of these changes was that the college became better managed: the fewer senior managers were more visible, accountable and exposed to challenge, while course teams had more accessible and informed managers at middle management level. Within a couple of years it became acceptable to distinguish four generic capa-bilities against which to assess senior and middle managers' performance: think-ing, achieving/self-management, communication, and influencing.

The organization and working methods of the middle managers have contin-ued to mature in keeping with the diversification of the college's products and services; indeed, our continuing expansion and diversification is largely occur-ring through the middle managers as they realize their own, and their area of responsibility's, potential. Thus one annually acquires getting on for £4 million from the European Union; another handles our corporate training services through a quasi-autonomous business unit; another has built us a world-class computer network, and so on. One runs several neighbourhood colleges in our rundown urban areas at arm's length from the main college because the residents still view the latter with antipathy.

The term 'middle manager' covers a very wide range of jobs and responsibili-ties now; their number is flexible according to the requirements, as are the arrangements used to link them to the organization. There is also considerable scope for the development of personal and group style and colour. The two main problems which arise from this and need constant monitoring are stress and overwork on the one hand, and uneven development on the other. Similar conse-quences among the senior management team are more easily managed since both heads of faculty and the principalship report directly to me and work substan-tially in teams.

Evidently in the world of further education there are internal reorganizations on average every four years, and these tend to coincide with the arrival of a new college principal. College staff are right to be cynical about organizational change in such circumstances. To inject some credibility into the review and reorganization until such time as its value could prove itself, I emphasized the following three points: that the aim was to build a dynamic organization which might then take change in its stride; that the new organization had both perma-nent and impermanent or organic elements; and finally that I would remain in the college for as long as it took to embed the new ways.

I am pleased that I made these points at the outset; the first two have provided the response to concerns that the structure is continually adapted in minor respects according to need. The third point has offered some assurance of personal and collective safety in an adventurous setting. However, it is also the case that in deciding to stay put for some time I chose to introduce a way of doing things which required, at least in the medium term, highly attentive and energetic management at all levels, and considerable trust and insight within the governing body/corporation board. The structure started to give student and client needs similar attention to that traditionally given to courses and qualifications. Given the continuing and helpful radical changes which colleges can now expect in their resourcing through Funding Councils, I feel increasingly confident that the college can soon adopt an even more overtly student- and client-led approach which may not face all the difficulties arising from being ahead of people's understanding and experience.

TAKING STOCK

Six years ago the college was complex in a bureaucratic way; however, its provision and services were fairly straightforward. The college is now much more complex in respect of its educational provision and services; however, the organization is itself reasonably clear and easily accessed by those who are not looking for it to act like a traditional further education college. For example, enrolment occurs throughout the year for much of the provision; managers are usually found working in mixed teams; the college's research arm is large and of a high quality. We give much time to new managers, especially those who may initially feel insecure because they cannot locate where power (as opposed to responsibility) lies. Both new staff and visitors may also need time to get up to our speed. Relaxation generally comes, though, once it is understood that dispersed power does not mean insecurity for either the individual or the organization.

The organization is actually now very strongly anchored in all the essential ways: governance, value system, planning processes, finance and resources, friends and supporters. While it is pretty honest and open, the college is not at all confrontational in nature, though. In 1992 it had to defend itself stoutly against asset-stripping by its LEA in the run-up to incorporation. Since we no longer looked like a castle or acted like gate-keepers we were thought to be a fair-weather organization which would collapse in the storm. In the event we proved to be remarkably strong due to a collective sense of ownership among our past, present and future students and clients, staff and others who knew us locally and nationally. We found that Wirral Met had attained some kind of symbolic resonance, no less!

The events of 1992 were wholly exceptional since they were a side-effect of the change of overall management from local government to national Funding Councils. Nevertheless the college had prepared itself to meet circumstances of equivalent seriousness because threats were never far off. The college's fearfulness prior to 1987 had been well-founded; its problem had been that no one knew how to manage vulnerable circumstances in a positive fashion. After 1987 the college had to learn that those who seek improvement in theory may dislike it in practice. While the college changed after 1987, its LEA did not, and I needed constantly to call upon my wider experience of local government, its purposes and qualities, in order to show leadership in acting with forbearance and sensitivity.

While it is reasonable to claim that its resilience in the face of adversity was a strength, the college has no reason to feel secure in its current state and context. Change has not permeated every staff group; with a workforce of 1,400 it is well-nigh impossible to make an impact for the better on everyone. While the college is cited by our main lecturers' trade union as having highly supportive management in industrial relations terms we are facing a period of inescapable strife. For reasons of productivity, accountability and quality assurance we must rearrange staff roles and relationships in a way that cuts right across the boundaries of the various trade unions; yet there is no immediate prospect of single union representation for the whole sector, or of helpful inter-union agreements. Thus, for example, the staffing of our ever-enlarging open learning centres, or of workplace assessment, creates territorial arguments as, for reasons of conditions of service not salary, we opt for non-teaching appointments. The long-cherished demand by the lecturers' representatives for continuing professional autonomy is being fought for through practices which can directly damage current students and turn off future ones. Disquiet about current trade union activity has led our ablest people to avoid involvement with it; thus a small group of people are having a disproportionate and unrepresentative braking effect on career and organizational development. We have to find a way through this problem, which may be long- or short-term, and in tackling it through the corporation board I am pleased that we have long-standing borough councillors with experience of public sector trade union issues. I have some concern that I may unwittingly have contributed to the loss of the internal trade union power of the lecturers by presenting a complex version of management which it is particularly difficult for them to deal with. However, I see no fresh ways of being helpful to the main lecturers' union (of which I am a member) in this respect at present.

The college is large and complex in many ways, including its staff, provision, traditions and coverage. It is therefore prone to error and inconsistency. I noted earlier that the current form of organization is very transparent, and enables senior management to get down to detail very quickly if the need arises. Before incorporation this was so mainly in relation to our core business students courses and associated services. We had learned to encourage our students to have high expectations of us and to voice their criticisms which were then conscientiously followed up. We knew we were communicating quite well the need for consistent and fair attention to students; however, our ancillary services were poor and served staff badly. To cope with incorporation we have now set up specialist units for finance, personnel, premises and management information, and their struggle to establish service standards and sub-systems shows us just how substandard we have been in these respects till now.

By regarding it as our duty to record and share our experience of change, the college has invited both justified and unjustified criticism of it. Overall this does not worry either my colleagues or me. We took the view that those who share most gain most, and this has proved to be so in many gratifying ways. We also believe that criticism of any kind helps to ensure that we stay alert. However, as indicated earlier, closer to home the effects of a high profile have been very unhelpful with the LEA, which has tended to see this as a challenge to its mastery and role. Thus over the last several years the college's ever-growing network of local partnerships with public sector, private sector and hybrid organizations has had to work around the Wirral LEA which has not yet come to terms with the college as an equal partner. This has required an urgent remedy for the LEA's sake as much as for the college's, and we have begun to address this problem in practical ways.

WHAT NOW?

The college is at present reviewing its organization form again, with a view to further changes. The reasons for this are to do with curriculum, students and technology. Having worked on a credit accumulation and transfer system for five years, we are ready to implement this across the college, and to do so must organize the provision as a single entity, rather than in faculties. To make the provision accessible and coherent, though, our students have to be supported on an entirely programme-free basis. We have also worked on integration of technology for learning, management and administration for five years and are now ready to become a computer-integrated organization.

It has in the last couple of years become easier to communicate these developments and their value because of changes in HE and industry. My personal Damascus in this respect was in 1990 when Professor Harold Silver noted the failure in the UK of the liberal imagination to seize the creative potential of new technology. More recently Louis Perelman's work, *School's Out* (1992) has convincingly warned us that schools and colleges which keep on doing what they have done before will become obsolescent, however well they are doing it. I am most of all preoccupied though by Peter Drucker's argument (1993) that all significant productivity gains are technology-led, and his subsequent question: when will education make its step-increase in productivity?

Underlying the current review, though, is a notion of a very different Wirral Met. We already provide the information technology for three geographically-spread colleges and a school, and are poised to add many more to our network locally and nationally. We have interesting commercial partnerships with the private sector due to our pre-eminence in new technology for FE. These developments have made us think hard about the practicalities of lateral and vertical integration between autonomous organizations. How does one ensure consistently ethical use of the system for example? We face new questions every day: how do our students and clients relate to educational discounts for software? What is a site? What service elements might fees relate to once costs transfer from end-use to systems maintenance? We tackle such questions with gusto despite their complexity for us, because they constitute the means of our realizing the new college as the hub of a local learning network, hopefully linked to many others over time.

In conceiving our likely future character I have been drawn to some of the work underpinning policy development in the USA. Robert Reich's *The Work of Nations* (1991) has helped me to consider changes in society and working lives, and Gaelder and Osborne's *Reinventing Government* (1992) has offered a glimpse of the 'third sector', the community, and their potential for empowerment if appropriately supported. With Merseyside now lagging behind even Northern Ireland socially and economically, there is every reason and need for Wirral Met to try to offer its residents something special.

A PERSONAL REFLECTION

I find it quite difficult at this time to evaluate my own contribution to the college and its development over the last few years. Of course I pulled it out of its previous mould and set it on a new path. That took a lot of energy, organization and independence of thought which I had gained as a mature student, a college lecturer and manager, an education officer, and a single working parent. However, when I opted to set up a lean organization managerially, using the senior management team which largely predated me, I did not carry through fully my tenet that almost everyone can be a good manager if given the right setting. I failed to offer sufficient explicit training for my nearest colleagues and tended to use example, coaching and monitoring techniques as the situation dictated. I fear this means that some of them rarely feel in adequate possession of their circumstances, and indeed they often will not be. Every year I resolve to do better in this respect and do not do so simply through lack of time. With any luck our new appraisal system will now ensure that I make good my promise. On the positive side, though, after six years I believe I have largely embedded the giving of feedback and support as a conscious management practice.

I value enormously the opportunities I receive to work with various national bodies, and never forget the fact that I am there as a reflective practising manager, whose usefulness would disappear were I not with the college. My national roles help me identify my essential reading and generally feed me mentally. But though I am adequately fed with ideas and network, I need to look again at the use of my time overall and the skills I need to use to maintain the college's position in the new setting. I am alert to the college's inability to produce firm management information precisely when I require it; the newness of our support systems generally; and the knowledge that the scope for error is much more limited than hitherto. I console myself with the thought that these concerns stem from internalized standards which are keeping in touch with the legitimate increasing expectations of the sector and know that, comparatively, we are doing well.

I feel good about having unlocked the careers and expectations of many staff and students who needed that. Though regarded as demanding and sometimes forthright, I believe I have also fostered a supportive environment and largely removed institutionalized unkindness. Most of all though I feel good about the support and forbearance which I receive from the college and its associates, and about my ability these days to recognize and appreciate it.

References

Drucker, P (1993) *Post-Capitalist Society*, London: Butterworth-Heinemann.

Gaelder, T and Osborne, D (1992) *Reinventing Government*, Reading, MA: Addison-Wesley.

Perelman, L (1992) *School's Out*, New York: William Morrow and Co.

Reich, R (1991) *Work of Nations: Preparing ourselves for 21st Century capitalism*, London: Simon and Schuster.

Reich R (1993) *Work of Nations: A blueprint for the future*, London: Simon and Schuster.

Chapter 9

Change and Stability: From 'Poly' to 'Varsity'

Michael Harrison

This author gives the reader considerable insight into the kinds of legacies – both helpful and less so – that those 'at the top' of former polytechnics have had to manage in the transition to independence. He gives numerous examples of how political passions and predilections and various forms of passive resistance confounded any attempt at strategic management in a Local Education Authority environment. Harrison clearly illustrates the values that can also be part of that local authority inheritance. These have proved central to the institution's identity and critical to its success. These values have driven a powerful alternative model of higher education that places access and accessibility, as well as flexibility and choice, at the core of its strategy and operations. The author illustrates in some detail the sheer complexity of what has been established at the University of Wolverhampton to support a truly alternative higher education. Increasingly, the new wine does not fit into old bottles, and the interconnectedness of cultural change processes in every corner of a pluralist system must be managed. For example, new relationships and new ways of working between academics and service/support staff become essential. Equally, wholesale imports of industrial practices also are now being subjected to a critical rethink, an example being team briefings. This is having an increasingly damaging effect on later stages of cultural change in many institutions, whereas it may have served a purpose at earlier ones.

Like others who are introducing change from the top based on similar such clearly defined values and commitments, such as Webb, Shackleton, Flint, Bull and Binks and Roberts, this author describes the struggle entailed in spotting and managing the contradictions between the rhetoric and reality of government policies. For example, institutions that were at the forefront of the expansion of higher education (see opening chapter and Appendix) and have fully committed themselves to student flexibility and choice via modular credit-based systems are now struggling with signals sent to academic staff by external assessments of quality and teaching that favour single-subject concentration. Much of cultural change is like pushing a boulder up the mountain: you are constantly alert to the possibility of slipping back to the old culture. Alternatively, there is the metaphor of the sponge that absorbs the change, but fundamentally does not change. The cultural change processes that have been initiated in support of the vision that is still supposedly upheld by all political parties can all too easily be subtly undermined by comparative performance evaluations that still favour traditional universities. The challenge posed by this contributor, along with others in this book, is at what social cost can this continue to occur?

INTRODUCTION: WHAT'S IN A NAME?

A new era

Amongst the many absurdities which accompanied the transition of Wolverhampton Polytechnic to the University of Wolverhampton was my being asked to cut the tape commemorating the renaming of the pub next door to the main entrance to the university from 'The George' to 'The Varsity'. The George had enjoyed a reputation as one of Wolverhampton's roughest pubs – no mean feat this – and, after a substantial investment in its conversion, emerged under its new title attended by a rumble of bouncers whose size alone guaranteed the deterrence of the displaced clientele. The polytechnic had almost doubled its size in the past six years, become independent of the local authority and had a long tradition of service to the community. Indeed, whilst titled 'polytechnic' it had made a major contribution, as its third largest employer, to the town's economy. It took, however, the designation as university to trigger this titular metamorphosis from our neighbouring hostelry. Did this diaspora of the low life from next door signify the dawn of a new era? Would a new title bring a similar status and respectability? Would research assessments bring cargo? Would life ever be the same?

An alternative approach

The collapse of the binary-line (see Appendix and glossary) was something I did not expect to witness during my working life. It was, and remains, of major significance for higher education institutions (HEIs) such as Wolverhampton, whose immediate history has been geared towards the development of an alternative approach to higher education. This alternative sees the creation of mixed modes of attendance, multiple points of entry and a plurality of access qualifications as fundamental to its mission. It is all too easy to stereotype the binary system as being divided between, on the one hand, 'elite' full-time biased, research-orientated institutions and, on the other, 'mass' open access, part-time-orientated, predominantly teaching institutions. Traditional universities include admirable pockets of part-time provision, rigorous commitment towards vocational sandwich provision and, in some cases, proven track-records regarding equal opportunities and local provision. Most ex-polytechnics have pockets of good research, the capacity to recruit internationally and have demonstrated comparable 'quality' when judged against more traditional universities. It can then be demonstrated that the binary line did not in itself represent a strict demarcation in the nature of provision or reflect unambiguous differences in and between the nature of institutions. In spite of this empirical blurring of binary arrangements there is, nevertheless, a major question of institutional identity posed for HEIs which have pursued a mission based upon distinctiveness of mission and purpose.

Managing contradictions

The insistence of the funding regime upon homogeneous criteria of performance and methods of research and teaching evaluation, poses a dilemma for universities which have forged an identity based upon a philosophy of difference from the traditional – more elitist – models as to what constitutes the idea of a university. An alternative identity is in itself an implicit critique of mainstream HE provision. Attempts to sustain this are exacerbated by the apparent failure of the 'system' to conjure a methodology which is able to express, measure and thus evaluate 'value-added' in the HE process.

In a society in which 'satisfactory' means inadequate and in which performance tables have undoubted media salience, HEIs which have celebrated difference as their kite mark are seriously questioned.

It may, then, prove expedient for those HEIs which have developed an identity based upon difference to keep their powder dry and wait for conditions more conducive to the tolerance of institutional pluralism to present themselves. Alternatively, the pressures toward conformity in a society which implicitly touts 'gold standard' criteria as the benchmark for high performance in the academy are considerable.

TAKING STOCK

Threats

In this chapter I will outline, from an entirely subjective perspective, some of the processes and pressures that accompanied the formation of Wolverhampton's mission that is premised upon institutional 'difference'.

It came as something of a shock for Wolverhampton Polytechnic to find that it was one of the most expensive public sector institutions in the country (1984/5). Changes in local authority funding resulted in a marked reluctance to continue with the considerable subsidies with which it had traditionally supported its polytechnic. The National Advisory Body for Public Sector Higher Education was into rampant planning and the institution recognized that radical changes were needed. I had just joined the polytechnic as assistant director for staffing as well as being dean of the faculty of business and social science. It was snowing, the mainframe computer staff were on strike and I wished that I was somewhere else. In liaison with a senior colleague I conspired to impress upon the director that 'something had to be done'. He agreed but the unions, NATFHE, NALGO, the administrative, clerical and technical staff union, and NUPE (manual staff) (see glossary) did not! Reluctantly the local authority felt enough was enough and a substantial programme of early retirements was negotiated. The authority, who took union agreement very seriously, required a 'consensus' to emerge. As assistant director for staffing, I spent a turbulent period imploring Scotty to 'beam me up'. A prolonged period of staff reductions, helped by a generous local authority scheme, meant that the more chronic financial excesses of the past were behind us. The price was demoralization and the loss of key staff in significant areas of teaching and research. Since the scheme was voluntary the results were arbitrary. At least we had backed away from a severe financial crisis.

The creation of the Polytechnics Central Admissions System (PCAS) confronted the institution with yet another blow to its corporate pride. We were one of the most under-chosen of the, then, polytechnics. I became director in May 1985 following a mini-crisis of a building-induced nature. The art school had to be closed, asbestos stripped out and the whole academic year for the staff and students staggered and then elongated.

Strengths

The manner in which the polytechnic, unions and local authority rallied and coped with this crisis led me to recognize that for all the gloom and doom the institution had real strength and resilience.

Part of this strength lay in a genuine commitment by a large number of staff, especially amongst those most unionized staff, to giving students new opportunities and life chances. Part-time modes of study were genuinely valued as an institutional strength, commitment to serving the community viewed as a worthy aspiration. The local authority was highly committed to access in the broadest sense and insistent upon its agencies, which very much included the polytechnic, demonstrating its credentials in terms of equality of opportunity. Some of this was rhetorical yet it did provide a real source of institutional strength and identity.

My predecessor had encouraged and created a serious springboard of course development. Consequently the institution had a highly developed diploma in higher education programme which enabled access to full-time HE for mature students with alternative entry qualifications. This diploma allowed students who had successfully completed to transfer into the final year of a number of degree programmes without loss of time. The staff who created and subscribed to this development constituted an enclave of radicalism and innovation for the whole institution. The, then, science faculty had developed, due to the sheer leadership capability of the dean, a sophisticated and accessible modular programme. Modularity was also pursued in the social sciences and humanities. Unfortunately, all three modular programmes were almost discrete, self-contained and unrelated! The polytechnic also had a large and successful department of modern languages and European studies with all the links with European academic and commercial institutions that accompany large language departments in the public sector.

Weaknesses

What was needed was a strategy that allowed the polytechnic to build upon and develop these strengths and which simultaneously made the course portfolio more attractive to potential students. There was little doubt that the music hall status of Wolverhampton, which itself had suffered disastrously in terms of unemployment and recession, made the marketing of the polytechnic more difficult. We had to look to a product-led marketing strategy.

To add to these difficulties NAB, in its infinite wisdom, decided to 'close' engineering. This was not entirely unexpected as this had been in serious decline in terms of student numbers for a number of years. It was typical of the institution to kid itself that this (a) was not happening (b) would go away when the market 'picked up' and (c) did not matter anyway! It was the polytechnic's outstanding ability to avoid rather than confront 'bad news' that was one of its most endearing and fatal characteristics. Having been a member of the previous directorate I was convinced that it was a mixture of the veto-group nature of this body as well as the intrusive nature of the authority that accounted for this curious corporate myopia. I was particularly hacked off because the reclamation of engineering was already upon my personal agenda. We launched a political campaign which led to the National Advisory Body backing-off, although it was probably more a result of the news that the body was itself under threat rather than any political perspicacity on the part of the polytechnic that led to the stand-off! It was clear, however, that if engineering were to resurrect itself, the traditional mechanical engineering path had rendered itself redundant.

INHERITANCE

Interference

A combination of the availability of the early retirement scheme and my own odious presence as director in some mysterious way led a large number of senior personnel to retire, gain promotion elsewhere or revert to private practice. This was not an even process. It did result in a situation that by 1986/7 I had a school, faculty and directorate structure of my own making filled with people of my own choice. I had no one else to blame.

The local authority however remained stubbornly intrusive. This did not, in all fairness, manifest itself with regard to the academic profile of the polytechnic. It was never a question of academic freedom, rather an issue of interference in financial and personnel matters. This involvement created immense difficulties for the polytechnic as it attempted to establish itself as a profit-making operator in the open market. There was still a pervasive ideology which sought to inhibit, regulate or, at worst, discourage activities not related to the core business of teaching publicly-funded students. This led to a range of bizarre financial arrangements (fudging/subterfuge) which were a major source of ambiguity until independence from the authority was achieved in April 1989. The chair of governors, himself an authority appointment, was wonderfully supportive of the polytechnic and, indeed, myself. He probably did himself no good politically by being seen to 'go native'!

Cultural legacies

While the impact of the authority's preoccupation with the polytechnic varied according to the political majority in control it did have cumulative consequences which are still felt, to varying degrees, in the institutional culture today. For example, there were disproportionate concerns with the minutiae of remuneration; numbers and conditions of service of the support staff were motivated by a concern with comparability of employee numbers and conditions in the rest of the authority. It was far easier, for example, to get the necessary permission to employ three animal biologists (difficult to establish comparability with an authority employee) than it was to regrade a secretary (all local councillors 'know' about secretarial functions and gradings).

This seemingly trivial emphasis upon the service/support functions of the polytechnic had a quite disproportionate impact upon its development, such as the development of a complicated academic profile without the depth and quality of support systems to underpin such an entity. The current scenario characterized by a highly developed modular multi-choice structure without an equally sophisticated management information system to aid and abet the planning, assessment and tracking that such a system necessitates can be partly attributed to the authority's baleful influence. I equally believe that my own political weakness in failing to confront the authority with the consequences of their own absurdities is as much to blame as is their own original sin.

The political agenda of the local authority led to a 'don't rock the boat' series of 'no go' areas within the academy. For example, catering had long been subsidized directly by local authority subvention. This was in turn a function of (a) a genuine commitment to the welfare of students by offering low price meals (b) a curious belief that students vote and that 'happy' students would vote for them (c) an admirable wish to offer conditions of service to catering staff superior to those in the private sector (d) the extrapolation to the polytechnic of a common practice in local authority agencies of subsidizing the meals service whether for schools or the staff in their employ. Even as the authority's willingness and ability to subsidize declined, the majority on the governing council and the web of committees and pressures which limited autonomous managerial action within the institution prevented the issue of catering prices and staffing from coming clearly onto the political agenda. This was but one, more dramatic, example of the authority's creation of politically 'ring-fenced' areas within the, then, polytechnic. Similar arguments could be made for the impact of this inheritance upon other areas of the polytechnic's activities such as the maintenance crew, computer services and the control and discipline of caretakers and cleaners.

Equally the management of industrial relations was highly circumscribed by the local authority's perceived interests. Although implicit, it was clear that there were severe limits upon the degree to which management could change the internal structures and staffing levels, or even to redeploy personnel in the institution without the direct agreement of the authority.

There were also legacies in terms of how capital stock was understood and treated. The view of the authority was that the physical premises were part of the stock that they owned and not surprisingly should be treated according the same criteria, priorities and management as the rest. This is both fair and politically expedient. However, it shows a total failure to recognize that its polytechnic was involved in a national competition for students and staff, in which the condition and appearance of the estate was of considerable significance. It does however encapsulate the key tensions which rendered incompatible the mission of the polytechnics as national providers of HE, albeit with a local/regional bias, together with their substantive status as agencies of local authority.

These comments seem highly critical of the local authority regime. In a sense they are not meant to be. For all the difficulties there were many instances, which far outweigh these adverse comments, that indicated a true commitment to the polytechnic and a genuine concern for its success and welfare on behalf of the self-same authority. The genuine commitment exhibited by members of both political parties when the existence of engineering was threatened, the quick and financially generous support given when the temporary closure of the art school threatened incipient chaos, provide some examples. The ultimate magnanimity in allowing undisputed carry-over of reserves and the great help given so as to enable the polytechnic to acquire new premises (fully aware that the final severance from the authority was inevitable) provide other indications of this support. The same can be said of the Metropolitan Borough Council (Dudley) whose support for the polytechnic was, and is, outstanding in spite of the fact that they had lost control of 'their' site since 1978.

A matter of values

I have always found it difficult to believe that collective entities such as 'institutions' have values. Whatever these values are, I am sure that the best of them at

Wolverhampton Polytechnic were inherited from its experience as a local authority agency.

Attempts at engineering changes in cultures are not conducted in abstract terms. They are actions which take place upon deeply sedimented historical inheritances. Understanding these is an essential part of management.

I believe that the best that was in Wolverhampton Polytechnic – its commitment to broaden opportunities through extending access, its emphasis upon adding value for the student by way of learning opportunities and mixed attendance modes and its concern to involve itself academically in the community, if you like, its core values – arose out of its origins as a local authority college. It is no coincidence that the institution's declared mission, once the vision/mission statement became fashionable, is no more than a refined distillation, an embellished extension, of these 'values'. These were derived, in turn, from the old civic concerns of the municipalities to provide a seamless web of educational and life-enhancing opportunities for their citizens. While I recognize that Wolverhampton's experiences are not necessarily typical I nevertheless believe that some understanding of the local authority inheritance, which manifested itself in a large variety of ways in different places, is necessary for the understanding of the differences between the cultures, attitudes, priorities and problems of the 'new' when compared with the 'old' universities.

Understanding what managers thought to be their inheritance, however misguided their perceptions of these may be, is essential for understanding their deluded behaviour! It was against this inheritence that a major phase of institutional development, quite literally, took off. I shall discuss this in two stages: pre-incorporation and post-incorporation.

BOOM

Seizing opportunities

The period from 1986 to 1990 saw unprecedented growth in student numbers combined with the rapid development of the academic programme towards a full-blown modularity. This major diversification programme included a growth of European study opportunities outside the school of languages and European studies and the development of continuing education into companies and public sector agencies using the accreditation of prior learning and experience machinery. Engineering started the long haul back to solvency. They built upon a slender, externally-funded project, based on computer-aided design and engineering and developed this into a full-blown undergraduate programme. Characteristically, the staff sought new, less traditional student markets amongst Business and Technician Council (BTEC) qualified and more technically minded students who were considering art school as an alternative. The limited liaison between engineering and art and design was indicative of new levels of cooperation between previously isolated departments. The thrust towards Europeanization was the product of a similar alliance between languages and business studies. A whole range of developments were the product of a wide range of coalitions between pockets of the academy that had hitherto enjoyed a splendid isolation. The reorganization facilitated by early retirements resulted in the radical reduction of the number of departments into fewer large multidisciplinary schools.

Polytechnic-wide modulating: named versus flexible routes

The move towards full blown, integrated modularity was centrally driven by the new deputy director for academic affairs. In retrospect one of the big mistakes made during this boom period was the acceptance of a gradualist, evolutionary approach towards the achievement of polytechnic-wide modularity. Against the advice of the deputy director I incorrectly decided that the framework should emerge from the variety of models available in the institution with newcomers to modularity (eg, art and design, business studies) adopting modular structures and frameworks through the process of cyclical revalidation. The key to this development was the evolution of combined studies which allowed students a wide variety of choice across the institution's academic offerings which involved, in turn, the creation of a large number of named routes. This grew into the 'Modular diploma and degree programme' which allows choice and the diversification of main routes across the board.

The key tension to be managed by this evolutionary approach was the division between those who correctly argued that a large number of students opt for clearly defined named programmes, eg, computing, business studies, art and design, that had become the 'tradition' in the polytechnics, and between those who equally plausibly argued that students were attracted by choice and flexibility as to what they could study once they accessed into the polytechnic. The 'solution' in an institution whose recruitment profile insists that developments must be product-oriented and consumer-led is to have a system which offers both – this is after all the true potential, the real pay-off in having a modular system.

One of the current ironies emerging from the logic of modular evolution is the development of *subject*-specific named routes, eg, psychology, sculpture, electronics, which in the context of the polytechnic's traditional strengths in offering integrated programmes, eg, business studies, social sciences, creates a whole new range of tensions. Primarily, the re-emergence of subjects with all the traditional 'old' university connotations poses a major set of issues for the modular ex-polytechnics whose rationale is built upon the multidisciplinary department/school and the integrated multidisciplinary programme! The number of subject routes to prove acceptable to the institution and the number that can be academically sustained will have profound effects upon the nature of power and identity in the university. Obviously the re-establishment of 'subject power' will pose interesting questions for the more managerially-driven leadership of the ex-polytechnics. Wolverhampton is still working through the full implications of containing such a large number and variety of structures for study.

I believe that a more bullish seizure of the nettle earlier, by way of imposing a singular academy-wide modular framework, would have made the process less confusing and painful. The process of introducing radical change in academic provision is always politically difficult. In retrospect, greater clarity of purpose and precision on my part could have helped the senior staff to achieve these changes quicker and with far less ambiguity.

Diversification: managing complexity

It became clear that the inherent weaknesses of our central administrative and management information services meant that we were quite incapable of managing such a complex course portfolio, with radical increases in student numbers on a multi-site basis. The system was creaking, the staff demoralized and the tensions between the 'boom' go-for-growth elements in a senior management and the more cautious concerns with quality and sheer manageability of the institution came to the fore. The modular degree and diploma programme which offered a wide range of choice appeared to be paying dividends in terms of student recruitment. The polytechnic was beginning to show a slow, yet largely consistent improvement in its ability to attract students. The problem was the imbalance between an increasingly comprehensive and sophisticated modular programme and the lack of an appropriate support structure, planning machinery and informational services to underpin them.

Adding to these problems was our own success at expanding both in size and the diversification of our activities. Complexity brings a new set of problems. A whole range of new entrepreneurial activities had taken off. This was in a context in which the Wolverhampton local authority took a rather dim view of such activities at best and at worst lacked a financial management system to sustain and encourage them. Not surprisingly it was in the institution's interests to mystify the situation but this did nothing for clarity of objectives and firmness of managerial purpose!

While this vibrant process of diversification, fostering new activities in the cause of external funding, and of internationalization of the academy was taking place, we were successful in being one of the first tranche of HEIs to win an Enterprise in HE award. This gave the diversification process an immense boost. It provided a margin of extra income which allowed a wide range of experimental activities and new ideas to come to fruition. More importantly, it offered a large number of staff the space and time in which to innovate. It also provided, I believe, a much needed focus which brought new combinations of staff together and further broke down the paralysing tendency to compartmentalize that had long bedevilled the polytechnic. In concrete terms it resulted in polytechnic-wide offerings in languages, business studies, law and information technology which strengthened the range of choices available to students whilst simultaneously breaking down barriers to cooperation.

Image and communications

Governors were persuaded that we needed an external consultancy in order to review our image and communications problems. The result was a new logo, the emergence of a house style for publicity and, perhaps most importantly, the recognition internally that marketing, publicity and image were important, vital and necessary (if not respectable) parts of the modern academic institution. The consultancy confirmed my own view that internal communications were in a deplorable state and rectification of the problem was essential if we were to develop a real corporate culture. The result was a regular house magazine (although this 'regularity' took several years to achieve) and a system of monthly team-briefings. This was a case of the importation of so-called industrial practices into the academy of which there were many more to come. It seemed to me that it was worth experimenting with since we were bereft of ideas on how to solve the chronic communications issues on our own. I believe that the development of information technology may now have rendered such techniques outmoded. However I am sure that, in spite of the cynicism the system causes, it proved an invaluable tool during the process of change induced by the severance from the local authority. Not surprisingly this period was one in which fear, rumour, innuendo and misinformation were rife. Team briefing was of some value as a mechanism by which management could 'set the record straight'. To my mind the consequences of the communications consultancy were of profound significance for the organization since they brought home to the pre-incorporation governors (who were still local authority dominated) the vital importance of image in the context of highly competitive markets. I think there was a general failure to recognize that higher education is essentially a market-driven phenomenon.

A major institutional visit from the Council for National Academic Awards – our accrediting body – brought home the degree to which we had a fundamental internal communication problem. By and large, the report from council was fairly supportive, noting the innovatory nature of the institution. CNAA, however, refused to grant the polytechnic extended delegated powers to accredit our own programmes. We had recently reorganized the quality control machinery in order to establish a two-tier system which gave increased powers to the faculties; this was felt to be more compatible with the polytechnic's modular programme. The fact that CNAA, after a period of discussion and modification, found the new system robust and granted us delegated powers suggests that there was nothing fundamentally flawed with the system. Their basic objection was that our own staff did not seem to fully comprehend the new system! This was indicative, not just of our communications problem, but was also the result of the aggressive change process being driven from the top. The centre had lost touch with the periphery – the real source of delivery in the institution. The narcotic buzz which accompanies rapid change had outstripped the corporate capacity to absorb and assimilate the injection.

Partnerships

Another major development at this time was our academic liaison with the then West Midlands College. The view taken by the management of both the college and the polytechnic was that a full merger was both appropriate and in the interests of both institutions. The polytechnic fully recognized that such a merger would considerably strengthen the quality and viability of the teacher training portfolio and diminish some of the chronic spatial problems resulting from past expansion, while building physical capacity for future sustained expansion. While the authority accepted the values of merging the college's and the polytechnic's teacher training portfolio they held back concerning full merger. Since this merger was on the horizon for several years it did lead to delays in implementing our much needed plan to geographically rationalize the deployment of schools and central services throughout the polytechnic. This delay exacerbated the feeling of pressure and overcrowding on the main sites in Wolverhampton.

INDEPENDENCE AND SYSTEMATIC GROWTH

A bit of hindsight

I am convinced that this period of rapid growth and change had been essential for the health and, possibly, the survival of the polytechnic. I am also convinced, in retrospect, that this could have been managed far more intelligently. While the authority had placed constraints upon the degree to which some of these problems could have been ameliorated (ie, upon the amount of investment in the quality and quantity of support staff, investment and use of information technology) I could have been far more upfront in pointing out to the politicos the adverse consequences of their position on these matters. Rather I had opted to 'go for broke' in terms of innovative academic development, diversification of the funding base and a rapid and radical expansion and to ignore the organizational and human consequences of this one-sided strategy of change. The severance of the polytechnic from the local authority system in April 1989 made it possible to address overtly these imbalances, distortions and disruptive consequences of past changes.

Managing the transition: the importance of strategy

When it became clear that government legislation would inevitably bring about the autonomy of the polytechnic from the local authority, the chairman of governors, with characteristic generosity, relinquished his post in favour of a member of the industrial community. My new chairman helped to establish a strategy which addressed the fundamental weaknesses and problems which confronted the polytechnic as an incorporated body and has continued to support the tradition of critical questioning of strategy and tactics, supportiveness once decisions of principle have been made, together with a hands-off approach concerning the day-to-day management of the institution. Above all the post-incorporation board of governors as a whole has so far recognized the importance of the polytechnic maintaining a sense of identity and mission based upon historical strengths and difference from the traditional university system.

The somewhat grudging acceptance by the local authority of the facts of separation led to delays in the appointment of key support staff. The issues were those of salary rather than substance. The creation of two 'shadow governing bodies' (two were necessary since it had been agreed that merger with Walsall would coincide with the day of incorporation) did allow the directorate, now with the support of the governors, to prepare for independence. This simultaneously meant a start towards the correction of the chronic imbalances which distorted the institution. This process included a reorganization of the directorate, reverting to a somewhat old fashioned system of deans of faculty being full members of the directorate while having a set of central functions as well as faculty duties. I was determined that the rift between centre-periphery and the problem of the directorate becoming disembodied from the rank and file concerns of staff would, at least, be diminished. The merger with Walsall also created the need to face up to the realities of being a multi-site HEI. The establishment of 'a centrally regulated, locally delivered set of campus services' was established. Although a less than ideal set of arrangements, it does at least create the conditions for a genuine feeling of ownership, responsibility and control for delivery of services of our various sites – so essential for the recapturing of a sense of pride in the physical environment in which services to students are delivered.

THE EMERGING DEVELOPMENT AGENDA

These issues concerning the delegation of responsibilities to campuses are indicative of a whole series of changes necessary if the polytechnic were to achieve some kind of match between its ambitious, complex academic programme, its commitment to increased accessibility, flexible modes of attendance, enhanced equality of opportunity and service to the various communities which we served, and its capacity to deliver these in a high quality learning environment. A number of major themes suggested themselves in these early days of independence. An agenda which the management of the institution is to this day still working through was set in these early days of independence from the local authority regime. Contingent factors have altered the timing, the priority given to any single item and the ordering of these priorities. I will merely enumerate some key themes and make limited comments on them.

Personnel

It was clear that most of our problems could be analysed as fundamentally issues concerning the management of human resources. The new independence allowed us to define 'Personnel' as a major management function together with all consequent implications for the remuneration and staffing of this key area.

The establishment of a businesslike relationship with the teachers' union, and more latterly UNISON (a new national union created by merger which represents all non-academic support staff), has stood us in good stead. I did, and I continue to, recognize not just the importance of good working relationships with unions, but of the crucial commitment of union members as 'custodians' of the institution's 'values'.

The post-local authority experience has led me to recognize the crucial significance of having sound, well-documented personnel policies and procedures. It is with some regret that I failed to achieve this insight during the previous regime. While changes in contractual arrangements have been of great importance in enabling the productivity accompanying subsequent expansion in student numbers, the real advantages of these changes in the management of human resources have been more covert and subterranean. The severance from the local authority, in conjunction with firmer management of human resources, has meant a change in atmosphere in which managerial direction is no longer defined as inherently threatening, nor work discipline an impingement on personal autonomy. Part of this has been the creation of a systematic development programme which, while still fairly primitive, at least supports development in line with the institution's corporate direction.

Finance and devolution

The establishment of sound financial procedures and practices was of overarching significance. Until incorporation the polytechnic had never had its own cheque book. Part of this process was the devolution of considerable financial autonomy and accountability to the teaching schools. The public exposure of school balances and deficits has offered a considerable incentive to heads to adopt the disciplines of financial management. One of the key issues which confronts the university in the light of recent government consolidation of student numbers is the degree to which radical financial devolution is compatible with institutional policies (ie, modularity) which require a high degree of central corporate control.

The new financial disciplines, the freedom to make financial plans (in spite of the government's propensity to change the rules annually) has led to the creation of reserves for development projects. This has been the vital element in creating planned, systematic growth, as opposed to the 'let it rip' developments of earlier years. It does however create a major problem, in the context of consolidation, concerning the control of central costs and the legitimacy of corporate strategies which tend to override devolved school autonomies. I think this will be a major issue for the financial management of the university over the next few years of consolidation, rather than growth.

Support structures and systems

Deployment and control

The freedom over personnel and financial management of the institution has allowed for some of the major problems concerning the deployment and control of the major support services to be addressed. Grading has become more equitable and we have made a major investment in both the quality of, and the career ladders for, senior support staff. We have given responsibility for the deployment of most support staff unambiguously to the heads of school and to the major line managers of the service departments. Additionally, we have created a separate planning office tasked with the production, distribution and analysis of student numbers on behalf of the institution's management. Nevertheless, the issue of the quality of management information remains a major problem in spite of the considerable improvements over the last few years. I feel that in our desire to break down the massive bureaucratic monolith of the past and to clearly define and locate managerial responsibilities, we have fragmented the services to the extent of creating another tier of coordination problems. I am sure that this, together with issues concerning devolution, will constitute the immediate managerial agenda over the next few years.

Estates strategy

The requirement of the Polytechnics and Colleges Funding Council to present strategic plans created an environment in which testing of the mission and strategy against the 'external' criticality of governors has proved most useful. The major input of governors concerning our planned development of a new site at Telford provides a good example. Governors' awareness of the importance of developing new markets, their perspicacity concerning questions of marketing, property issues and legal intricacy, has proved a major strength in bringing this project to fruition. The need to integrate the 'academic plan' with the 'resource/estates strategy' has created a new sense of internal discipline and forward thinking which has allowed us to overcome some of the incipient chaos of the pre-incorporation growth trajectory.

Quality issues

It became clear, once the immediate post-incorporation problems had been settled, that we had to look again at our whole strategy with regard to the monitoring and improvement of quality. We had certain endemic problems due to the ambitious nature of our academic programme. A wide-ranging, choice-driven modular system in a multi-site organization has its own discrete potential for cock-up. Furthermore, the newly emerging 'quality business' was unlikely to favour universities such as Wolverhampton that had taken 'alternative' provision as the key to their distinctive mission. There seemed a 'solution' to both problems. BS5750 offers an internal discipline which forces those who seek such accreditation to confront their own inadequacies. I am convinced that the pursuit of the British Standards kitemark has, and will increasingly allow the university to overcome some of these endemic problems. It will, once achieved, provide a baseline upon which a true total quality management regime can be built. TQM also provides an alternative view of quality development which may be better suited to mass HE than the inherently conservative deliberations of HEFCE. It may offer a quality alternative which facilitates pluralism rather than induces conformity.

BS5750 (Doherty, 1993) provides no more than a baseline upon which to build a more complex total quality management system. I believe that the British Standard (when we eventually get it), when added to the measures we have already taken with regard to programme monitoring (highly devolved to give producers a sense of ownership) and student feedback, does provide us with the beginnings of a strategy which is better suited to the purposes of mass higher education than the course dominated Threshold Model inherited from the CNAA. The advantage of BS5750 is that it provides quality standards for the whole university and not just for academic staff. In this sense it is promotive of team-building rather than divisive. This baseline must, of course, be supplemented by a genuinely developmental human resources policy if we are to convert the procedure-driven skeleton of BS5750 into a real quality culture.

In my opening comments I indicated that the pressures emanating from the current quality debate may lead to universities, such as Wolverhampton, to reconsider their position as providers of alternative models of HE. I hope that I have given some impression as to how an institution such as Wolverhampton has grown, developed and responded in the past. It is one of life's ironies that now we are independent of the local authority apparatus we enjoy excellent relationships with the various boroughs in which we are located. I hope the university is now capable of being retroactive in a changing world. I also hope that I have given some impression of how a certain continuity of institutional purpose has survived and evolved through all this change. I would also hope that this 'alternative' concept of a university is sufficiently robust to withstand the growing seductiveness of the conventional wisdom concerning what a 'varsity' is all about.

Reference

Doherty, G D (1993) 'Towards total quality management in higher education: a case study of the University of Wolverhampton', *Higher Education,* **25**, 321–39.

Chapter 10

Survival is not Compulsory

Ruth Gee

Ruth Gee, like Chris Price, has written this chapter from the perspective of having moved on, and here is a similar exploration of the difficult realities and choices facing the person introducing change 'from the top'.

She provides considerable insight into the tensions entailed in knowing when best to act and when best to consult, and in managing shifting patterns of support and resistance. Within this, she underlines the value of ensuring that big visions remain linked to tangible and incremental signs of success. The symbolic can spur the real, as was the case of this institution's significantly improved comparative performance within the sector. (This theme also figures in Wilson's and Shackleton's chapters.) Like Bull, she places considerable emphasis on the importance of timeliness and careful phasing, also with a major institutional restructuring. They both describe processes that seek to work 'with the grain' but at its edge, so potential is continuously being developed.

Her frank treatment of relationships with the governing body, and her analysis of their ambivalence about the nature and pace of change despite an ostensible commitment to radical leadership, is especially welcomed, and takes further issues introduced in the chapters by Price, Webb, Edwards and Bull.

She places much emphasis on attention to formal and informal communication, and rightly sees a communication strategy as guiding processes of consultation and involvement and not merely information sharing. These themes are also picked up by Shackleton and Price. She also explores the values of an external facilitator.

The attention she gives to learning and development, her own as well as that of others, is likely to prove salutary to those who are committed to creating leadership and change management styles 'at the top' that are far richer than 'command and control' modes of operating.

INTRODUCTION

The arrival

'You don't need to change: survival is not compulsory.'
'If you are not part of the solution, you are part of the problem.'

As the words bounced from the walls of the college theatre, I felt a combination of tension, exhilaration and excitement which was to mark the next four years of my leadership of the college. Some were stunned, others outraged, a few were delighted.

This was my first staff meeting. Prior to my arrival I had sent a letter with everyone's pay packet introducing myself and inviting them all to a meeting in the second week of my appointment. It was the first time that both teaching and non-teaching staff had been invited to the same meeting. Hitherto the groups of staff had been regarded as distinct, the purpose of one being to serve the function of the other. I was very clear that while their roles were different, their value was equal. One group could not function effectively without the other and we were all there to serve the needs of the students. It sounds so simple, almost clichéd and yet that was a message that was going to need repetition many times.

I had intended to be direct in my first meeting with staff but had I overdone it? Was the challenge likely to alienate more than it attracted? I recognized the value of, and was committed to the principle of, consultation and action based on consensus but I sensed that a strong lead from the top, within a short time-scale, would be essential to future survival.

Defining leadership is difficult and in 1989, the immediate post-incorporation period for public sector higher education, it was a relatively new concept. Successful management as the expression of clear leadership was looked upon by many in academia with suspicion, because although consultation was well established within colleges and universities, decision making usually followed a leisurely period during which consensus had to be achieved. The tradition of higher education was after all one of academic freedom and the encouragement of diverse ideas – the new culture which the government sought to impose was seen as threatening that environment. It was to be done through the domination of public sector higher education governing bodies by nominees of business, industry and commerce. An immediate tension was imposed through this legal framework, and in many higher education institutions a power struggle of cultures took place. In my own case the supremacy of the business approach on the governing body resulted in the principal's post being redesignated as that of 'Director and Chief Executive'. Defining roles and ensuring the appropriate separation of the executive from the legislature was essential. I was required to set objectives, to direct and to execute matters.

That required a game plan. Mine was straightforward – I had to generate a recognition that the college needed to change if it was to survive, and a commitment to an improved, relevant and flexible student experience. In this chapter I shall explore how I approached this challenge and created substantial change.

Background

There are some common characteristics of institutional change wherever it occurs and I believe one is that individuals do matter; the interpersonal relations of the inherited staff team as well as the strategies and tactics they adopt in any given situation will impact on outcomes. Given this starting point, I believe an understanding of my personal characteristics and cultural context is essential if there is to be any meaningful analysis of the process of leadership which I experienced. A simple pen portrait might be useful.

I was 41 years old, mother of a 10-year-old son and a 12-year-old daughter and the wife of a man whose work prospects were based in the south east of England. Moving house and relocating to a semi-rural part of north west England after 17 years spent in an inner city London borough was a radical move. The energy that went into my role as director had to be matched by support for the family unit. It was not easy but it worked. It was my professional drive which led to the relocation. The feeling of liberation at being at the top was real and exhilarating. At the end of the day any mistakes were my responsibility but I took the opportunity to shape, lead and manage in a way which enabled me to feel comfortable about myself. My advice to anyone considering an application for a chief executive post would be to be clear and positive that it is what you want to do. Never apply for a job to which you feel less than fully committed.

The semi-rural college I had moved to was not known for its innovation. Many of the staff had been there for a long time and had enjoyed a comfortable existence under the control of the Local Education Authority (LEA). The majority felt that a new culture imposed as a result of government intervention was repressive and retrograde. They did not wish to be exposed to the market place and competition. The staff who did recognize that change was inevitable were able administrators but management was not a skill that had been necessary when the LEA took all the policy decisions. It also did not come naturally to many.

INITIAL STEPS

Towards a shared purpose

It is relatively easy to reflect on process retrospectively. Living and shaping events at the time was less clear. Tom Peters (1993) has said, 'a tolerance for ambiguity will be success tool number one for line workers, politicians and corporate chiefs alike'. There are no certainties of outcome. It is unclear how staff dynamics are going to work and in the first instance leadership requires a recognition that the only certainty is the uncertainty of the future. What is required is a clear personal vision and commitment which forms the bedrock for leadership and action.

I did have a clear idea in my own mind about what needed to be done if the college were to survive. There was much speculation at the time of incorporation in 1989 that only the big institutions had a long-term future and I was in a college which was relatively small. Somehow or other we had to generate a sense of identity and a clarity of purpose which differentiated us from our competitors.

Creating a vision owned and shared by the majority is essential in all organizations and higher education is no exception. Yet there is a history within it, and a culture of academic autonomy, of freedom of thought. Managing a factory of ideas is very different from managing a production line of tangible goods. Although I shared (and still do) the staff's sense of a need for local and open accountability, their hope was that things would go away. How could I generate a sense of reality and from that a shared vision?

I found that focusing on the simple question, 'What is our purpose?' was an enormous help. Many had not thought strategically before and the question also forced an analysis of what the future held. 'What do we want to be in the year 2000?' I raised the question in that first staff meeting and subsequently set up a number of meetings and residential away-days which were to focus the minds and hearts of many. Clarity of purpose focused attention on the organizational structure and the question about whether structure was serving or dictating purpose. It took 18 months before there was a majority view that structure was dictating purpose and that we had to change. By then the staff were able to propose the solutions.

Needs for immediate action

But while I waited for that support to develop, I felt frustrated. Things were not moving as quickly as I felt they ought and I saw the external pressures mounting against us. The higher education sector funding methodology was based on assumptions about expansion. It was clear that teaching group size had to increase and that teaching methods had to change. The introduction of technology to support both learning and teaching was essential. The college had to market itself and position itself against local competition.

I offered no choice to staff about the establishment of a discrete personnel office, the effective functioning of the finance office nor the establishment of a marketing and communications office. I introduced a college newspaper and formed an access and equal opportunities unit. The opponents of change were worried. Those first actions had been neither consultative nor slow to implement. I acted decisively and introduced the new.

PROGRESS AND RESISTANCE

Trade unions

When it came to the more radical change that I felt to be necessary to alter the culture, provide the founder for the future and bring the student experience into the 1990s, I encouraged greater staff involvement. Over an 18-month period the shift started to happen. Ironically, at the same time the trade unions decided to object. Although the activists within the unions were a small minority of staff, the majority were apathetic about formal union activity and did not get involved. I had a personal history of valuing trade union involvement and I found myself with a terrible dilemma. Yet I was convinced that to concede to their demands for no structural change would be ruinous for the college. I looked to the governors for support.

Governors

I made many assumptions in those early months. Governors had made a bold choice in appointing me. I was not a traditional higher education chief executive and indeed that role itself was evolving. I had a history of teaching in secondary schools rather than higher education; I had been a local government councillor, and had entered the senior management team of an inner London polytechnic as a consultant prior to being offered a substantive post as an assistant director. I recognized that I had a lot to thank the governors for. They took an act of faith in appointing me and I assumed they would want to support my recommendations once I was in post.

Despite my past political experience I had underestimated the key individual opponents on the staff and within the trade unions, and their individual political power with certain governors. Birch wrote in 1988 that, 'what is required above all from managers is an awareness of complexity and an understanding of context, notably its micropolitical and cultural dimension.'

Individuals with an axe to grind or an anxiety to indulge will do so if they feel the climate is right and no educational manager should underestimate the personal and political networks that operate in all communities. I recognized their existence but I assumed that because it was in the best interests of the college to move quickly, they could be overcome. Little did I reckon with the power of the sports club, the party political groupings, the church and the pub – networks that for a woman in the north west were hard to penetrate and were in any event at a considerable remove from our multi-faceted student body. I had made an understandable assumption – that within an organization dependent upon market forces and fitness for purpose, logic and rationality would prevail. The governing body was persuaded that I was introducing too much change too fast and although they supported my proposals for structural change after two years of my being in post, I felt a sense of lost opportunity. I recognized four out of five assistant directors deciding to retire faced governors with the prospect of having no one on the inside to defend the status quo, provide a sense of historic continuity and preserve custom and practice. It was too great a threat, and therefore they asserted their control, through the deferral of this support.

I learnt a lot about relationships with governors in that episode and I believe that any college manager needs to consider the personalities and processes involved very carefully. It is the job of the chief executive to work well with the chair of the governors and indeed the board as a whole. I always took that as axiomatic. There may be a tendency to overlook the group dynamics of a number of individual governors, many of whom have competing views and perspectives. Experience of other higher education institutions has taught me that governing bodies *can* be generally business-like, supportive of the organization yet critically constructive; but if there is a danger in your college that those competitive forces may get out of hand for whatever reason then you need to be particularly vigilant. The Education Reform Act gives enormous powers to boards of governors. All chief executives should be aware of these powers and try to 'manage' them in the best interests of the college.

Learning and development

The college moved from a traditional hierarchical line-management structure to a functional management structure based on a matrix. The sceptics remained but an increasing number of staff were assuming ownership and the culture felt as if it was shifting. I tried to encourage a new 'no blame' culture in which individual initiative was welcomed and there was a sense of personal responsibility. A holistic staff and organizational development programme seemed vital and we decided to increase the budget allocation as a reflection of that importance.

Working with an external facilitator

I found the involvement of an external facilitator an invaluable tool to the activity. An independent consultant in whom I had great professional confidence, she understood the sector and the needs of both funding council and students. I was able to look to her for personal support and I believed she would generate confidence in the staff. I used her in structured sessions with senior staff and the decision to do so was initially very controversial. Some wanted to interpret it as a sign of personal uncertainty; others were nervous about another woman joining the group – this had been a men's team for so long and things were in danger of getting out of hand! Others were just a little nervous of the novelty.

The presence of a facilitator allows the chief executive to play an equal role within the group; to lead or not to lead as need dictates. It helps to elevate the views of other team members and a skilful facilitator can soon overcome initial reservations. Her involvement allowed me to observe process as well as to participate within it. That opportunity rarely exists in an increasingly pressurized educational world yet the need is becoming greater and greater. She provided an essential sounding board for some of my more radical ideas and helped me to keep a sense of perspective, necessary when trying to pace change. She also helped me see how inactivity could be the result of a positive decision, something that was novel to most.

Learning from elsewhere

Many of our competitors had introduced changes in the 1980s such as modularization, credit accumulation and transfer schemes. In deciding where we wanted to be in the year 2000 we decided to make a virtue of the omissions of the past; for example, to take the best of modularization schemes elsewhere and avoid the mistakes of others; to use technology as the hallmark of the future.

Analysing and anticipating the changes of others was also an essential part of the process. For example, we decided that we were not going to develop links throughout the region but focus instead on developing strong links with a selected group of further education colleges. Recognizing that time and tide wait for no one and trying to translate that into everyday practice is a challenge all managers face. We should decide to leapfrog certain steps in a change process more often!

Learning 'at the top'

The sense of personal exhaustion can be real. Initially, I was so anxious to succeed to prove my professional virility to my team of male colleagues that I worked very long hours. Once the children were in bed, it was out with the thought pad and on with the creativity. Then at one of our away-day sessions on team building, our facilitator introduced the notion of a structured feedback technique. Although it became a source of humour, it became adopted into the culture of the senior management team. As a result, I was sensitively advised that my energy, hard work and commitment were in danger of developing into a detrimental role model. Could I please send out some signals that taking a holiday was acceptable?

The obvious had not occurred to me. I was colluding with the male model. I took heed and subsequently made very public declarations that I expected staff to take their leave entitlement and that there was no virtue in long hours in the office if short ones would do. I distinctly remember the occasion when, on a day's leave, I was called on my mobile phone and advised that there was an emergency and I should return to campus immediately. I remembered the feedback, assigned the task to someone else and tried to sound calm as I announced that I could not return until the end of the day. I spent the next few hours continuing my shopping, including the purchase of an office coffee machine (I never drink coffee!) and tried to pretend that I found the art of delegation and relaxation easy. Simple incidents like that often provide a personal breakthrough. By my fourth year I started to convince other over-conscientious staff of the wisdom of the argument and the need to recharge the personal batteries in the interests of students and others.

COMMUNICATION

Sharing information

Effective communication is essential in any organization at any stage of its evolution. There is a truism about information and power and I tried quite genuinely from the start to share information as widely as possible, both formally and informally. In-house newspapers, the distribution and accessibility of formal documentation for committees, the regular formal opportunities to meet in various groupings of staff and students, the open door sessions, strategy days and away-days, which I introduced, were all important parts of the internal communication process.

Although I am not a technician of information technology, I realised its enormous potential for democratization and speedy sharing of information and in many respects this was the most significant area of change which I introduced. The college was definitely well ahead of the game at the time I left. By the end of the second year, computers were standard for both administrative efficiency and learning support. I wanted to introduce e-mail throughout the campus and that in itself created a communication revolution. Everyone soon had access to a terminal, if not initially on their own desk, at least through the staff common room and the library. The fact that the chief executive would send electronic mail encouraged others to gain their own passport. Indeed it did not take long to realize that if you tried to contact me by phone, you had to pass my secretary who was an effective gatekeeper, whereas if you used e-mail then you made direct contact and usually got a very prompt reply!

Communication as involvement

Yet in my experience there and elsewhere, staff never feel as if communication is good enough. The appointment of a new assistant director with a communications background was indispensable. She dealt with the criticism very effectively by drawing together existing practice, recommending some new ones and drafting a coherent policy framework which was adopted by the academic board and the board of governors.

Many people confuse communication with decision making and can feel disaffected because they are not part of the formal decision-taking process. Good information sharing which is multi-faceted, formal and informal, helps to engender a sense of participation in decision taking even if others take the final decisions. That differentiation needs to be clearly stated and understood. I would recommend that all colleges adopt a communication policy which is formally adopted by the academic board and the board of governors. It also makes it easier to demonstrate that effective communication is a process which operates in many different directions and is not simply top down.

External communication

External communication usually benefits from a professional input but the successful chief executive needs to be able to maintain good relations with the press and the media, should be an effective public speaker and seek to exploit such public relation opportunities as arise. This he or she will need to do at local, regional, national and occasionally international level.

If you need to leave a lot of the work to the press or marketing officer, ensure that he or she is strategically located to take a regular brief. This activity is too sensitive and important to relegate to a distant site.

SIGNS OF CULTURE CHANGE

Feeling good

Such developments were important in the changing of the college's character and the creation of a distinctive ethos. It took four years for me to feel that the ship was sailing in the right direction and not simply blowing with the wind. Visitors started to comment that the 'feel good factor' was strong and that the college had its own identity and buzz. Such culture changes are hard to define and difficult to manage but the results were due, I think, to the holistic strategy for change which began in the first year.

Looking good

Cultural change in a college benefits from some tangible expression. Lack of capital investment is commonplace in colleges and universities and my college was no exception. There had been no major capital investment in the college for 20 years. Much of the teaching space was dowdy and many communal spaces gave the impression they had seen better days or were 'time warped'. Alongside the restructuring exercise, we had to create a more up-to-date and purposeful environment for students, visitors and staff. It began with a decision to change the appearance and function of the main entrance. I had to demonstrate to the sceptics my capacity to generate the income to pay for it.

Performing well

Throughout the first two years we increased the student intake according to our targets and reduced our teaching costs. We became the second most space-efficient college in the sector: an essential ingredient in persuading the Funding Council to allocate a capital grant. Learning to anticipate the thinking and the rules of those who controls the purse strings is now essential to any successful college manager. It sounds so obvious but I realized that to many it was not.

By 1992, the front entrance had been refurbished; there was high quality teaching space in the main building and we had won a major capital grant from the Funding Council for a new learning resources centre.

Governors had recognized the need to invest in the college's capital infrastructure if it were to be attractive to future students. We obtained financial support for the building of 300 new student residences and catering facilities and student common room facilities. Just before I left, I signed a partnership agreement with a major international computer company to ensure that college IT equipment could be kept up-to-date. We did not want to lose our competitive edge.

The effect on staff and student morale was enormous as they realized that the fine words of managerial promise were becoming deeds. I recommend the value of physical manifestations of change. Many low cost, relatively superficial environmental improvements bring real added value. Fresh paint, the absence of graffiti and clean corridors and teaching space reflect a concern for the learner which should be the hallmark of all institutions. Culture and ethos change with individuals and group dynamics but buildings go on for ever!

LOOKING BACK, MOVING FORWARD

It is wise to acknowledge that versions of reality are frequently constructed after the event. I freely admit to being proud of the changes made. Of course they were the result of many people's effort and I am proud of that too. I still regret that I was not able to persuade everyone of the values of change.

The need for allies

From the first term I identified those staff members who genuinely wanted to help the change process. I spotted the untapped yet ambitious talent and, despite the recruitment of excellent new staff from outside, demonstrated that change could be directed by staff with a long history in the institution. Several of these were women who, although cautious at first, became more confident in their own ability and the value of their contribution. As 72 per cent of the student body were women, I felt the existence of positive role models was very important and adopted specific strategies to encourage the development of women staff and students. By 1993, there was in place a senior staff team (about 20 in total) of high calibre and committed staff. I had learnt in the early 1980s that one of a manager's greatest skills is the ability to appoint others with different but complementary skills.

Setting an example

Generating staff confidence can be a long-term process although a few discerning judgements in the early days are essential. Staff want to feel that you are going to be a good judge of ability and character, that the rewards go to the deserving. This is a delicate balance to strike when you are simultaneously trying to show everyone in the college that they are truly valued. Appreciating role and application was important in the development of the college appraisal scheme but it took time to persuade staff engaged in a national trade union dispute that my motives were honest.

Again I felt that I needed to provide a positive role model. My appraisal was conducted by the chair and vice-chair of the board of governors. I decided at short notice to ask senior staff for their honest views about my performance. The spontaneous request resulted in six submissions, some apologies and one refusal. The texts are still in my possession as are those of the two subsequent years. They proved to be an excellent tool for future planning for myself and a useful personal development technique for the contributors. One told me that it was one of the most difficult exercises she had ever done. Amongst other things, she reminded me that a chief executive will always be viewed by her staff in hierarchical terms, whatever the matrix structure and however personable the individual.

Planning for your own support and development

It is important to recognize and manage constructively the occasional period of loneliness and isolation of the job at the top. I tried to arrange a week's work shadowing every year. I became wedded to a personal development concept which I spread amongst other senior managers, especially the women, a number of whom subsequently held senior posts. I also talked regularly to someone who had no connection with the college yet was able to offer support or sympathy or a direct word as appropriate. This counsellor was to support me through many an occasion and, just as importantly, our relationship was fun.

Moving on

I often underestimated the subtleties of being a woman in a man's world. In a small and sometimes small-minded community, these can lose their subtlety. This had to be kept in perspective. When I was given the opportunity, after four years, to take the top job of a new national association for colleges I could not resist the temptation. A return to London, to a policy making and lobbying role was a positive career move and had domestic attractions too.

I believe the college was stronger when I left than when I arrived. I am however writing in retrospect.

Despite the frustrations, I never felt disabled, and it is the personal pleasure, sense of satisfaction and feeling of liberation at being at the top which I prefer to remember.

In conclusion, if I had to offer one single piece of advice, I would suggest that personal enjoyment and the generation of fun opportunities is vital along with keeping a sense of proportion throughout the process of change. As one of my senior colleagues reminded me, 'Just remember that if you comment on the stormy weather, at least one person will interpret it as a sign of impending redundancies!'

References

Birch, D (1988) *Managing Resources in FE,* Staff College publication, Bristol.
Peters, T (1993) *Independent on Sunday*, 19 September.

Chapter 11

Focusing the University: The Changing Role of the Vice-chancellor

Kenneth Edwards

Ken Edwards offers a historical perspective on the 'perpetual revolution' that has so fundamentally changed the role of vice-chancellor in traditional research universities. Prior to the government-imposed reforms of the last decade, he describes the seemingly genteel but highly politicized world that characterized what was essentially a confederation of loosely affiliated academics. Change evolved slowly, if at all, and decision-making processes reinforced inertia more than action, as well as professional self-interests. He describes the challenge of trying to focus points of light in three-dimensional space into an image. He uses this metaphor to capture the essence of the balancing act now required by vice-chancellors who must protect the fundamental mission of a university while ensuring its survival through constant change. Leading 'from the top' rather than from the centre becomes essential. On the question of mission, he differs from Webb, Harrison and Shackleton who are actively questioning taken-for-granted understandings of college or university for the 21st century.

He captures the interplay and consequences of traditional university 'collegial' politics and governance through committees. He discusses the advantages of devolution, citing in particular the value of decision making remaining collegial but responsive to external pressures. As in Wilson's and Webb's chapters, he is not preoccupied with the tensions generated by devolution between corporateness and autonomy in the same ways that Harrison and Bull are. The latter are operating in different managerial and institutional cultures.

The author asserts that managing change 'from the top' of a university is still as much a leadership role as ever. He emphasizes that creating a climate of anticipation and preparing for change are as important as achieving particular outcomes.

A delightful embellishment in this account on managing change 'from the top' is the citing of Cornford, and his principles of the wedge, dangerous precedent and unripe time. Drawn from a pamphlet written long ago, their continued usage as arguments against change may be familiar.

INTRODUCTION

It is part of the fundamental nature of universities that they will be constantly changing. New ideas arising from the advancement of knowledge will create new research fields and new subjects for teaching. External forces, such as expectations of governments, employers and students, will also create change. Much of this change may be barely perceptible to an external observer. For considerable lengths of time there may be very little in the way of external factors which will create change, and for quite long periods universities may be substantially isolated from their surrounding communities.

But every now and then there will be something of a revolution in the attitude which the community takes to the universities in its midst. Such an attitude change may be a reaction to perceived undesirable characteristics; for example European universities in the Middle Ages experienced strong action against them as the result of the riotous behaviour of students. The 1960s have probably been a factor in the great interest which many governments now take in what goes on in universities in their countries. The particular form of this interest will be shown in very different ways. There may be greater demands that the universities contribute more in an overt and direct way to the needs of society as perceived by the government. Interventions may be designed to generate courses of instruction which are more 'relevant', or research that is more related to wealth creation. Today we are indisputably in a phase of a major concern by national governments in how universities are run and what they do. As they have in the past, universities are finding ways to adapt to the changes that are being thrust upon them. In this chapter I will offer my own perspective on such developments, drawing on my experience as vice-chancellor of Leicester University.

THE HISTORIC VIEW OF THE UNIVERSITY

In considering how universities are able to organize themselves to respond to vigorous campaigns which arise externally we must first consider evolutionary or internally generated change. It is a basic organizing principle of a university that it is an association of professional academics. Like many associations of professionals, the reason individuals belong to such an organization is a matter of convenience. The opportunity to practise as professional academics outside a university is severely limited. Membership of a university affords two principal benefits: the costs of overheads (such as libraries, computer services, provision for making arrangements for students) and the degree of specialization allowed so that the group is able to attract customers much more readily than could an individual practitioner. Thus academics may regard the university as a necessary evil, and would not wish to receive much direction therefrom. There is an interesting tension between the desires of individual academics to pursue their subjects according to their own professional standards on the one hand and the concept of academic collegiality of the community of scholars on the other. In such circumstances the role of the vice-chancellor is seen as one of providing the appropriate framework within which his academic colleagues can pursue their interests of teaching and research.

This confederation of academics, loosely affiliated in a university, would place the vice-chancellor at the 'centre' rather than at the 'top'. In other words the process of change was traditionally one of attempting to arrive at a consensus within the university with the vice-chancellor having a responsibility for achieving that consensus, possibly exercising some steer in so doing. To be effective, such steers had to be subtly applied and in fact anything that was seen as an obvious attempt to influence the direction of the university would probably be resisted by the academics as a matter of principle.

EXTERNAL PRESSURES ON THE ACADEMIC GUILD

As a loose confederation of academics, a university which existed without any external pressures would evolve slowly and be subject to considerable inertia in making any changes in its organization. But of course, universities are never entirely devoid of such external pressures. The force of such pressures varies over time; in the last decade or so they have been very considerable in many countries 'legitimated' by the dependence of universities on funds provided from tax revenue. In recent years in the United Kingdom government has essentially attacked what it perceives as groups of academics protecting their self-interest against the legitimate interests of customers and tax-payers.

A consequence of this perception in recent years has been a requirement for constant change, presumably based upon the assumption that any association of professionals would very quickly re-erect barriers to protect its own interests. Thus the government's strategy has been two-pronged. The first is a greater demand for accountability, including demonstrating that university teaching and research are relevant to the community. This goes beyond the non-controversial requirement for demonstration of financial probity. The second is what appears to be the principle of a Maoist perpetual revolution, presumably based on the premise that only by such constant externally-induced change will the organizations be kept on their toes.

Government policy may operate either by a *dirigiste* planning mechanism or an interventionist market system. Change will also be stimulated by student demands and employer demands; these two groups are likely to become more self-aware and therefore more active when the government is taking a politically overt stance of influencing what goes on in the universities. This high level of intervention by government has produced a totally different atmosphere surrounding the way in which a university is organized to make decisions itself. The issue becomes one of how to deal with such externally generated pressures for rapid change while maintaining the internal requirements to protect the fundamental mission of the university. Therefore we must ask the question: what is the fundamental mission? It is even more important at a time of great change to reflect on these fundamentals than when the institution is left largely to its own devices.

THE CHANGING ROLE OF THE VICE-CHANCELLOR

In this context, the task of the vice-chancellor is to try to balance the need to ensure the university's survival, by being able to respond adequately to external pressure, with ensuring that the university is clearly able to develop policies in line with its fundamental mission. This requires a vice-chancellor to be much more proactive and to recognize his or her responsibility as a leader, helping the university to interpret the fundamental aims in the light of the changed world in which it now exists.

One way of describing this interpretative role is through the metaphor of focusing. The academic activities within a university can be regarded as many points of light of varying brightness arranged in three-dimensional space. In order to create an image a lens is required. A lens will have a particular focal length which will determine which of the points of light can be brought into focus on a single image. Reducing the aperture through which the light passes can increase the depth of field and so bring more points of light into simultaneous focus, but at the cost of reducing the total amount of light transmitted to the image. Unless all the light sources are very bright, it will be very difficult to create an image at which they are all in focus.

The role of a vice-chancellor can, therefore, be regarded as ensuring the university makes decisions about the choice of lens and the size of the aperture to create an image which is most appropriate for the institution, both internally and externally. If the external world has very little interest in the nature of the image it is likely that the decision will be made that the image produced maximizes the range of light sources which can contribute to that image. This may well be at the cost of generating an image which is in 'soft' focus. However, pressures in the external world may make it necessary to adjust the system so that a very clear image is produced, although at the cost of excluding from the contribution to that image some of the sources of light. Indeed, the process may go further by removing the source of fuel from some of the activities so that the remainder can be better resourced and, therefore, generate more light and make a greater contribution to the image of the university as seen by the outside world. An alternative strategy would be to reposition some of the sources of light so that they too are in focus.

STRATEGIES FOR MANAGING CHANGE

Anticipating and focusing

The process of managing a university requires, therefore, both an acknowledgement of the existence of a variety of stakeholders: staff, students, government (representing the society as a major funding source) and employers, and also an adaptation to the different pressures applied by several stakeholders. When the pressures from the external stakeholders or from students become very great, it will be necessary for the university to ensure that its activities have a clear institutional focus, which may impose some constraints on the freedom of individuals. Nevertheless it is vital to recognize that it is the activities of the academic staff in teaching and research which create the light for the institution to produce any kind of image.

Where the rate of change is very fast, one of the most crucial elements in management is to anticipate the nature of such events as far as possible, thus allowing time to prepare the institution for the adaptations which will be necessary if it is to be successful and retain academic and intellectual vigour; the vice-chancellor must be particularly responsible for leading such foresight exercises. The second stage is to ensure that such thoughts on what the future looks like and how it could be responded to are adequately and fully communicated within the university. Many will be suspicious of change and that change will certainly be hurtful to some. Others will be excited by the prospects and in fact may have to be restrained from over-enthusiastic responses.

A key element both in preparing for change and in ensuring successful internal communication is to identify key people, give them clear responsibilities and allow them to exercise those responsibilities without undue interference – while ensuring that contact is close. Clearly, pro-vice-chancellors, deans and heads of departments will fall into this category, but so will many others. An institution must have a network to ensure that information flow occurs in many directions and that the reasons for changes are well appreciated, accepted and, ideally, enthusiastically supported. Rapid change also makes it necessary to replace some part of a cumbersome committee system with less formal networking and methods of communication. At the same time, a dynamic and vital university must provide very clear channels of communication.

Consensus versus management

A major difficulty in managing change lies in setting up structures which can combine the capacity for rapid response to external changes with a high level of involvement and commitment of the members of a university. Structures which universities have inherited from the past tend to be slow, having developed within a culture of leisurely and thorough consideration. Indeed, the underlying assumption was that consideration could be thorough only if it were leisurely. What was important was to ensure the maximum chance of getting the decision right rather than making that decision by any particular deadline.

But did these processes ensure that decisions were 'right', and what were the criteria for determining correctness? The emphasis was on process, underpinned by a faith that collegiality and achieving consensus would lead to a 'right', or at least an acceptable, decision. Processes of decision making are political and it is important to understand what the political conventions of any particular group are.

Collegiality is indeed a laudable aim, at its best attempting to ensure that the whole group (whether this be a department, a faculty or an entire university) agreed wholeheartedly on a certain course of action and then enthusiastically implemented that decision. On the other hand, collegiality could be regarded as requiring a *complete* consensus leading to the expectation that nothing should be done unless everyone agreed. Cynics see collegiality as self-serving and self-protective. Adam Smith regarded collegiality as the willingness to accept poor performance by one's colleagues in the expectation that they would return this tolerance.

Academic politics, like any other system, is subject to its own conventions and pressures by which some groups try to create change and other groups try to stop them. Are these political processes any different in academic communities from those which occur in any other society or activity? At a fundamental level, the answer is almost certainly no; the difference is that academics love to develop arguments and to conduct debates and while they are no less likely than anyone else to have prejudices, their training has made them expert at rationalization. So academic politics tends to have a longer time-scale.

Such conventions of decision making will achieve formal expression in a particular system of governance. An important element of academic politics is the difficulty of changing a long-standing system of governance. But it is legitimate to ask whether these elaborate committee systems achieved the objectives of democratic decision making based on collegiality and working consensus. Did they permit any changes at all? Changes have occurred, but perhaps despite the system rather than because of it. New activities have developed and new courses of action have been undertaken because of the interplay of the political system within the system of governance. Power politics will clearly have operated in such decisions, with well-organized groups prevailing. But there are costs to such political processes which may well have left some parties extremely disgruntled while the secrecy surrounding the decision making alienates those left outside. Furthermore, the political processes became very elaborate and time-consuming so that many academics wishing to concentrate on teaching and research were disinterested and consequently may have been disenfranchised.

Thus it is reasonable to argue that these elaborate systems did not necessarily work very well, even in what I have called 'leisurely' times. Nevertheless, they did have a certain credibility with their members and, what is more important, they did create a framework for individuals or groups to have an input into the decision-making processes should they so wish.

This analysis highlights two important features of decision making in a university. The first is that the members must believe that whatever structure is in place is the most appropriate for the circumstances in which the university finds itself at any particular time. The second is that there should be clear channels of communication so that any individual or any group with a view to express is aware of how to do so.

A SOLUTION: DEVOLUTION

The dilemma

So, I return to the vital question of how can we create a system in which there is a strong feeling of involvement but which also allows the university to respond quickly to changed circumstances. A system which takes detailed decisions centrally cannot possibly be *both* quick and collegial. A centralized and highly 'managerial' system can achieve speed but not involvement, while a highly 'democratic' system cannot possibly be quick. A solution which accommodates both needs is to devolve decision making to component parts of the university. I believe that the creation of an acceptable system of decision making is an outcome of devolution at least as important as the claims for improved efficiency and responsiveness which are the elements of the more orthodox arguments in favour of devolution.

Devolving decision making does have difficulties and dangers. Difficulties arise from the transfer of power: those asked to give it up (whether they are the senior management teams, a well-entrenched bureaucratic system or a board at the pinnacle of a complex committee system) may be reluctant to do so; while those asked to receive power may be concerned and apprehensive at the responsibilities. The latter group will certainly require initial training and continuing help. The vice-chancellor must be willing to become personally involved as a consultant and to ensure that there is an input to each part of the university from the institution's strategic aims and objectives.

Maintaining control

The dangers of devolution are that there will be a loss of control, particularly with regard to finances. This risk can be minimized by ensuring efficient systems for providing financial information and for exercising financial control are in place. A significant danger is that there will be a loss of coherence of academic strategy throughout the institution. This concern may well be one of the reasons underlying the development of mission statements, strategic forward looks and so on, which have become so prevalent. The benefit of creating such statements is at least as much in the process which has created them as in the products themselves, and if they have genuinely involved wide consultation, the statements will have commitment and a better chance of being realized. Part of the process must be creating an understanding that change is to be expected; strategic statements and plans are only a framework for the development of the university in a changing world rather than immovable targets. Managing change is as much concerned with creating a climate of anticipating and preparing for changed circumstances as it is with proposing specific responses.

The devolution of a high degree of budgetary control does not mean that the university as an institution washes its hands of the development of a strategy for each faculty and department. There must be shared ownership between the centre and the unit and the vice-chancellor has a crucial role in generating this joint involvement. In fact, the first step is to create a commitment to the sharing process.

A case in point

In 1988 Leicester University had been through several years of financial cuts involving, in particular, a large number of academic staff posts being left unfilled when they became vacant. This necessarily opportunistic policy had created a situation in the arts faculty in which the 80 or so members of academic staff were distributed in 13 different departments, some of which contained only two or three academics. There were only two professors in the whole of the faculty. Furthermore, it was known that the University Grants Committee was undertaking national subject reviews in classics and music and there was a strong likelihood that the university would have funding withdrawn for both subjects. Not surprisingly, morale in the faculty was very low.

I formed a small informal team consisting of myself, the senior pro-vice-chancellor, the dean of the faculty and the staffing officer. We had extensive discussions with the faculty, both formally and informally. The first step was to persuade them of the need for change and of the crucial importance of the faculty accepting responsibility for finding a solution. There was much agony but eventually a shared ownership was created between the faculty and the university's central management. The plan so generated was – and this was crucial – also acceptable to the UGC who allowed us to redeploy the available resources. The plan involved closure or amalgamation of several departments with some staff taking early retirement and a few accepting transfer to other universities. The transformation was also a springboard: the arts faculty has subsequently acquired a number of new staff including several professors and is now growing, vibrant and healthy.

It would have been irresponsible and unfair to have handed the whole problem of dealing with the crises to the faculty and it would have been disruptive and ultimately unsuccessful to have tried to solve it solely from the centre. While it was clearly necessary for the faculty to accept ownership of a solution it was also essential for the centre to be actively involved. The success of this partnership, or at least the subsequent recognition that it had been successful, helped to create the climate for the later development of devolved budgeting on a faculty basis throughout the university.

CONCLUSION

Observers of the academic life would do well to remember that while the issues and the players have changed over the years, much has remained the same. No one has described academic politics with greater brilliance than F M Cornford in his *Microcosmographia Academica: A guide for the young academic politician*. Although this was first published 75 years ago, the statements and analysis remain equally valid; indeed, because they concern consequences of change, they are perhaps even more important now. This brief, highly entertaining but ultimately serious pamphlet deserves reading in its entirety. However, the flavour can be identified from the opening chapter:

> *While you are young you will be oppressed, and angry, and increasingly disagreeable. When you reach middle age, at five-and-thirty, you will become complacent and, in your turn, an oppressor; those whom you oppress will find you still disagreeable; and so will all the people whose toes you trod upon in youth. It will seem to you then that you grow wiser every day, as you learn more and more of the reasons why things should not be done, and understand more fully the peculiarities of powerful persons, which make it quixotic even to attempt them without first going through an amount of squaring and lobbying sufficient to sicken any but the most hardened soul. If you persist to the threshold of old age – your fiftieth year, let us say – you will be a powerful person yourself, with an accretion of peculiarities which other people will have to study in order to square you. The toes you will have trodden on by this time will be as the sands on the seashore; and from far below you will mount the roar of a ruthless multitude of young men in a hurry. You may perhaps grow to be aware what they are in a hurry to do. They are in a hurry to get you out of the way.*

Cornford identifies a number of 'Principles' which are frequently used in argument against any proposed change. Among these are the 'Principle of the wedge', the 'Principle of the dangerous precedent' and the 'Principle of unripe time'. I am sure that any reader of Cornford's book will easily recall from personal experience occasions on which these principles have been invoked. Cornford's satire subtly uses the academics' attachment to 'principles'. The concept of the importance of the principle is dear to the heart of academics although I always suspect that when a member of a committee announces that the argument which he or she is about to develop is a 'matter of principle', I am about to hear a thinly disguised case of special pleading.

Reference

Cornford, F M (1908) *Microcosmographia Academica: A guide for the young academic politician*, Cambridge: Main Sail Press.

Chapter 12

Bringing about Cultural Change in Colleges and Universities: The Power and Potential of Story

Susan Weil

CHALLENGING THE TAKEN-FOR-GRANTED

Changes in society as well as in government policies and practice have transformed public sector management. Those at the head of educational institutions have been anything but immune. As illustrated throughout this book, they have had to introduce and support sufficient change to ensure that their institutions could survive and indeed prosper through the 'grotesque turbulence' (Webb, Chapter 3) of recent years. Simultaneously, they have had to manage their changing role as chief executives.

Role models and raw material to stimulate debate

There are different ways in which this book might have revealed the complexity and problematic nature of these emerging challenges for those 'at the top' of universities and colleges. It would have been customary to do this through a more traditional academic mode where the emphasis would have been on the analytic, informed by an historical and detached perspective. Given that the contributors are 'at the top', the result would most likely have been panoramic, indeed Olympian, and tending towards the authoritative.

Instead, the ten different contributors in this book have given *personal* meaning and weight to introducing change 'from the top'. By putting themselves at the centre of their narratives, each author has illuminated how he or she understands what it means to work to best effect with the pressures of the external environment and the hidden processes that either create or undermine the life-force of an institution. By revealing internal landscapes, they have provided access to the actual dilemmas and paradoxes of effective management and leadership in today's colleges and universities. They have had the courage to take off the mask that is afforded by the third person narrative and to bring the Olympian and panoramic perspective down to earth: perhaps the most challenging task of all for those 'at the top'.

The narrative thus becomes more than a way of speaking. It becomes a metaphor for a way of perceiving, feeling and existing as a manager (Hillman, 1975, p.332). In this, the contributors become much needed role models. They offer the possibility of developing deeper understandings at a time when there is much pressure to posture behind masks, within and outside institutions. The capacity to forge living connections between the different realities being lived out and shaped within institutions is at the heart of effective management. The contributors have provided here raw material to assist our exploration of the role of the chief executive and change in the management of colleges and universities.

Pushing the boundaries of current understandings

Many of the current government's interventions into the public sector have tended to reinforce private sector understandings of effective management and organizational change. In the early years of 'reform', it was as if management practices in the private sector were 'all good' and in the public sector, 'all bad'. This was the more interesting, in the context of Britain's declining economic performance internationally.

Effective management has tended to be understood at government level in mechanistic and controlling terms (Morgan, 1986). A business approach has been reinforced through the appointment of governors from a wide cross-section of industry and the tightening up of their legal responsibilities within the new universities (see Appendix). The increased influence of traditional management consultants who reinforce such understandings at institutional and government levels has also had its effect. For example, it is assumed that segmentation and fragmentation of wholes into parts (such as with Funding Council definitions of acceptable cost centres for accounting purposes) make institutions and people therein more manageable. The tightening up of controls, contracts and accountability is expected to improve professional performance.

Such 'reforms' are made in the name of the need to increase efficiency, extend accountability and transform existing relationships and processes. These are intended to serve new educational purposes and arrangements for a broader range of economic, social and technological needs. These may well be valid starting points for redefining public service management but increasingly the means are being disconnected from purposes and the means themselves are making the purposes defined by the rhetoric unachievable.

More traditional approaches to the management of change have stressed the linear, the panoramic, the grand strategy and mission 'at the top', and quick-fix solutions and blueprints for bringing about change successfully. In reality, this is not how change happens. Webb's metaphor (Chapter 3) helps to capture the more elusive reality that managers must handle:

For me, management (even, perhaps especially, forward planning) is not a jigsaw in which everything has a precise place into which it must be slotted, but a watercolour painting in which a general intention is transformed as liquid colours collide and merge in unpredictable ways. The task is to spot the 'accidents' which can be worked on to create valued passages, while subjecting others to damage limitation. More formally, I am intrigued by the complex interaction of the planned and the serendipitous.

Resonances that connect stories of change

There is much resonance between my many years experience of supporting people and organizations through significant learning and change processes and the themes that have emerged in this book. Future states *cannot* be neatly described, carved in granite and then pursued, past a clear set of targets and milestones. The creation of meaningful mission or vision statements takes time and investment, and necessarily involves many iterative processes, up, down and around institutions. This does not mean that the person at the top does not play a role in determining the parameters for such dialogues. It *does* mean that they are managing the process. Further, this requires imaginative handling, so people can begin to build a sense of personal connection between their own past and present and that being envisaged for the future. Starting states also cannot be easily defined, except in the most simplistic and mechanistic of ways. Many people's stories must figure in descriptions of 'present states': there is no one starting position.

Strategies cannot be devised at the top and then 'neatly' implemented. Strategy formation at its best is approached as a process of organizational diagnosis and development that focuses and shapes future effort from the outset through active involvement. The processes used need to be designed so that what is envisaged begins to be experienced during the formation stage. They need to be dynamic and iterative, connecting continuously the experience and intelligence-gathering capacity of the periphery with the centre. The approach itself must actively forge links between, and give real meaning to, the five key starting points for any significant change effort: identity, mission, culture, key relationships and ways of working (Beckhard and Pritchard, 1992).

These authors have illustrated that new structures can be useful in supporting change. Notwithstanding when and how they are introduced, however, they can only influence in a limited way actual individual and group behaviours, processes and attitudes. The intended outcomes of a restructuring effort can also be severely undermined if institutions do not have the means of continuously identifying the tensions and dilemmas (both new and old) that inevitably surface under the changed circumstances. The partnerships that enable these to be worked with creatively and constructively, in ways that remain linked to shared purposes and values, provide the essential connective tissue in making any new structure work. The interplay of formal and informal processes, of diagnosis and development, needs to be orchestrated sensitively, in ways that remain attuned to internal and external realities.

Many of those here have also learned that communication is about far more than information. There is recognition of the importance of communication processes being kept attuned to different learning needs, relationships and stages of change. Many varied and carefully targeted approaches are required to foster awareness, understanding, favourability, involvement and commitment of professionals and service/support staff. The same approach for all purposes and all people cannot be used, as has so often become the case with the introduction of private sector team briefings, for example.

Releasing talent, potential and enthusiasm in academic communities is hard work, and has little to do with financial rewards, hands-on command and control management and logos or mission statements. Their involvement in change cannot be nurtured in colleges through statements about values and purposes made from on high that remain disconnected from actual experience. Nurturing vision and creativity and engendering commitment and community – essential ingredients in improving performance and efficiency – require sensitive and creative 'unsticking' processes.

Pluralist professional cultures are characterized by multiple loyalties, often extending beyond the institution. The identities of colleges and universities are entangled with the critical, the conflictual, the well-argued position and the controversial. These offer both challenge and resource in any organizational development effort (Pascale, 1990). Effective managers ensure that challenge and conflict remain at the heart of any change effort, recognizing that herein lies the energy and muscle that can drive needed developments. An organization that is at ease with itself can, as Jenny Shackleton says, 'provide personal scope for the development of personal and group style and colour' (Chapter 8).

Fitness for different purposes

The production of goods for the sole purpose of yielding profits for shareholders is not the task of a public service manager (Parston, 1992). In colleges and universities, people and relationships are at the heart of a complex set of processes that are intended to yield outcomes to the benefit of both individuals and society. The outcomes need not, nor should they, be achieved inefficiently, nor in ways that eschew accountability to multiple stakeholders. Nor should they be pursued at enabling such relationships and processes to be understood or enacted differently in support of mass education, diverse community interests lifelong learning and socioeconomic aims. What I am concerned with here is the gross oversimplification of such change processes, in both managerial and educational terms. These can ensure, as Morgan (1986) argues, that change remains illusory and merely cosmetic. Underneath, patterns of traditional power and control will continue to be reinforced and sustained.

Paradoxically, the limitations of more mechanistic and control models of management have increasingly been recognized within the private sector itself. Companies that have turned themselves around have transformed their taken-for -granted assumptions about the management of change (eg, Kanter, 1983; Morgan, 1986; Nohria and Eccles, 1992; Pascale, 1990; Pascale and Athos, 1981; Peters, 1992). I believe that we now need to do the same in universities and colleges, but on our own terms. Creating change needs to evolve fitness for new purposes. But to do so, the approaches we adopt need to do justice to the hidden processes that undermine mechanistic, control-oriented change efforts and to the complex nature of our distinctive 'business'.

THE POWER AND POTENTIAL OF STORY AS A MEANS OF UNDERSTANDING ORGANIZATIONS

Extending the metaphor of personal narrative

I believe that the usage of story in this book is more than merely a particular form of narrative. It can also be understood as a metaphor that can underpin new understandings of organizations and, indeed, specific strategies for creating change. Story takes us away from mechanistic and instrument-of-domination explanations and solutions and provides different ways of making sense of the key themes in this book, as reviewed above.

Stories can be understood as events retold from experience that 'appear to carry meaning, however small' (Reason and Hawkins, 1988). Many different stories are at play within colleges and universities: educational stories, knowledge and research stories, community stories (including those shaped by politicians), institutional stories, managerial stories, group stories and individual stories.

Seeing organizations as machines or management as domination and control leads to particular kinds of actions which, in self-fulfilling ways, create certain kinds of responses. People within institutions are not spectators to the story being written by those 'at the top' – they are 'spect-actors' (Boal, 1979): they actively make their own meaning when a radical new departure is taken. That experience becomes the raw material from which new stories are created or old stories are reasserted with a vengeance.

Bringing Olympian perspectives down to earth

The notion of story provides a means of bringing Olympian and detached perspectives at the top into play with the more earthly and human elements of colleges and universities, and the emergence of shared educational purposes and values. It helps us to envisage creative engagements within institutions that can give rise to new forms of story and simultaneously guide processes of organizational diagnosis, learning and development. These in turn can build the capacity of institutions to write their own stories and become less reactive to external pressures and constraints.

The idea of story could easily be dismissed as peripheral, fanciful, as something that has little to do with the real business of change. But storytelling lies at the heart of any institution and any significant change process. Stories are part and parcel of everyday life within organizations. People constantly make meaning out of bits and pieces of stories. Managers may communicate policies, report decisions, assert what is right and what is misunderstood, but what is spoken about, in a myriad of ways, is the dramas, the feelings, the passions, the power, the pain, the values, the celebrated, the respected and the despised. In a professional and academic culture, these explorations of self in relation to a changing world are distinctive and challenging.

The creation of unnecessary problems 'at the top'

Those at the top of colleges and universities can generate unnecessary problems for themselves when they are seen to be pushing information and policy from Olympian heights, with few mediating processes of direct engagement (outside the formal committee system). 'Getting the message across' requires more than the firing of memos, or linear and mechanistic approaches such as team briefings. The intelligence of the 'Receivers' of such communications deserves more respect. Reactions against such simplistic processes needlessly fuel hostile understandings of management. There are many processes at work within colleges and universities that encourage professionals to actively disassociate themselves from, and not identify with, what are seen as the invasion of managerial practices.

How stories are understood and transmitted says much about an organization's style and culture and the potential of those at the top. For example, if a senior team tends to push things 'down the line' from the top, they can fuel storytelling to which they lose access. Refractive layers of politics, personalities and distance make listening nigh impossible. Senior managers become shielded from many of the dramas below, both by those in the middle, but also by virtue of their perceived abuse of power and control. Stories get stripped down into descriptions; pattern and relationship become divorced from context. Shouting louder does not work either. Myths only grow bigger and stronger, and bubble away in the heartland of the different tribes and territories that cover the landscape of a college or university.

Consequently, seemingly sudden blow-ups can startle. If buffer zones between the top and elsewhere in the institution are well-defined, messages up and down the line become increasingly distorted and managers increasingly run the risk of having no access to the very data they need to make sound decisions about how best to manage the process of change.

Recognizing different kinds of 'making sense' processes

Reason and Hawkins (1988) suggest that explanation and expression can be understood as two different ways of reflecting upon and making sense of experience. Explanation lays emphasis on 'classifying, conceptualizing and building theories from experience'. The person seeking to make sense of his or her experience uses distance to evolve concepts and models that map out the reality being experienced. Analytic and experimental approaches depend upon explanation. Both seek to manage the uncertainty that characterizes experience. On the other hand, expression puts emphasis on the further discovery of meaning. Rather than standing back from seeming disorder, subjectivity and dissonance, the alternative is to delve deeper into it. In this way, we begin to surface and make sense of the intricacies and delicate texture of interwoven meanings, and to understand their relation to other forms of experience and 'meaning making'.

In colleges and universities, we tend to privilege explanation that in turn becomes codified as propositional knowledge: that which Heron (1988) describes as 'learning about' a subject, learning that 'something is the case'. We ascribe a lower status to practical knowing, imaginal knowing and experiential knowing. Explanation and an emphasis on propositional knowledge tend to dissect experience into manageable parts. Expression aims to understand and work with pattern, messiness, complexity and richness.

These two approaches to understanding have further meaning within colleges and universities. The first approach is associated with traditional science as taught; the latter with the humanities, social sciences and creative arts. These have traditionally been understood as polarized paradigms within such institutions where many other dichotomies freely reign: theory versus practice; pure versus applied research; corporate versus autonomy and collegiality. These oppositions are not only problematic when it comes to relationships and communication between managers and professionals. They also constrain and distort relationships and communications between professionals and more heterogeneous groups of learners who participate in higher education for many reasons. Actual experiences of learning and creating knowledge, as lived, do not fit neatly into such boxes. Similarly, learners do not merely enter colleges and universities to know conceptually or to explain (Weil, 1989a, 1989b).

Effective management in today's colleges and universities needs to begin to heal these splits and create the possibility of learning and change processes for staff and students alike that do not reinforce or create further dichotomies that fragment our experience. Introducing change from the top needs to be 'more like art than teachable science'. Schon (1983) captures this paradox aptly:

> *We might begin to heal the split in the field of management if we were to recognise that the art of management includes something like science in action. When practising managers display artistry, they reveal their capacity to construct models of unique and changing situations; to design and execute on-the-spot experiments. They also reveal a capacity to reflect on the meanings of situations and the goals of action.*

Story provides a means of bringing together these different ways of knowing and being, and healing the splits that can cripple our colleges and universities and are too often being played out in the managerial arena, in response to government interventions. The use of story as means of understanding and creating change can provide a means of managing both the absurdities and the more exciting challenges of the external world, while harnessing the power of different forms of knowing within, and the considerable talent of all staff.

The act of telling stories involves both agency and communion. These two forces are central to organizational effectiveness. Those 'at the top' continually despair that those 'below' will not be accountable, will not take responsibility. But maybe this would prove less of a dilemma if a different starting point for their own, and the organization's, development were adopted.

The challenge is to channel intelligence and creative energy in directions that serve the organization well. But this is not possible if staff have not had the opportunity to establish meaningful points of connection between their own individual and various group stories with the broader organizational and educational story, so that collectively, there is greater capacity to manage the political stories. If colleges and universities are to be developed to fuller potential as dynamic and vital forces within society, 'rending them asunder' is no longer an option. There are enough external battles to be fought without having to create unnecessary battles within.

STORY AS A BASIS FOR CREATING CHANGE

In this section, I shall extend the general ideas above into an exploration of the power and potential of story as a means of supporting cultural change within colleges and universities. I shall explore six sets of processes that interlink with each other and need to spiral forwards and backwards like a double helix.

I will consider story as a basis for creating change through the first person narrative, rooting my explorations in my current experience as a consultant.

Moving to story

When I first work with an individual or institutional client, description of a situation, not story, often provides the starting point for our interaction. Clients outline structures, draw charts and produce mission statements and policy documents. They assert what they are trying to do and they then identify key players' roles and responsibilities and how these are relevant to achieving intended ends.

They also explain how things are 'supposed to work'. The rational, the intended, the desired and the (too often) mechanistic solutions that have been implemented are the dominant emphases.

The problems are familiar: communication, resources, external pressure, unclear structures, poorly defined roles and accountabilities, inadequate systems, and so on. I am then told about people: how they are supposed to act, and how they are not acting as desired or as intended. Throughout, I listen attentively to the ways in which they define others' stories. This person is too old, this person is bitter, this person is climbing fast up the career ladder, this person is excellent, this group has always been a powerful barony, this group has good people in it but they are silenced by certain people who are against what we are doing. What I am offerd are catalogues of explanations, with a counterpoint of player profiles. The problem is construed as being 'out there, with them'. It is the exceptional manager who from the outset expresses his or her doubts about different approaches and who displays, as Bull emphasizes (Chapter 6), a concern with failure in process and not merely control.

At this point, we are still 'stage setting'. The real challenge is to move to stories that take us closer to the core of the onion. Description sheds little light on what is particular, what is uniquely a play in this particular organization's story, its different group stories and individual stories. What are the many influences which shape the meaning given to particular acts of, for example, strategic planning or information sharing?

At this stage, I know little about how broader 'community stories' are being read by different players within. Equally, how do different values about education play themselves out in the institution and what processes have been used to connect them to new educational purposes and processes? Nor do I have any grasp of how intended purposes are being mediated by the organization's own myths, style, and structures. I am keen at this stage to learn more about who else has been involved in helping this person make sense of the stories that I am being told. Who and what is mediating these interpretations? What listening processes have been used by this person, and how have the processes themselves – in the ways that they have been designed and approached – enhanced or constricted hearing and understanding? How have they built up or undermined mythologies? Equally, who has been involved in the emergent institutional story? Is it just those at the top and, if so, what processes of engagement supported this? For example, did just the 'top team' go away for two days, and brainstorm, and then return to 'send it down the system'? Did they then label as resistant to change those who unlike them had not had the luxury of 'bashing things through'? Or did the process involve people up, down and around the institution?

My focus on these things goes well beyond the list approach of a 'SWOT' analysis (strengths, weakness, opportunities and threats). I am seeking pattern and essence as handles for our work together and defining ways forward.

The same litany may characterize my first few hours in many colleges and universities. They have all lived through the same external conditions. It is only when we get into what these mean in terms of that particular institution, and those people's lives and the various things that mediate institutional experience, that I can begin to hear distinctive differences that need to be worked with during these early stages. It is working *with* the organic processes, not against them, that makes the critical difference in a major change effort. This doesn't imply that a clear executive steer must be relinquished.

I am frequently told that I afford the first space for any kind of genuine reflecting on action and 'knowing in action' (Schon, 1994), but my point of entry into institutions is usually through a single person. The next challenge is to extend the possibility of moving from explanation to expression, and therefore to 'hearing story' from other key players. I need to see at this stage those who would define themselves as storytellers and audience in relation to the 'problem' that is being outlined.

Hearing stories

I begin to get a feel for how we might best approach my hearing of stories else-where within and outside the institution. These decisions will be guided not only by the quality of the listening, mirroring and conceptualizing processes I have used until then, but also by the expressed aims and felt needs that brought me into this relationship with the institution in the first place. The values, metaphors, trust and indeed prejudices we both bring to this encounter, and the resources available, must also influence this conversation.

Part of exploration of the story of the organization will entail learning who has an important story to tell me. It is essential that I begin to hear different stories in the organization and the resonances and dissonances across them. Some of these may be constructive, others may not be.

Ways of hearing and gaining access to stories can take many different forms as, 'there are many languages in which meaning can be created and communi-cated' (Reason and Hawkins, 1988). Often, at the beginning of an intervention with an institution, the best approach is to work with groups who represent different functions – sometimes called 'slice groups'. Two hours with 12 to 14 people representing a broad mix of backgrounds and perspectives can open multiple windows on an institution's key stories and the ways in which meaning is made of them at different levels. The process itself sends a signal that some-one is listening.

The aim is to get at essence and pattern. Questions can be direct: for example, over the past year, what changes have been handled well, and what not so well, and why? This enables storylines to begin to open up. In turn, patterns can be played back. Equally, questions that get at meaning and key storylines more obliquely are as valuable. These, for example, might ask people to reverse roles with students, employers, people in the community: you are at a party in town and people are talking about this institution – what are they saying?

Similarly, metaphors are powerful tools for surfacing meaning: for example, if this institution were an animal, what would it be and why? The animals may vary, but if the question is asked repeatedly, patterns begin to emerge. For example, with one senior team all but the CEO chose animals that were capable of fast forward movement, but each was held back in some way – by a tether, excessive weight, a cage, etc. This signalled a clear pattern in his leadership style that needed attention if talents were to be released. It was also clear that there was now need for attention to process, especially in the context of a merger. The use of photos with the team revealed that three people with the greater power in the group tended to see future ways forward in terms of task, the others in terms of development planning and more iterative processes that broke down barriers

across the institution. The surfacing of these patterns in an otherwise highly effective team in turn led to a rethinking of priorities. In another institution, the dominant pattern across animal metaphors was one of disarray: the pattern, revealed
over time, was that it was not worth doing anything collectively as it always fell
apart, either by the force of someone's intervention or sabotage, or because there
was insufficient management support and attention to wholes and parts.

These patterns provide invaluable reference points for later stages of working
together, when the first flushes of excitement die down and setbacks need to be
understood and confronted. Echoing back to these earlier patterns can help
people make constructive sense out of what is happening, despite intentions to
the contrary.

When I begin to search out meaning, to hear the stories that shape people's
experience of an institution, especially in groups, they always begin with the
most negative. I am seen as the messenger who may be able to 'make those
managers hear'. I have learned over many years not to take this backlash at face
value. First, I do my best to listen sensitively to the messages and patterns in
what they are saying. I seek to demonstrate that I understand the different
languages of expression and concern that are used by different groups. I also
begin to mirror back their meanings and the key patterns, in ways that illustrate
points of possible connection as well as difference.

This kind of hearing frees up the space for moving beyond the solely negative.
As importantly, I often find that they themselves initiate the move into more
constructively and creatively focused expression. Someone in the group will
always help to turn the tide with, 'It is not all bad, though. What about ...' What
is most important, however, is the quality of the relationship at these early
stages. This has a major influence on the quality of the stories that are offered to
me as data. Similarly, the quality of the relationships and communication
processes built between those at the top and those on whom change depends, has
a major influence on the validity and reliability of the data they obtain and, in
turn, the quality of the decisions that influence the change process and its
success.

What I am essentially describing here is a kind of conversation that is all too
rare within institutions. In my own experience, the time and space allowed for
this kind of listening, which goes beyond simple headlines, and does not leap to
conclusions or solutions, is seldom legitimated in the formal arena of relationships within institutions. Organizational investment in learning networks and
action learning sets that can embed these processes in an institution is still rare.
Those that have started have often had to do so without the resource of external
facilitators. Too often they then falter in the welter of politics and histories that
can undermine new forms of encounter. They may offer a valued space for
listening but, without support, they often fail to make full use of possibilities for
learning that connects individual and institutional stories (McGill and Beatty,
1992).

Listening also needs to be valued as an essential dimension to leadership and
management style. It need not be expensive, in either time or external resources.
I often use the metaphor of the GP's surgery. Years ago, even before the restructuring of the National Health Service, there was a nominal seven minutes per
patient allowed per GP consultation. This fact stayed with me, and over the years
I have been very struck by the considerable difference between the quality of one
doctor's listening power as compared with another's. With one, I can feel as if I

have had 30 minutes and I have benefited; with another, you can feel rushed through, agitated and as if no listening whatsoever has taken place.

Mirroring stories

The process of listening is often in itself developmental, but it also raises expectations and fears. Many of us have learned the risks of describing reality as we genuinely experience it. As the outsider, it is possible to hear resonances and dissonances, to suggest patterns beyond the filters of personalities, histories and politics. But equally, the outsider becomes all too aware of the walls that are deeply resistant to change, in the form of cynicism, mistrust, resentment and threat. This is why the next stage is so critical. If the outcomes of listening are dealt with too rapidly, with leaps to explanation and action, it is likely that opportunities for collective focusing will be lost.

Mirroring stories refers to processes whereby patterns, key storylines, and important commonalities and differences are held up, and worked through. It entails people recognizing and becoming ready to work with these as a basis for prioritizing and shaping ways of moving forward. This stage requires that others have the courage to listen, to learn and to be challenged with alternative world-views. They require the wisdom to trust that the 'Dunkirk' reaction is necessary, but is only a part of a change process.

Wise organizations bring outsiders in to listen *not* when things have deteriorated to a negative state, but as part and parcel of organizational learning and continuous improvement. In such cultures, there is a hunger to understand and know better how best to move forward. Stories are deeply embedded in the culture. In such cases, the desire is both to strengthen connections between institutional stories and those of individuals and groups, while at the same time creating the corporate space for autonomy and diversity in the living out and writing of new stories.

Managers' fears about investing time in such processes can all too often be expressed in the form of fears about others: for example, 'Do we run the risk of ignoring poor performance if we do something like this?' On the contrary. The shaping of accountabilities and responsibilities becomes central to this process, and far more easily than if imposed from above. Such issues cannot be divorced from the whole.

In this I am reminded of the famous story of the trip to a Japanese company by a group of Western business people. As they encountered workers and supervisors working in teams, challenging their managers, taking initiative and finding solutions without having to ask permission from above, the comment was made, 'If only we had people like that back home'. The teamleader was later heard to remark just as the group was moving out the room, 'Sad that they do not realize that they do!' As Bull (Chapter 6) says, 'a failure in structure must be seen as a failure in process'. Shackleton's story (Chapter 8) helps us to apprehend a different kind of organizational reality, where issues such as performance are tackled from an entirely different starting point.

In any process of cultural change, where new forms of listening, hearing and acting together are to be created, space to build confidence is essential, away from the immediate pressures that beleaguer institutions. Away-days can be extremely valuable, if they are linked to an overall organizational development strategy. The intensity of such events often requires teamworking on the part of the facilitators.

My colleagues and I try to devise programmes that build a constructive foundation to support the mirroring and making-sense processes, and hold participants
(and especially managers) back from the all too common premature rush to 'quick
fix sure to backfire' solutions. Away-days need to begin with a process that
echoes those used in previous diagnostic stages, and make a wide range of meanings accessible to the entire group. This can then be deepened through a more
incisive feedback process. For example, the use of photos can offer metaphors for
exploring strengths, weaknesses and key issues for people as individuals while
also establishing a foundation for recognizing commonalities and differences. The
questions must be tailored to the needs, issues and aims of the away-day process.
To illustrate, choose three photos: one that captures an important strength on
which the institution is now building; one that captures something that you
believe needs to confronted openly; and one that offers a key to how you might be
more fruitfully engaged in these processes of change.

The process of individual selection is then supported by a structured listening
process, governed by strict rules. This deliberately interrupts processes of everyday discourse from sabotaging the possibility of 'fresh hearing'. In turn, one
person speaks, another listens, another takes notes and coaches against slippage
in terms of time or process. Each trio is therefore compelled to listen to three
alternative worldviews, as mediated through the metaphors offered by the
photos. This kind of process begins to create its own mirror across different individual, group, organizational and educational stories. Its outcomes provide the
basis for a feedback process that can deepen and extend this initial picture.

There are many different ways of holding up a picture of what has been
discovered through consultations, slice groups, interviews, questionnaires and
other processes of prior data collection: pictures, diagrams, overlaid transparen-
cies illustrating matches and mismatches. The point is that the process needs to
offer to the group the possibility of seeing the world of the institution in a different way, from a variety of perspectives. Often, what has been learned beforehand
chimes with what they began to discover for themselves, and allows new forms
of valuing. They discover what is shared in common and, as importantly, they
begin to break down the mythologies that often have built up between different
role groups within an organization.

Making sense of stories

Moving to story, hearing stories and mirroring the multiple stories that obtain in
an institution, and learning more about how these are mediated, provide essential
starting points in a change effort. There can be many different languages. Getting
the balance of agency and communion becomes central to success. Phillida
Salmon, who explores story as a metaphor for living, and who was my inspiration for this chapter, captures it thus:

> *Agency lies not in governing what shall happen to us but in creating what
> we make of what happens. We ourselves construct the meaning of our story.
> And because it is we who live out that story, the kind of meaning we give it
> has [...] serious consequences for how we live. In our perspective on our
> own past history, in our anticipation of the future, in making our way
> through the infinite complexity of encounters and events – we have only
> our personal story to guide us. Though it is we who shape our stories,
> those stories also shape us – ourselves and our lives (Salmon, 1985).*

What has gone very wrong in many institutions is that, for example, the funding council story, or the manager's story, is 'living the people'. The story becomes one of being 'done to' rather than 'making sense and doing with'. The spect-actors required to carry through changes become reduced to spectators (Boal, 1979). Such positions become reinforced by paper-dominated top down communication processes. The essentially creative character of life is thus denied. Institutional stories that have sufficient resonances with individual and group stories offer the opportunity of vision and new forms of action. Processes of 'making sense' need not rest on the assumption that total consensus is essential, nor that an executive steer must be loosened. On the contrary, in the current public sector management context, such activity must be framed by clear para-meters and priorities. Executive responsibility is essential. Making sense enables institutional members to recognize key dilemmas that have been jointly identi-fied, and to believe that at least some of these are being understood and 'owned' by all concerned. On the basis of such stepping-stones, however small they may be, meaningful action can proceed.

Processes of making sense as a means of strengthening communion and generating a stronger basis for action inevitably involve conflict. If people are helped through this well, the energy that has gone into suppressing or inappropri-ately expressing conflict can be redirected into the very lifeblood of the change effort. Efforts to make sense, to name what is happening, surface power strug-gles. Explanation and rational argument will be used to ride roughshod over meanings and resonances that must first be respected. If managers have the courage to tackle such genuine difficulties, there is likely to be more forgiveness than blame when they are forced to act without consultation, due to pressures of time or the exigency of external agencies.

Many of the changes that are being demanded of professionals in today's colleges and universities challenge them to stand at the brink of two different worlds – one that is familiar and another that is uncertain and threatening. The shedding and transformation of taken-for-granted ways of thinking, behaving and attaching value inevitably require time and support. We are not asking professionals merely to learn a new skill; we are often asking them to make sense of assumptions and paradigms of both management and education that are totally unfamiliar. It is up to managers to build recognition and acceptance of the need for change, and to support people when they flounder. But it is when these normal processes of 'colliding' are misunderstood and labelled as evidence of resistance to change, that a very different story begins to be created for an insti-tution. This will severely undermine its capacity for change. On the other hand, when the anger and conflict that go with making sense of differences are handled well, resilience and robustness can be generated.

Processes and skills of listening, reflecting and sense-making need to be culti-vated deliberately, so that they become part of the repertoire of an institution that is facing change. They need to be supported by management and leadership development programmes and processes that do not reinforce mechanistic under-standings of organizations. An investment in time and resources must be based on a widely shared recognition that managing the process is of vital importance to the success of any change effort.

Enacting and retelling stories

The approaches described above offer another way of understanding the adage in change management: know your starting points. They require imagination, vision, leadership – and a belief in human, group and organizational potential. They place an active value on agency and communion, and not just 'at the top'.

As Salmon (1985) argues, to ask people to change their stories within organization is to ask them to change their lives. In the metaphor of life as story, and of organization as story,

> *'human practices are not fixed, but rather are potentially open to infinite variation. It is because we tell ourselves certain kinds of story that we come do to things in particular ways, to give our lives the particular forms they take. Yet through the metaphor [of organisation] as story, the most far reaching, the most profound changes are possible in human life. This does not mean that they are easy.'*

Enactment is about doing, about testing out. Rehearsals for this, however, can be of vital importance to subsequent success.

Often on away-days, my colleagues and I will involve subgroups in working through a challenging framework of questions that focus development and action planning around key priority issues that the group collectively has identified as important. This framework has within it many cycles that involve them in designing and experiencing many of the above processes: diagnosing the current situation, envisaging attitudes, behaviours and activity that would define significant progress, considering what is known, assumed and unknown about others who need to be involved, planning for their participation, anticipating difficulties, generating a range of options and defining next steps. At various stages, 'cross-groups' form, and 'visit' the work of every other group and offer guidance and information. In this way, a group can begin to experience iterative processes of consultation and action planning, and to realize that a momentum of forward movement can be sustained without leaving people behind. The process of working on specific institutional issues on behalf of the entire group, in mixed-role groups, is also itself often a novel and rewarding experience. It is still rare for heads of departments, both academic and services/support, and members of the vice-chancellor's or principal's team, to have this opportunity. The outcomes of this work provide the foundation for the clarification of responsibilities, accountabilities and targets. In turn, it becomes important to plan for review and monitoring, both of the process and task dimensions to continuing work. Such an approach releases considerable energy within a senior group. As importantly, it helps them to begin to realize how and why people are often needlessly disempowered in the name of 'managerialism'. A different worldview, and the seeds of an alternative culture, can begin to be shaped. Those involved become better equipped to involve others.

There are many different ways of getting people to enact new stories, and through the process of enacting to in turn retell the past and reshape the present and future. In particular, there are enactment processes that move beyond familiar, 'Define your future vision' approaches. Too often, in a college or university, the latter can be seen merely as word games that operate at the level of rhetoric with little connected meaning across the institution. Visions, however, can be given meaning through the exploration of different futures.

I have used a number of different enactment approaches for many years in organizations, drawing on a variety of sources (see, for example, Weil *et al.* 1985; Boal, 1979; Freire, 1970; Moreno, 1947). Enactment approaches test personal and strategic assumptions about future visions and policy intentions in actual practice. They enable people to live out different future scenarios *as themselves* and to explore the range of options open to them within these. The approaches allow personal, role-based and institutional dimensions of change to be surfaced, which in turn can be supported by development planning and activity. As importantly, enactment approaches enable people to explore the future without severing connections between educational, managerial and organizational stories. Shared values can be given shape and meaning.

A variation on such approaches is provided by the Office for Public Management's usage of soft futures methodologies (OPM and University of Portsmouth, 1994; Parston and Liddell, 1990). One member of a family of techniques is 'open simulation' whereby new roles, relationships and structures can be tested to the limits in simulated dynamics of future situations:

> *Hard quantitative approaches to anticipating the future are excellent in some circumstances. They are of little benefit, however, when used to try and anticipate how the shifting maze of relationships and systems that typify a large organisation will react to a major change. Much more helpful in these circumstances are 'soft' techniques which rely much more on the experience and judgement of those actually involved, since only they understand how people might react in the new circumstances (Office for Public Management and University of Portsmouth, 1994).*

This approach has been used to test the effects of the contracting arrangements introduced into the National Health Service (Parston and Liddell, 1990). It has been pioneered within the colleges and universities sector in Britain by the University of Portsmouth. Two years had been spent on negotiating a new structure that was to make curriculum development and responsiveness to the external environment and clients primary forces in the institution. An open simulation was designed to capture the dynamics of the proposed restructuring, based on much hearing, mirroring and making sense of stories beforehand.

Throughout the country, colleges and universities have placed a disproportionate and inappropriate emphasis on restructuring as a strategy for cultural change. Such efforts, if well handled, can release energy, new talent and potential. Continual restructuring, however, can produce discontinuity, disorder and dissonance. This was something that this university did not want to happen; it was also recognized that 'rewiring' an institution does not guarantee success. Instead, 'making it work' depends on the,

> *passion and perspiration of people, and how they communicate and negotiate with each other through changed and everchanging circumstances.... Such relationships do not just happen, they must be built. The pace and nature of changes confronting universities do not make it possible to predict clear solutions; instead capacities for organisational learning and leadership must be conscientiously nurtured....It would be impossible to 'imagine' all the potential consequences of the restructuring. Yet this...is important to the future of the institution. Waiting to see what happens and then muddling through is unacceptable (OPM and University of Portsmouth, 1994).*

Such approaches provide powerful vehicles for organizational learning and help to guide development and action planning. They recognize that for all the time that managers spend on defining new policies, writing new visions and missions and shaping strategic objectives, their translation into actual practice depends on far more. Words and exhortations have limited impact. The simulation provides a foundation of shared experience that can be channelled into collaborative planning and action by key players.

I am continually reassured that creative and well-supported approaches to enactment, that have at their root an appreciation of story and the processes described above, enable institutions to retain their pasts in forms that remain dynamic and supportive of future directions. They can draw strength from the former 'landscape to which there can be returns, to make sense of the further living that has been done, to lend it richer meaning' (Salmon, 1985). In other words, retelling stories from the past from new points in the future becomes central to processes of embedding changes in attitudes, behaviours and ways of seeing the world.

FINAL REFLECTIONS

Changing the story of an institution always involves changes for other people. Every player in an institution is both storyteller and audience, both spectator and spect-actor, engaged in different acts of communion and agency. But how these come together to create a greater whole that is vibrant, has purpose and is effective on the many fronts now demanded of colleges and universities is the biggest challenge facing those at the top of colleges and universities.

Changes that are convincing can only be made jointly with others. A leader who works well with story – although he or she may not define it as such – knows the value of moving beyond mere explanation. She or he listens for patterns and clues that can guide the design and management of developmental processes. The telling of the stories that inspire is encouraged. The value of involving as many people as possible in making sense of external pressures and constraints, and determining and enacting future options will be expressed in many forms.

Those at the top need to remain accessible to the stories that are important signals of things that are potentially damaging but unintended. The orchestration of constructive and creative engagements to support these processes can then give rise to the development of appropriate and fluid structures that can be shaped as the institutional story evolves – themes in the chapters by Wilson, Bull, Shackleton and Webb. The connective tissue of relationships and new ways of working, that bring both communion and agency together, can be simultaneously nurtured.

The shift from the administrative to the efficiency paradigm (PMF, 1994; Richards, 1993) keeps those at the top of colleges and universities under continued pressure to be the politicians' 'agent for reform' by those below, as discussed in Chapter 1. Within such a context, suggestions that there are alternative managerial and organizational change strategies for tackling these concerns can all too easily be read as 'resistant to change', or as 'too soft'. Hard, fast-driven solutions remain popular antidotes to what is seen as professional resistance. The longer-term consequences of these are ignored.

Even the space provided by the rhetoric of 'consumer responsiveness' can seem severely constricted. When mechanistic and control-oriented understandings of management are combined with traditional understandings of educational processes and outcomes in universities, the reverberation 'down the system' can become deafening for those who are daring to explore alternative purposes for colleges and universities. The difficulty of managing such contradictions in truly alternative institutions has been well illustrated in the chapters by Webb, Harrison, Flint, and Shackleton. For example, the government's emphasis on 'diversity of mission' to support the shift to a mass system of post-school education becomes undermined by the means adopted to enhance efficiency, accountability and new forms of service delivery.

Notwithstanding the difficulties imposed by such political constraints, those at the top must work through, with key players within, the harsher political stories without. These need to be more broadly owned. This working through, however, needs to be approached on the assumption that creative alternatives can be generated. The institution's own self-determination of purpose need not be undermined. Mechanistic understandings may bombard the institution's walls, but an alternative music can be composed within whereby the worst and best effects of the 'beast' outside can be managed on the institution's own terms.

It would be all too easy to regard this exploration of the power and potential of story as a metaphor and approach to cultural change as far removed from the world of funding councils, politics, power games within institutions, the defence of professional self-interests and the splits that so often obtain between academic and services/support staff. I would obviously say, not so. Seeing organizations as machines, or management as domination and control leads to particular kinds of actions and responses. A different framework approach to tackling such challenges allows the possibility of different outcomes.

The kind of work suggested above *is* about art and science in action. It is about creating organizations where learning and self-assessment become their lifeblood, supported by effective listening and connecting processes through which ways forward become illuminated and can begin to be enacted with enthusiasm – that most precious resource identified by Price (Chapter 2).

The personal narratives that form the foundation of this book illuminate a larger story about learning, development and organizational change processes. Each author has taken off the mask, and put down the Olympian shield. Each has acknowledged in different ways the possibilities of creating more resonance than dissonance between the story that the institution wishes to tell and the people on whom the success of such a story depends. Story becomes a metaphor for beginning to see how processes for building internal capability can create new capacities for dealing with external pressures and evolving new forms of institutional and educational story:

To create a story which is credible, which allows development as well as continuity, which tells a tale worth telling – this is the task that, as human beings, we must all attempt. It is a task which, essentially, demands imagination. If we are to construct a coherent account – an account which encompasses rather than denies, all the phases we have lived through, the vicissitudes, the pain as well as the joy – then we must approach our experience and that of others, with the greatest possible imagination. The story-teller commands the audience (Salmon, 1984).

I therefore close by urging those introducing change at all levels to be story-tellers, as well as co-creators of story. In practice, this means having the courage to be role models for others. This entails challenging mechanistic models of management and managing change and creating new institutional and educational stories that can serve diverse student, staff and constituent communities wisely. We need to shape an alternative paradigm for managing change in today's colleges and universities. This requires us to bridge the dualities between theory and practice, between art and science, between past and future, between the third and the first person narrative, and between explanation and expression. We must bring things down to earth and create and enact the kinds of stories that provide a centre of balance in the Twister game of public service management that was described in Chapter 1. Those who do this well will stand out as leading managers, thus serving as powerful role models for others. But the power and potential of story helps us to remember that every new departure involves a host of characters whose stories are inextricably interlinked.

As we open up colleges and universities to more and different students, and push the boundaries of our understanding about giving expression to educational opportunity, there are many stories still to be written. What stories do you need to hear to write and enact new ones with others? And in the telling of such stories, will you keep alive dynamic possibilities for further knowing?

References

Beckhard, R and Pritchard, W (1992) *Changing the Essence*, San Francisco, CA: Jossey-Bass.

Boal, A (1979) *Theatre of the Oppressed*, (trans C A and M L McBride) New York: Urizen Books.

Boal, A (1992) *Games for Actors and Non-actors,* (trans. A Jackson) London: Routledge.

Freire, P (1970) *Pedagogy of the Oppressed*, New York: Continuum.

Heron, J (1988) 'Validity in Co-operative Inquiry', in Reason, P, (ed) London: Sage.

Hillman, J (1975) *Revisioning Psychology,* New York: Harper Colophon.

Kanter, R M (1983) *The Change Masters*, New York: Simon and Schuster.

Mcgill, I and Beatty, L (1992) *Action Learning,* London: Kogan Page.

Moreno, J L (1947) *Theatre of Spontaneity,* New York: Beacon House.

Morgan, G (1986) *Images of Organisation,* London: Sage.

Nohria, N and Eccles, R (1992) *Beyond the Hype,* Boston: Harvard College.

Office for Public Management and University of Portsmouth (1994) *Making it Work,* London: OPM.

Parston, G (1992) *A New Framework for Public Management,* London: Office for Public Management.

Parston, G and Liddell, A (1990) 'How the Market Crashed', *Service Journal,* May.

Pascale, R (1990) *Managing on the Edge: How successful companies use conflict to stay ahead,* Harmondsworth: Penguin.

Pascale, R and Athos, A (1981) *The Art of Japanese Management,* New York: Simon and Schuster.

Peters, T (1992) *Liberation Management*, New York: Alfred Knopf.

Public Management Foundation (1994) *Public Manager in the middle,* PMF, London: Office for Public Management.

Reason, P (ed) (1988) *Human Inquiry in Action,* London: Sage.

Reason, P and Hawkins, P (1988) 'Storytelling as inquiry' in Reason, P (ed) London: Sage.

Richards, S (1993) *The Consumer Paradigm,* London: Public Management Foundation.

Salmon, P (1985) *Living in Time,* London: JM Dent.

Schon, D (1983) 'The art of managing', in *The Reflective Practitioner: How professionals think in action,* New York: Basic Books.

Schon, D (1994) *Organisational Learning,* Conference 10, London: Office for Public Management.

Weil, S (1989a) *Making Sense of Experiential Learning,* Buckingham: SRHE/OU Press.

Weil, S (1989b) 'Influences of lifelong learning on adults' expectations and experiences of returning to formal learning contexts', unpublished PhD dissertation, University of London.

Weil, S (1992) 'Learning to Change' in *Managing Fundamental Change,* London: Office for Public Management.

Weil, S with Annamonthodo, P, Brandt, G, Chung, D, Douglas, C, Gunning, M and Phoenix, A (1985) *Through a Hundred Pairs of Eyes,* London: CSDHE/LGTB.

Appendix

Growth and Diversity: A New Era in Colleges and Universities

Rhodri Phillips

Views expressed in this chapter are personal and do not necessarily reflect the views of CVCP.

INTRODUCTION

Higher education in Britain has rarely been in a steady state. It has continuously been pushed by two conflicting pressures: to maximize its contribution to society and the economy, and to control public expenditure. Nevertheless the changes that have taken place since the mid-1980s have been the most momentous since the period following the publication of the Robbins Report in 1963, and have changed the face of higher education.

The purpose of this chapter is to provide a broad context of the changes that have and are likely to take place in higher education. It examines the interrelationship of three factors: Quantity, quality and funding. In teaching, for example, there has been concern that the growth in student numbers but a decline in funding per student has lowered quality. This chapter concentrates largely on teaching within a simple model, shown in Figure A.1, and on universities and colleges of HE.

The distinction between HE and FE is a legal and administrative convenience, based on the educational standard of the course, but in reality the two are closely intertwined. Many colleges of further education run higher education courses and vice versa. The Further and Higher Education Act 1992 did not only complete the reorganization of higher education; it also gave colleges of further education their independence from local government and set them on the path followed by polytechnics and colleges of higher education four years earlier after the 1988 Act. Although their roles may differ to some extent, the issues they face are very similar.

GOVERNMENT POLICY FRAMEWORK

The Conservative government that came to power in July 1979 saw itself as engaged in a mission of reform and renewal but in its early years its policy

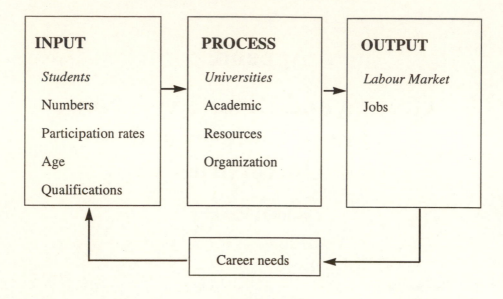

Figure A.1

changes in education concentrated largely on schools. This changed in 1987 with the publication of the White Paper *Higher Education: Meeting the Challenge* (DES, 1987) which proposed major changes to the organization of higher education:

- a growth in participation rates among young and mature students in higher education and some growth in FTE students numbers;
- the replacement of the University Grants Committee by the Universities Funding Council (UFC) to fund all British universities;
- the creation of a Polytechnics and Colleges Funding Council (PCFC) to fund polytechnics, colleges of higher education, voluntary and other grant-aided colleges in England (those in Scotland and Wales continued to be funded by local authorities).

These changes were enacted in the Education Reform Act 1988 and the UFC and the PCFC took on their new responsibilities on 1 April 1989.

The increase in full-time student numbers proposed in the 1987 White Paper was relatively modest. A radical policy was introduced in 1989/90 when tuition fees paid by local education authorities were sharply increased as an inducement to institutions to expand faster, encouraging a growth in student numbers and reducing the cost per student, while maintaining quality. The target was one in three young people in higher education by the year 2000.

The 1987 White Paper set out the government's agenda which runs as a continuous thread through subsequent years:

- wider access to higher education for young people with qualifications other than A levels, and for mature people;
- continuing part-time higher education for those in employment who wished to improve their professional knowledge and skills;

- improvements in the design and content of courses and in quality of teaching;
- greater emphasis on quality in research;
- increased efficiency of institutions, measured by performance indicators.

The 1991 White Paper, *Higher Education: A New Framework* (DES, 1991) made more radical proposals to reorganize higher education and to continue the drive to increase efficiency and quality.

- separate Higher Education Funding Councils (HEFCs) in England, Wales and Scotland funding all higher education institutions in those countries;
- the upgrading of polytechnics to university status and the extension to them of degree-awarding status with the consequent winding up of the Council for National Academic Awards (CNAA);
- the introduction of new measures on quality assurance, including a quality assessment role for the HEFCs and a quality audit unit developed by institutions.

These changes were included in the Further and Higher Education Act 1992.

By 1994, the government saw itself as having 'solved' the issue of higher education. The sector had been reorganized, numbers of students had grown and issues of quality were being addressed. As the government saw it, the onus was now on the universities and colleges themselves – cajoled by the HEFCs – to make a mass higher education system work efficiently and effectively. A policy of 'consolidation' was introduced tentatively in 1993/4, but it is the government's intention that it will be rigidly enforced in 1994/5 and subsequent years as part of the containment of public expenditure.

GROWTH IN TEACHING

It is worth examining the extent and pattern of growth in student numbers since the late 1980s as a mass higher education system has been created. The rate of growth in home student numbers exceeded the forecasts of both the 1987 and the 1991 White Papers, and targets set for the end of the decade had already been achieved by 1993/4.

The total number of students rose by over 50 per cent but there were wide variations between levels and modes (full and part-time). Postgraduate numbers, particularly on part-time and distance learning courses, grew particularly fast. At undergraduate level, the big increase was in numbers on full-time courses (see Table A.1)

The increase in numbers on undergraduate courses was achieved by increased participation in higher education by all age groups, but particularly by mature students aged 21 and over when they entered courses. The age participation index of 18–19-year-olds (ie, the proportion entering higher education) rose from 14.6 per cent in 1987/8 to 31 per cent in 1993/4 (close to the target that was planned to be achieved by the end of the decade). But numbers of older entrants grew faster, and in 1993/4 formed over half the undergraduate students at some new universities in urban areas (see unpublished statistics).

Growth in undergraduate numbers was not evenly spread among subjects. Despite the popular view that growth has been largely in the humanities and social sciences, numbers in science subjects as a whole grew at the same rate –

Table A.1 Growth in home student numbers (in thousands)

	1988/9	1993/4	Growth %
Undergraduate			
Full-time	517	866	68
Part-time	233	276	18
Open University	82	97	18
Total	832	1239	49
Postgraduate			
Full-time	47	76	62
Part-time	59	111	88
Open University	3	11	267
Total	109	198	82
TOTAL	941	1437	53

Source: DfE unpublished statistics

31 per cent – as non-science subjects. But this masked wide variations. Among the large academic areas, growth was particularly high on undergraduate education courses but below average on physical sciences and engineering.

The proportion of 18–19-year-olds in England and Wales achieving two A level passes – the basic entry requirement to degree courses – rose slowly but steadily in the late 1980s and early 1990s to 21.8 per cent in 1991/2 but this was well below the current rate of entry to higher education in 1993/4. Many enter full-time and sandwich first degree courses in England without A levels but – surprisingly, in the perception of most staff within universities – the average score of those entrants with A levels has risen (DfE, 1994).

The evidence on wastage rates on first degree courses is inconclusive. In England, they have fluctuated between 14 and 17 per cent from year to year, but there was no evidence by 1991/2 of an upward trend, although more recent figures may be different when they are published. The academic quality of entrants does not appear to have declined, which would have contributed to the stability in wastage rates. Indeed the evidence of degree standards is that the proportion of students on full-time and sandwich courses achieving good degrees (defined as first and upper second degrees) rose (DfE, 1994).

Looking to the future, the government's policy on consolidation means that there will be only small growth in full-time student numbers on higher education courses funded by the HEFCs. Those institutions which wish to continue to expand their teaching provision will have to look for growth in other areas:

- *full-time*: nursing and other courses funded by health authorities (which accounts for why many universities are seeking to take over nursing colleges), self-funded professional courses, overseas students;

- *part-time*: undergraduate and particularly postgraduate courses provided they are run in twilight hours or at weekends (the evidence is that day-release is disappearing in the face of employers' reluctance to release employees during working hours).

Part-time postgraduate, or rather post-experience, education may provide one of the most important expanding markets over the rest of the decade. The notion that individuals take responsibility for the education and training linked to their career development, as set out in the CBI's careership proposals (CBI, 1993), appears to be gaining ground. Those who have already taken an undergraduate course are increasingly prepared to study further on masters, advanced diploma or non-assessed courses. Lifelong learning will require employers to become learning organizations and universities to provide more individually-oriented teaching and learning approaches (Lloyd, 1992).

The projections of the Department for Education (DfE) and the Committee of Vice-chancellors and Principals (CVCP) of undergraduate and postgraduate numbers to the year 2000 envisage some continued growth, particularly after the end of the current public expenditure planning period in 1996/7. DfE/CVCP projections for full-time undergraduate numbers are based on the planning assumption that the age participation index among 18–19-year-olds will gradually rise to 33 per cent by the end of the decade. This would give some 220,000 entrants aged 18–19 with a further 100,000 mature entrants aged over 21. However the proportion of 18–19-year-olds entering higher education could be much greater if numbers of young entrants expand at the expense of older entrants within the overall planning total. Whether such a shift in the age of entrants would take place would depend to a large extent on the central policy of each university and the decisions of admissions tutors.

It is expected that the expansion in 16–19 education and the introduction of General National Vocational Qualifications (GNVQs) will increase the number of 18–19-year-olds with suitable qualifications for entry to higher education. The national training and education targets envisage 50 per cent of the age group achieving GNVQ level 3 by the year 2000 (DES/ED, 1991). The development of GNVQs has been criticized (Smithers, 1993), for such things as the lack of syllabuses, time limits, written examinations and external tests, and changes are likely. The lack of scores on GNVQs for admissions tutors might limit GNVQ students to the local university with which their college has links (in contrast to A level students with a 'portable' qualification leading to entry at any university).

TEACHING FUNDING

The funding regimes under which universities and colleges have operated have changed twice – from 'stop' to 'go' and then back to 'stop' – in the last five years to reflect changes in government policy on student numbers. However, it is fair to say that the change from 'stop' to 'go' has been easier to implement than the reverse, because institutions have entered long-term commitments in the growth period (principally on staffing and property) which must continue to be financed.

When the UFC and PCFC were set up, new funding arrangements were introduced with two objectives: to increase the numbers of publicly-funded students and to reduce the public funding per full- and part-time student while maintaining quality. This was to be achieved in three ways:

- the grant and fee per student rose by the Treasury's internal inflation index (called the GDP deflator), which was always less than the retail price index increase each year;
- efficiency gains were required each year;
- the UFC and PCFC introduced bidding systems to enable institutions to bid for additional funds placed at the margin below the average grant per student.

The first two have been central to all government expenditure programmes over the past decade and are not unique to higher education; the third operated differently within the UFC and PCFC sectors. The UFC published a guide price at which all universities bid so that funded numbers and grant per student remained largely unchanged. In contrast, the PCFC required polytechnics and colleges to bid a small part of numbers funded in the previous year. The polytechnics and colleges responded with aggressive bidding down of the marginal grant per student.

While the UFC and PCFC were devising their new funding methodologies, the government announced a very large shift of funding from grant to fees and non-cash-limited funding for fees. This provided a big financial incentive for institutions to take on additional students at the margin. The recruitment of fees-only students had a much greater effect in reducing the total funding per student than the Funding Councils' competitive bidding mechanisms. Over 30 per cent of the students at some institutions were recruited on a fees-only basis.

Universities on the one hand and some polytechnics and colleges on the other, adopted different strategies. Universities were concerned at the effect of declining funding per student on the quality of teaching and at the effect of increased student numbers on research quality. They were therefore cautious in their growth plans. Polytechnics and large general colleges (small specialist colleges were different) took the opposite view. They were committed to widening access to higher education and saw growth as desirable in itself. They also wished to increase their market share and maximize their teaching income (their only major source of income at that time) before the government ended the period of growth. With marginal revenue being greater than marginal cost, growth yielded larger surpluses which could be ploughed back into the institution. The result was a growth of 68 per cent in the amount of public money in real terms devoted to higher education between 1988/9 and 1994/5; but funding per student has declined and will continue to do so (DfE, 1994).

The creation of the three new HEFCs in 1992 coincided with the government's decision to end the period of growth in student numbers because its targets had been met. There have been three changes in the funding mechanism to ensure that institutions maintain their present numbers of students but do not increase them:

- In 1993/4 the HEFC in England incorporated fees-only students into funded numbers at each institution (with a consequent fall in the grant per student depending on the number of fees-only students in that institution). This grant per student was called an Average Unit of Council Funding (AUCF) and differed among 11 academic subject categories. The result was that institutions could not reduce their intake without losing HEFCE grant.

- The classroom-based course fee rate was reduced marginally in 1993/4, with little effect on recruitment. It will be reduced by 45 per cent in each of the three fee rates in 1994/5. Existing students will be protected by an increase in HEFC grant but any financial incentive to recruit fees-only students will be removed.
- To reinforce the message of the fees reduction, the HEFCs will penalize any recruitment above 1993/4 levels in 1994/5.

The abrupt change from growth to consolidation caused many problems for those institutions which planned to grow fast in the mid-1990s, principally in the former PCFC sector. The strategic plans of polytechnics and colleges prepared in 1992 (PCFC, 1992b) envisaged a substantial growth in home student numbers between 1991/2 and 1995/6. Income was planned to grow by 43 per cent during this period, and tuition fee income (including that from overseas students) by 75 per cent. Polytechnics and colleges planned to invest heavily in premises and staff and some had begun to do so on the basis that growth would continue. For example, large increases in teaching accommodation were planned in this period: 20 per cent across the sector and 137 per cent in larger colleges; an increase of 15 per cent in full-time academic staff was also planned. Those institutions which had to service long-term commitments without the growth for which these had been entered into found that they had to make radical readjustments in their financial forecasts.

As university and college funding has changed under public expenditure constraints, so has the funding of students themselves on full-time undergraduate courses. Student loans were introduced in 1990/91 and from 1994/5 maintenance awards will be reduced by 10 per cent a year for three years and the equivalent amount of money added to the maximum student loan. By 1996/7, maintenance awards and loans will be approximately equal. This will mean a sharp increase in student indebtedness.

Looking to the future, there is common ground between the government and the CVCP that the effect of public expenditure constraints on the quality of higher education will require an increasing financial contribution from full-time students in future. A report commissioned by CVCP from London Economics (CVCP, 1993) set out various options for a student contribution to tuition fees. There is no indication that the government will require a contribution by full-time students to tuition costs in the next few years; instead it is pursuing the switch from maintenance awards to loans described above.

TEACHING EFFICIENCY

An important item on the government's agenda is an increase in 'efficiency'. The latest government expenditure plans (DfE, 1994) acknowledge that institutions have:

> *achieved significant reductions in unit costs in recent years as student numbers have grown. These reductions have been accompanied by maintained or increased quality, and thus represent productivity gains...The scale of the gains has exceeded those planned by the Government as a result of institutions' decisions to recruit at or above the level of the Government's plans.*

them or to top slice and encourage research in other departments (McVicar, 1994).

The 1992 research assessment exercise resulted in a wide distribution of research funding (wider than for teaching funding). The biggest recipients fell into two main groups: Oxbridge and the biggest London colleges, and the older civic universities. Most of these are well represented in the more expensive medical, science and engineering research. There is evidence that most universities are now positioning themselves for the next assessment exercise in 1996 and seeking to recruit senior research staff especially in social sciences and humanities, where barriers to entry are low because they are a people business. While positions at the top of the research funding hierarchy are unlikely to change much, the positions in the middle order may be very different by the end of the decade.

A long-term consequence of research assessment may be to concentrate research in fewer universities. The American model of graduate schools has been seen as a means to focus not only postgraduate research education but also research effort as research is increasingly concentrated in a small number of 'research universities' within a mass higher education system (Phillips, 1994).

Running alongside the development of research assessment by successive Funding Councils have been changes in science research funding. The 1993 White Paper *Realising Our Potential: A Strategy for Science, Engineering and Technology* (OST, 1993) made several proposals that directly affect universities:

- a reorganization of the Research Councils, most importantly a split of the Science and Engineering Research Council into the Engineering and Physical Sciences Research Council and the Particle Physics and Astronomy Research Council;
- the creation of a technology foresight programme to identify emerging developments and inform government policy;
- a reorganization of postgraduate research training.

Changes are now also being made to the funding of economic and social research.

Funding for postgraduate research students is provided by the Research Councils and the training is carried out in universities; typically an award is made for three years for training leading to a PhD. The proposals for reorganizing research training (OST, 1994) envisage two stages: a Masters year which should provide both training in research methods and the development of specialist knowledge, followed by a PhD. The intention is that the 'research' Masters degree should be distinctive from other Masters degrees and should be a qualification in its own right. There may be arrangements for 'recognizing' equivalent training in other degrees (eg, four-year undergraduate programmes leading to Masters' degrees) and other forms of flexibility.

CONCLUSION

Higher education has changed since the mid-1980s; it has not simply grown. Much of it has changed its character. The range of backgrounds of students, the range of courses they undertake, and the range of types of universities and colleges means that much more choice is available to would-be students. Some universities and colleges have remained little affected, but most have been changed beyond recognition. The successful way that these changes have been organized is a tribute to the management skills of staff at all levels in universities and colleges.

The key to the future is to balance two factors: the need for the imaginative delivery of education opportunities to meet the needs of lifelong learning and the pressures to conform to traditional standards in teaching and learning. The prospects for the next few years is that quality rather than growth will make higher education more inward-looking and conservative. The swashbuckling entrepreneurialism of the early 1990s may have been a passing phase, and there may be a retreat to conservation. Let us hope not.

References

CBI (1993) *Routes for Success – Careership*, London: Confederation of British Industry.

CVCP (1993) Review of Options for the Additional Funding of Higher Education, Report by London Economics for CVCP, London.

DES (1987) *Higher Education: Meeting the Challenge*, (Cm 114), London: HMSO.

DES/ED (1991) *Education and Training for the 21st Century*, (Cm 1536), London: HMSO.

DES (1991) *Higher Education: A New Framework*, (Cm 1541), London: HMSO.

DfE (1993) *Higher Quality and Choice: The Charter for Higher Education* London: DfE.

DfE (1994) *The Government's Expenditure Plans 1994–95 to 1996–97*, (Cm 2510), London: HMSO.

ED (1993) *Labour Market and Skill Trends 1994/95*, London: Employment Department.

HEFCE (1993) *The Review of the Academic Year*, Bristol: Higher Education Funding Council for England.

HEFCE (1994a) *An Overview of Recent Developments in Higher Education in the UK*, January 1994, Bristol: Higher Education Funding Council for England.

HEFCE (1994b) *Assessment of the Quality of Higher Education: A Review and an Evaluation*, report by the Institute of Education, University of London, Bristol: the Higher Education Funding Council for England and Wales.

HEQC (1993) *Some Aspects of Higher Education Programmes in Further Education Institutions*, London: Higher Education Quality Council.

Johnstone, R J (1993) 'Funding research: an exploration of inter-discipline variations', *Higher Education Quarterly*, 47, 4.

Lloyd, B (1992) 'Lifelong Learning: The real challenge for the 1990s, *Higher Education Policy*, 5, 4.

McVicar, M (1994) 'The 1992/93 research assessment exercise: the view from a former polytechnic', *Higher Education Quarterly*, 48, 1.

OST (1993) *Realising Our Potential: A Strategy for Science, Engineering and Technology*, (Cm 2250), London: HMSO.

OST (1994) *A New Structure for Postgraduate Research Training Supported by the Research Councils*, consultation paper, London: Office of Science and Technology.

PCFC (1990) *Performance Indicators: Report of Committee of Enquiry*, Bristol: Polytechnics and Colleges Funding Council.

PCFC (1992a) *Macro Performance Indicators*, Bristol: Polytechnics and Colleges Funding Council.

PCFC (1992b) *Polytechnics and Colleges Strategic Plans 1991–92 to 1995–96*, Bristol: Polytechnics and Colleges Funding Council.

Phillips, Sir David (1994) 'The research mission and research manpower', in *Universities in the Twenty-First Century: A Lecture Series*, London: National Commission on Education.

Roberts, D *et al* (1992) *Higher Education: The Student Experience*, Leeds: HEIST.

SBU (1993) *Student Satisfaction Survey Report*, London: South Bank University

Smithers, A (1993) 'All Our Futures: Britain's Education Revolution', Channel Four Television.

UCE (1993) *The 1993 Report on the Student Experience at UCE*, University of Central England in Birmingham: Student Satisfaction Research Unit, Centre for the Study of Quality in HE.

Glossary of Educational Terms

Academic Boards *see* Senate.

Accreditation The process whereby institutions are granted the power to award their own degrees. The CNAA previously played this role for the former polytechnics and many colleges (*see* validation). Universities also have the power to accredit colleges providing courses at higher education level.

AFE An organization set up in 1993 to promote and support FE colleges throughout the UK.

API Age Participation Index (previously APR – Age Participation Rate): the number of young people (under 21), home initial entrants, expressed as a percentage of the 'relevant age group', being half the total number of 18 and 19-year-olds in the population (see Appendix).

AUT Association of University Teachers: the union which represented staff in traditional universities and, after 1992, the union that is open for membership by all academic staff in HE institutions and which carries the responsibility for national pay bargaining.

Binary line the term used to distinguish the newly created public sector institutions (polytechnics) from 1965, and the traditional universities, established by charter under the Queen's Privy Council. The binary line was abolished in 1992 following the Education Reform Act.

BTEC British Technical Education Council: established in 1983 and one of the largest of the 15 national validating bodies. It is a national educational validating body for employment-related qualifications.

CAT Credit Accumulation and Transfer: the national framework established initially by the CNAA to enable comparable assessments of credits across FE and HE institutions. The government-funded elements of this are now overseen by a unit at the Open University.

CDP the former national body for directors of polytechnics, now merged with CVCP.

CEO Chief Executive Officer.

CNAA Council for National Academic Awards.

CVCP the Committee of Vice-chancellors and Principals.

DfE the Department for Education, created in 1993 out of the former Department of Education and Science, created in 1964; the government department, headed by the Secretary of State for Education, with responsibility for determining the educational budget and for policy.

EHE the Enterprise in Higher Education initiative, set up in 1988 by the Department of Employment Manpower Services Commission (now the Training and Employment Division of the DoE). This provided the opportunity for HE institutions to bid for £1 million over a five year period to develop more enterprising graduates through curriculum development and organizational change.

FE   Further education: sub-degree level post-school education and training.

FEFC   Further Education Funding Council.

Foundation year a year's preparatory course which has the equivalent of an A level on successful completion and therefore enables access to degree courses.

FTE   full-time equivalent (students and staff); one method of calculating total student numbers in an institution.

GMS   Grant maintained schools: established following the 1988 Education Reform Act. They receive funding in the form of a grant directly from the DfE.

Governors the body (called a council, board or corporation) to which the chief executive is accountable: by law in former public sector institutions, and by tradition in the chartered universities. Referred to as 'Board of governors' or 'Governing councils' in HE, or the 'corporation' in FE, these are comprised of both independent members (often representing industry) as well as representatives of the institution (staff and students).

HEC   Higher Education for Capability: the initiative set up by the RSA in 1989 designed to promote a broader interpretation of educational processes and outcomes in HE, aimed at developing greater capability for life and work directly through the curriculum. A key emphasis in this was on increasing learner responsibility, individually and in groups.

HEFC   Higher Education Funding Council: England (HEFCE), Scotland (SHEFC) and Wales (HEFCW).

HEI   an acronym often used to specify 'higher education institution'.

HEQC   the umbrella organization established by the CVCP to fulfil particular quality appraisal and quality enhancement activities for the HE sector. This undertook many of the functions of the former CNAA after the 1992 FHE Act.

HMI   Her Majesty's Inspectors: educational specialists attached to the Dfe who provided advice for schools, colleges, LEAs and the Secretary of State. This was abolished in 1992 and replaced by OFSTED, the Office for Standards in Education.

Incorporation Refers to the granting of autonomy to institutions formerly under the control of their LEAs by the 1988 ERA and the FHE Act, 1993.

LEAs   Local Education Authorities. There are 104 of these in England and Wales, each with its own education committee and a statutory duty to provide an education service. These were the bodies which managed polytechnics and, until 1993, FE colleges.

LET   Learning from Experience Trust: a charitable body set up by Norman Evans in the 1980s to promote the accreditation of prior experiential learning by FE and HE institutions.

LMS   Local Management of Schools: delegation to a governing body of management of a school's budget share from the LEA. Schools were granted the right to 'opt out' of LEA control by the 1988 Act.

NAB   National Advisory Body for Public Sector Institutions: this operated as the planning body for polytechnics and colleges from 1983–8. LEAs oversaw the administration and usage of NAB-determined funds.

NALGO   National Association of Local Government Officers: one of the unions for staff in local authorities and therefore for HE and FE institutions that were part of LEAs until incorporation in 1989 and 1993 respectively.

NATFHE   National Association of Teachers in Further and Higher Education, the union of which academic staff in further and higher education are eligible to be members.

National pay scales in both further and higher education, there are nationally agreed pay scales negotiated by the relevant unions.

NCVQ   National Council for Vocational Qualifications was set up by the government in 1986 to improve vocational qualifications by basing them on the standards of competence required in employment. It does not award qualifications but establishes the national framework for awarding vocational qualifications and for establishing their equivalence with other educational awards (see also NVQs).

NTET   National Targets, Education and Training, that have been set for the nation by a partnership of industry, further education and other vocational accrediting bodies.

NUPE   National Union of Public Employees: now part of the newly merged union, UNISON.

NVQs   these are issued by approved awarding bodies and reflect standards of work performance set by each sector of industry. Routes for career progression are defined by the NVQ framework which divides into five levels of competence.

OFSTED the Office for Standards in Education: a government agency with responsibility for schools inspection.

PCAS   Polytechnics Central Admissions System; prior to 1992, the body that handled all admissions to public sector higher education. This function has now been assumed by UCCA, the Universities Central Council on Admission.

PCFC   the Polytechnics and Colleges Funding Council, set up in 1988 to allocate funds to the non-university sector of higher education in England.

Polytechnics the former public sector institutions of HE established in 1968 to offer an alternative and more vocationally-focused route through higher education than that offered by the traditional universities.

PVC   Pro-vice-chancellor, the term often used to designate those who assist the vice-chancellor in the executive management of the institution. This is still often a rotating post in traditional universities, whereas it is a permanent appointment in the new universities.

Quality assessment introduced in 1993 [pilot exercise] by the HEFC, this seeks to provide assessments of teaching quality of individual subject areas in universities and colleges.

Quality audit introduced in 1992 by the Academic Audit Unit, the body set up by the CVCP to respond to increased demands for accountability. This unit has now become part of the Higher Education Quality Council.

RAE   Research Assessment Exercise (or Research Selectivity Exercise), set up by the University Grants Committee (the predecessor to the HEFC) in 1989, involving the universities and, from 1993, the former polytechnics when the new Funding Council was established (see Appendix).

ROA   Records of Achievement: one of the many new forms of assessment being introduced into FE and HE programmes, enabling students to document learning outcomes.

Semesterization the process of changing from a three-term academic year to a two 'semester' year. This is seen by some as a strategy for making better use of HE human and physical resources, since the long vacation can be used for a third semester.

Senate   the highest academic committee within a university with responsibility for ensuring the quality of its academic teaching and research. This can still be known as an 'academic board' in former public sector institutions, where the remit was often broader prior to the 1988 Act which specified its terms of reference in relation to the legal responsibilities of the chief executive and governing body.

Sixth form college 16–19-year-olds may transfer from a secondary school to a sixth-form college to complete their education. A wide range of GCSE at ordinary and advanced level are offered (ie, A levels and O levels), together with an increasing number of vocational and pre-vocational courses for students of all abilities.

SSR   staff student ratios: an input measure of a university's academic resources.

TECs   Training and Enterprise Councils: set up in 1990 in order to stimulate a better usage of education and training resources in order to support the development of local/regional firms.

Tertiary college an educational establishment offering sixth-form and further education through a full range of courses for the 16–19 age group.

UCCA   the Universities Central Council on Admissions, established in 1961 by the UK universities to solve some of the problems arising from the increased pressure of applications for admissions. UCCA has now been superseded by UCAS, which replaces both it and the former PCAS.

UFC   the Universities Funding Council, which superseded the Universities Grants Committee in 1988 with responsibility for administering funds subject to such conditions that the Secretary of State determines for education and research.

UNISON   The union formed in 1993 out of the former unions NUPE, NALGO and COHSE.

Unit of resource the amount of money allocated to institutions per full-time equivalent (FTE) student by HEFC.

Unitization the process of establishing a unit of academic currency across institutions that supports flexibility, student choice and accumulation and transfer of credits.

Validation the function undertaken by a range of agencies and professional bodies as well as HE/FE institutions to assure the quality of educational courses/programmes/ modules. Formerly, the procedure whereby the degrees of polytechnics and colleges were formally designated as CNAA degrees.

VC   Vice-chancellor: the term often used to designate the person at the head of a university. Other terms include rector, principal, director and chief executive officer.

Index